CASUALTY AND INSURANCE ISSUES IN COMMERCIAL LEASES

ALAN M. DI SCIULLO

ABA
AMERICAN BAR ASSOCIATION
Real Property, Trust and Estate Law Section

Cover design by Andrew Alcala

Printed in the United States of America.

26 25 24 23 22   5 4 3 2 1

A catalog record for this book is on file with the Library of Congress.

Dedication

To my parents, Peter and Marion Di Sciullo, who raised me; my aunt and godmother, Vera Kaney, who guided me; my siblings, Jean, Mary Beth, Katie, Mark, and Chris, who tolerated me; my wife, Mary Jo, and daughters, Megan and Corinne, whom I adore; and my granddaughters, Emilia and Zoey, whom I hope will take the wisdom and fairness reflected in these pages and incorporate them into their lives.

Contents

About the Author

Alan Di Sciullo, Esq. is the retired Director of Global Real Estate for Shearman & Sterling LLP. In that capacity, he directed the firm's worldwide real estate portfolio. He has been a Senior Vice President with a major global banking organization working on its corporate real estate merger and acquisitions activities and was of counsel with a New Jersey law firm. Mr. Di Sciullo served the largest portion of his career with Morgan Stanley as First Vice President and Senior Counsel responsible for real estate transactions and related litigation, such as the largest leases at the original World Trade Center totaling over 1.2 million sf, claims and relocations following the 1993 and 9/11 attacks on the Towers, development of the 600,000 sf Discover Card Headquarters in Riverwoods, IL, and over 200,000 sf for Dean Witter Trust's headquarters in Harborside Plaza, Jersey City, NJ.

Mr. Di Sciullo has been active in civic and professional activities. He was a member of President Reagan's Private Sector Survey on Cost Control (the Grace Committee) and was elected a fellow of the American College of Real Estates Lawyers (ACREL) in 2003. He has served as an Executive, Council and Planning member of the American Bar Association's Real Property Trust & Estate (RPTE) Section and Senior Lawyer's Division (SDL), and has been a long-serving committee chair and Council and Planning member of each. He also served as President of the New York chapter of the International Association of Corporate Real Estate Executives (NACORE), director on that organization's international board of directors, president-elect of its educational affiliate, the Institute of Corporate Real Estate, and an advisory member on the New York chapter of its successor organization, CoreNet Global. He received numerous leadership and planning awards as the chair of the West Windsor Planning Board between 1993 and 1997. He was a director on the New Jersey Planning Officials board from 1996 to 2014, and he is currently an advisory director for the Georgetown University Wall Street Alliance.

Mr. Di Sciullo is a co-author of a 2800-page treatise *Negotiating and Drafting Office Leases* (Full Court Press) now in its 28th year of publication. He is an adjunct Professor at NYU Schack, where he was recently honored for over 30 years of service to the University and has received Outstanding Teaching and Services awards. He has also received several Outstanding Faculty awards from CoreNet Global's MCR program.

Mr. Di Sciullo graduated *cum laude* in Government and Economics from Georgetown University. He holds J.D. from the Georgetown University Law Center and an M.B.A. in finance from New York University. He is listed as a Super Lawyer and in Who's Who in America and the World and in companion publications for American Lawyers, Finance and Emerging Leaders. He has been a frequent author and speaker on commercial real estate and insurance issues.

Preface

I was one of the lucky ones.

On the morning of September 11, 2001, I was rushing from an early doctor's appointment to get to my office on the 65th floor of Tower 2 of the World Trade Center (WTC) in New York City to be on a 9 a.m. conference call with my Morgan Stanley legal colleagues. Normally, I would be in the office well before nine, but even with the early appointment I was still making good time to be in the office for the call. I was on the PATH train that links New Jersey with New York at the Exchange Place station about eight minutes from the last stop at the Trade Center when the conductor said over the intercom, "Have you heard this one?" and suddenly the train stopped. We were instructed to go to the westbound platform to take a train now going to Christopher Street. When I exited that train a few minutes after nine, still hell-bent on dialing into the conference call, I looked up and saw what could only be a scene from a bad movie—the upper floors of Tower 1 of the Trade Center were on fire! A helicopter was circling the tower. It took a few more steps to see that the second tower was burning fiercely a few floors above my 65th-floor office.

I got as close to the buildings as possible. The way down to the towers was a mass of debris from the attacks. Parts of the plane from the initial attack were strewn all over the street and had torn away part of a construction canopy. Even from a distance, you could see people jumping from the burning and blackened Tower 1. I was lucky being on the north side of the towers. People with whom I spoke on the south side said it was nothing less than an indescribable war zone.

FBI agents and New York City police were all over lower Broadway, a block away from the burning towers, which was the closest I could get to see if coworkers and friends had escaped. Several fire trucks passed by us carrying with them many firefighters in their last hour of life.

The attack caught America by surprise. Even after the Trade Center was bombed in 1993 and many of us were fortunate then to escape from the upper floors, not enough precautions were in place to prevent the horror of what happened on September 11.

For nearly a half hour, I watched as the towers burned. The weather that day was perfectly gorgeous, in sharp contrast to the horrific events unfolding before us. The clear blue sky offered a perfect view of the towers for the perpetrators and for us to see the aftermath. I was able to get as close as St. Paul's Church in lower Broadway, which is behind 5 World Trade Center, to see if colleagues had made it from the buildings.

At approximately 9:48 a.m., someone to the right of the crowd where I was standing shouted that the building was collapsing. Weakened by the crash to its core by the airplane and the 3,000-degree fire flamed by the jet fuel, the top 30 floors of my building, the South Tower, start to twist and fall as a unit toward Church Street, in front of where many of us were standing. As this top unit began dropping, it crashed on the rest of the standing tower, causing floors to pancake on one another rapidly and violently. By the 40th floor, the tower resembled a brown waterfall as the concrete floors imploded on one another in rapid succession. A gray cloud puffed up over 1 Liberty Place, in contrast to the black smoke emanating from the burning first tower, as 2 World Trade Center kept collapsing. As the tower crumbled to the ground within a minute's time, the deadly remnants hit the ground and began rushing toward us like shrapnel in a debris-laden brown and yellow cloud. A police officer and I turned and ran up Broadway. When I gestured to the officer that we get behind some concrete barriers we were passing, he shook his head not to. He didn't think that they would stop the debris. We ran hard to escape the debris. As I told my best man and former track teammate, Gary Beach, a former state champion, I beat his best time that day.

We finally reached safety at City Hall and saw people emerging from the cloud crying and covered in yellow ash from the collapse. One soot-covered businessman emerged in a suit that looked like it had been blasted onto him. Those of us who had made it past the debris turned back to help those who were emerging from it. All around the WTC area, strangers helped one another the entire time after the attack until the second tower collapsed at 10:15. Instead of panic, I saw the same spirit of cooperation and assistance on September 11 as when the WTC was bombed in 1993 and we had to evacuate the towers from the upper floors.

Since cell phones were not working, we lined up at pay phones to call home. Again, people were cooperative and generally limited themselves to a single call, in consideration of others in line.

I walked the nearly four miles to Morgan Stanley's Midtown offices. I noticed that about a mile from the now-collapsed towers, it seemed as if nothing had happened. People were outdoors enjoying the day seemingly oblivious to the horror that was happening only a short distance away. Only when I got to Times Square did reality start to hit home. People were gathered around the street watching the large screen carrying news of the event and related tragedies at the Pentagon and in Pennsylvania as the terrorists' plot was reported.

I got to my company's offices at 750 7th Avenue and watched a near-miracle unfold as our IT and real estate groups had already begun placing employees and getting the firm's computers running. Workers who just hours ago had been in the towers and had escaped the worse attack in this nation's history were rebuilding their company. We worked until well into that evening, when I was able to catch a train home. The station reflected the tragedy of the day. Even at midnight, the parking lot in my town was still filled. I got home and hugged my family. I then did the only routine thing I remember doing that day—I took the garbage out to the curb for the next day's collection.

What is now being called "Ground Zero" was once a vibrant office and tourist complex rising nearly a quarter-mile high and totaling over 7 million square feet of office space. Nearly two decades of my legal career was spent at the World Trade Center. In 1983, Dennis Greenwald, Dean Witter's General Counsel, hired me to do the legal work in negotiating what would become the largest leasing deals in the Trade Center, covering nearly 1.4 million square feet in 2 and 5 World Trade Center constituting Dean Witter's world headquarters. When Dean Witter and Morgan Stanley merged in 1995, the executive offices moved to Midtown Manhattan, but Morgan Stanley still had the largest tenant roster at the Trade Center on September 11. Miraculously, only six members of our firm out of nearly 3,700 at the WTC were killed in the attack. I learned a lot in those Trade Center deals, and the experience resulted in the basis for my later practice, and subsequently, much of the material I have contributed to this book.

The World Trade Center was as much a home for many of us as our family residences. We spent more time in these offices than we did in our homes. Those of us who had offices in the towers took some delight in seeing tourists pay to wait, oftentimes for hours, to see a view very similar to the one we saw daily from our offices only 45 floors below the observatory deck. The south side had a tremendous view over New York Harbor and the Verrazano Bridge, and the north side—where I had my office—had a phenomenal view of Midtown Manhattan that came to life at night when the Empire State Building and the rest of Manhattan lit up.

The Trade Center was a source of my children's, Megan and Corinne, childhood memories as they attended my company's holiday parties on the 44th floor at 2 WTC and other company functions. Corinne would kick a soccer ball the length of one of the Trade Center floors with members of our legal staff. Megan and I spent a pleasant day three weeks before the attack doing college tours and having lunch at an outdoor restaurant in the shadow of the towers.

In the days following the attack, we all came to grips with what was being called the "changing event" of our lives. Our firm had a beautiful memorial at St. Patrick's Cathedral, and as many of us were still processing the events of the past week, our country was going to war to punish the perpetrators of the attacks and to prevent the occurrence of similar events. At a gathering following our memorial service, one of my coworkers, who had escaped from the 64th floor, commented, "At least we know who will attend our own memorial service," meaning that she was gratified at the outpouring of calls and concern she received about her well-being following the attack. I add my own feeling to that statement. In the minutes following the time they first heard about the attack, my good friends Tom and Barbara Frascella, Phil and Denise Dwyer, and Jerry and Debbie Schaller went to my home to help my wife, Mary Jo, until she received word of my survival. I appreciate all the calls we received in the ensuing days from all over the country, particularly, Dr. Cynthia Paulis from Texas; legal colleagues Kathy Martin from Minneapolis, Tom Fleming from California, and Mary Ann Scala calling from Alaska; Tim Graham, Hal Taylor, Jim Rothenberg, Jeff McCormick, and Bill Bain who kept me laughing about our former rugby exploits some many years ago at Georgetown; John Wood, Nancy Stein, John Lench, Bob Mc Gillicuddy, Gordon Wyllie, Phil Neuer, Bruce Bloch (himself a survivor of the attack), Susanna Fodor, and the many other people from NACORE; and many, many more friends and relatives who took the time to call in those awful hours following the attack. It is gratifying to know that there are so many people who have that concern even if it takes as horrible an event as 9/11 to bring it out.

September 11 will have a profound effect on the way we real estate professionals do our business in the future. It is significant that the terrorists chose an office installation to do their damage. Offices in America are where we still do the overwhelming bulk of our business and transactions, notwithstanding the technological advances of the past decade and the advent of virtual offices, hoteling, and other means of conducting business. Office buildings are where the greatest concentrations of people and businesses are located. That the terrorists didn't kill more of the 50,000 people who worked at the Trade Center was a function of both the time of morning when they hit and the floors in the towers into which they crashed their hijacked planes. It is not far-fetched that our generation's Pearl Harbor was a New York office building and our *Arizona* was the World Trade Center.

Unfortunately, security will be a pervasive concern in our leasing transactions, especially in the near future until terrorist activities are eliminated. Our usual concerns with fire, flood, and "sick building" syndrome are now heightened with measures that must be taken and incorporated into our leases against intentional and malicious attempts to hurt or kill us and damage or destroy our places of business. It becomes another dimension in the age-old negotiations between landlord and tenant, but one brought about from truly sinister and evil forces. It is an issue on which undoubtedly landlord and tenant stand on the same side, but they differ on their view of the extent of prevention to be offered, what is practical, and then who should bear the cost. John and I take these issues, examine them, and attempt to offer insights, clauses, and solutions to incorporate into our usual leasing transactions.

There were many heroes that day in New York. Rick Rescorla, who headed Morgan Stanley's security at the Trade Center, was one of them. Even before September 11, Rick was a hero to many of us who knew and worked with him. He was one of the most decorated soldiers in Vietnam and a hero of the bloody battle of Ia Drang, which is the subject of the movie and book *We Were Soldiers Once*. In the 1993 bombing of the Trade Center, Rick was one of the last people to evacuate the building, leaving only after he was assured that everyone else had left. Unfortunately, Rick had the same sense of duty on September 11. Many people passed him on the stairwell as he held a bullhorn to keep moving people out of the building. Once again, as he did in 1993, Rick went back through the building to make sure everyone else had left, and he was still in there when it collapsed. He is greatly missed, but he has been an inspiration to the rest of us.[1]

1. Alan Di Sciullo, Voices of September 11th Living Memorial Project, *A Comment on September 11*, https://voicescenter.org/living-memorial/911-stories/statement-alan-di-sciullo.

Chapter 1
Risk Allocation and Responsibilities

[1]—Introduction

When I speak about casualty and insurance issues on commercial leases at seminars and conferences, I begin with the statement, "This is the most boring part of a lease but most gut-wrenching when a fire, flood, hurricane, or other casualty occurs." My career in this area as an attorney has seen me handle not just the usual fires, floods, water leakages, and hurricanes but also more obscure events such as the bombing of the World Trade Center in 1993 and the more horrific attack of the Trade Center on 9/11.[1] My advice for anyone in this specialty is to try to anticipate any imaginable event that can occur and then think even deeper into the worst imaginable event. Nothing is outside the realm of possibility.

The process of reviewing the casualty and insurance clauses in a lease requires a specific knowledge of these esoteric areas; the ability to consult with experts, such as a risk manager, insurance agent, or experienced attorney in this field; imagining the worst possible things that could happen in a commercial leasing situation; and then drafting for those events to have insurance coverage to compensate for injuries and damages and assure yourself of the peace of mind that you have the event covered when it occurs.

One of the major issues arising under a commercial lease is the allocation of the risks and responsibilities for casualties, injuries, damage, or destruction on the leased premises.[2]

1. Alan Di Sciullo, Voices of September 11th Living Memorial Project, *A Comment on September 11*, https://voicescenter.org/living-memorial/911-stories/statement-alan-di-sciullo.

2. Another consideration is where the tenant will work while the premises are being restored. Will the landlord be responsible for relocation expenses and so on? Any restoration provision should address the issue of relocation during the restoration period. Such a provision usually addresses size, configuration, and monetary issues. Typically, the tenant willnot be required to pay additional rent or common charges if the new space is larger. Still, location and building reputation can be very important to a tenant. Therefore, tenant's counsel should be sure to address these issues in such instances.

Until the advent of modern insurance, under most leases, the common law governed who was responsible for these occurrences. To a certain extent, the harshness of the common law standards imposed upon a tenant for repairing the premises still exists in some modern lease and insurance provisions, although the insurance industry has been especially proactive in updated coverage and exclusions in the past quarter century.

[2]—Common Law Standards

At common law, the landlord was not responsible for repairing the premises or leased improvements. The medieval tenant typically rented agricultural lands. The improvements on these lands, such as a barn or a shed, were merely incidental to the leased property. Most often, the landlord lacked the necessary tools and skills to repair or maintain these structures. As such, the tenants took the leasehold in an "as is" condition, under the rule of caveat emptor.

Under the common law, the tenant had no legal obligation to restore a structure damaged by fire, flood, or other casualty. However, the tenant was frequently economically compelled to rebuild the damaged or destroyed structure if it wanted to receive the maximum benefit and use of the land and the premises it was leasing. Therefore, a tenant assumed considerable risk and liability in entering into a lease at common law.

Today, most modern leases involve urban and suburban offices and retail shops where the improved space is the main focus of the lease agreement rather than the underlying land. Moreover, most tenants do not have the time, skill, or tools necessary to repair or maintain a building or premises.

A few states have refused to follow this common law rule. In addition, recent cases have tended to repudiate the common law standard on the theory of commercial frustration.[3] In New York, for instance, a tenant may surrender possession of the premises and will be relieved of further rental obligations so long as the casualty was not the tenant's fault.

While most courts and modern leases are moving away from these standards, a few jurisdictions still retain these common law rules. Due to the variety of case law among the states, a tenant cannot be fully assured of what its obligations will be in a particular situation unless it is thoroughly familiar with the laws and cases of the

---

3. See Milton R. Friedman, Friedman on Leases at 133, 473, and 1404 (3d ed. 1990) for an extensive discussion on the case law and application and theory of commercial frustration and frustration of tenant's use. See also Robert F. Dolan & Joseph Rasch, Rasch's Landlord and Tenant §§ 19.1 et seq. (3d ed. 1988) for an examination of the common law and current obligations of the parties with respect to transferring control of and repairing the premises.

jurisdiction governing the lease. It is a tedious job for tenants and landlords with multiple operations in numerous states to keep abreast of the applicable law, but it is extremely important.

[3]—The "Hub and Spokes" View of Casualty and Insurance

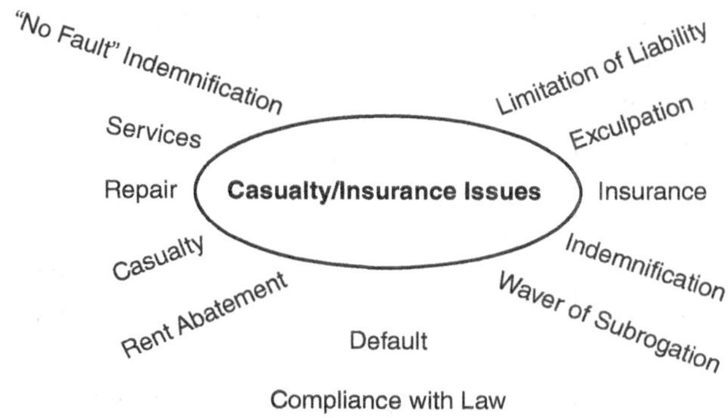

I have used the "Hub and Spokes" method of reviewing lease casualty and insurance provisions as a way of showing both the complexity of these provisions and the interrelationship of these provisions with other provisions in the lease. Within the scope of the casualty and insurance provisions are at least a dozen interrelated clauses, which are tied to the two main sections. Using the "Hub and Spokes" approach allows the negotiator to tie the chief concepts of dealing with a casualty event into a general scheme and to tackle all of the affected provisions at the same time. It also allows the negotiator to develop a consistent approach to these provisions to minimize the possibility of vague or ambiguous clauses addressing any of these sections.

Grouped under the casualty set of clauses are services, repairs, rent abatement, default, compliance with law, and the primary casualty provision. Force majeure can also go under the casualty clause.

These six sections are interrelated because when there is a casualty, the parties' rights and responsibilities with respect to each of these areas will be affected. The parties will certainly first go to the casualty provision in the lease to determine their rights immediately after the event. They will also go to the repairs and services sections to see if there are any suspension rights following a casualty, what rent abatement rights accrue following the casualty, termination rights following the event (which may be contained in either a default provision or a casualty section), and which party may have repair or other obligations following the event under the compliance with law section.

The casualty section should also set out a schedule to reconstruct the premises and building and each party's obligations to do so. Usually, this reconstruction schedule will follow the initial work schedule, with the owner being responsible for repairs and reconstruction of the common areas and structural and operational (e.g., HVAC) elements of the building and premises and the tenant being responsible for its own build out along the lines of its initial improvements and for replacing its own personal property. Usually, the parties will also want to continue the leasing relationship after the casualty. However, they need to find out how long it will take to rebuild the building and premises to help them determine whether keeping the relationship is feasible. The particulars of a reconstruction schedule usually get negotiated further after the destruction since all circumstances could not have been anticipated. Spelling out the parties' respective termination rights gives each party an idea when that party will be free to seek alternative space, defuse the emotion following the event, and form a basis from which to proceed.

Insurance issues and obligations tie in closely with the casualty section, especially in developing a "no fault" indemnification scheme. In reviewing the contract and determining the rights and obligations, the parties should first go to the insurance clause to see which types and amounts of coverage apply. Typically, parties are required to maintain a form of property insurance (e.g., the basic form, CP 10 10; the broad form, CP 10 20; or the special form, CP 10 30), commercial general liability, workers' compensation, and automobile liability. Next, the parties should determine the types and extent of indemnification they each must provide, whether there is an exculpation clause,[4] and whether there are any limitations of liability.[5] Damages are usually limited to the landlord's equity in the building, and tenants often negotiate to supplement that limit with building cash flow and insurance proceeds. If the parties want to set up a no fault indemnification scheme, there may also be a separate section or preamble to the insurance section stating that intent.[6]

Insurance coverage should define each party's specific coverage requirements. The casualty section should specify each party's rights and responsibilities for an event covered by that section. At the onset, the casualty section should define what constitutes a casualty under the lease, namely, a sudden unexpected occurrence, natural disasters, or an act of God ("force majeure"). These are sudden, unanticipated events, not expected events such as Year 2K. The clause should spell out each party's termination rights and to what extent and when the tenant may be able to expect to receive a rent abatement if the premises and building cannot be occupied.

---

4. If there is an exculpation clause, it is undoubtedly written to relieve the landlord from liability for its gross or ordinary negligence.

5. The limitations of liability clause differs from an exculpation clause. A limitation of liability usually limits the extent of damages a party—usually the tenant—would receive following a judgment in its favor.

6. Such a clause appears at Chapter 7, section 2, *infra*.

As noted in this section, there are interconnections of several casualty and insurance provisions. Since these provisions are inherently interconnected, in a badly drafted lease these provisions may be drafted as if they stand alone. If so drafted, the casualty and insurance provisions can conflict with one another.[7]

Beat Steiner points to these intertwined areas that create, as he calls them, "Pretzel loops." These are insurance, exculpation, and indemnifications clauses; tenant improvement, maintenance, casualty loss, insurance, and surrender clauses; and operating expense inclusions, exclusions, and landlord repair and maintenance provisions.[8] Since most leases require the parties to carry specific insurance and the tenant to release the landlord from certain liabilities (exculpation clauses), mutual indemnification, and waiver of subrogation provisions, these clauses should be drafted together to achieve a sensible allocation of risks and responsibilities.[9] Ideally, these clauses—which constitute a "no fault indemnification" schedule—should work together and maximize the possible benefits from insurance that the landlord and tenant carry.

While it is common for a lease to impose certain insurance obligations on the tenant, since many leases do not address the landlord's insurance, this could create duplications or, worse, a void in coverage. When both landlord's and tenant's requirements are stated in the lease, these clauses should be able to work together. Steiner states that it will not make sense for the tenant to be required to carry property insurance on all tenant improvements of the premises if the landlord has an obligation or intends to carry property insurance for the entire building, including tenant improvements.[10]

In the usual lease, a landlord might disclaim all liability to a tenant for the condition of the premises or events related to the premises. This release, according to Steiner, is overboard if one of the effects is to deny the tenant the benefit of insurance that landlord is carrying, and the cost is then passed through to the tenant.[11]

Steiner notes that an effective waiver of subrogation in favor of the tenant keeps the tenant from being sued by the landlord's insurance company if, for example, the tenant's negligence causes a covered casualty loss and the insurance company pays on the policy. According to Steiner, the term "waiver of subrogation" is a misnomer since it is really a waiver of claims, usually limited to property damage claims.[12]

At a minimum, the lease should contain a landlord's waiver for the tenant's liability for property damage to the extent such damage is covered by the landlord's

---

7. Beat Steiner, *Three or More Pretzels in a Lease: Sorting through Intertwined Provisions*, 32 Probate & Property 46, 46 (July/Aug. 2018).

8. *Id.*

9. *Id.* at 47.

10. *Id.*

11. *Id.*

12. *Id.*

insurance. The tenant should make sure that the landlord's carrier will agree either to waive any subrogation in this circumstance or that the landlord's coverage is not impaired, because the waiver effectively eliminates the insurer's subrogation right. According to Steiner, a waiver of subrogation clause in favor of the tenant makes sense when the tenant is paying all or a proportionate share of the landlord's property insurance; in fact, a mutual waiver of subrogation makes sense in most leases.[13]

To avoid inconsistencies, related lease clauses should be made subject to or consistent with the waiver of subrogation provisions. The waiver that the tenant obtains should have no exceptions that will reduce the waiver's scope. For example, there should be no exceptions when the tenant is negligent, since that flies in the face of the purpose of the waiver, which is to prevent the insurance company from bringing a claim against the negligent party.

It flows that the insurance provisions of the lease also need to be consistent with the subrogation waiver. For example, the waiver will be meaningless if the language applies to claims covered by property insurance that the landlord carries but the landlord has no such insurance. It is much better to tie the waiver to claims covered by insurance that the landlord actually carries, but it would still be useless if the release does not require the landlord to carry any specific insurance or the landlord fails to carry the required insurance.[14]

Indemnification clauses from tenant to landlord should not be so broad as to make the tenant thereby responsible for damages covered by insurance and to which the waiver of subrogation would apply. Clauses in which the tenant agrees to pay for repairs and replacements related to the premises should carve out an exception to such losses due to a casualty that insurance covers. Steiner says that the landlord's waivers should only apply to the extent that the landlord is able to recover under the usual causes of a loss of property insurance policy.[15] Steiner notes that a good rule to follow is that the party who owns the improvements and is obligated to remove them after a casualty should be the party that maintains the property insurance for that property.[16] While generally the landlord should not have to insure the tenant's improvements or trade fixtures, an exception would be if the landlord is concerned about the tenant's financial ability to restore fixtures that are not insured.[17] Casualty and insurance clauses should be aligned.

Replacements of tenant's work in the event of casualty loss should be consistent with other provisions of the lease, and as such, the casualty loss provision should

---

13. *Id.*
14. *Id.*
15. *Id.* at 47–48.
16. *Id.* at 49.
17. *Id.*

contain language that is consistent with both the insurance provisions and waiver of subrogation, as well as the ownership of improvements.[18]

[4]—A Modern Perspective[19]

September 11, the coronavirus disease 2019 (COVID-19) pandemic, and Hurricane Katrina and other natural disasters have brought to the forefront the importance of the lease casualty clause. What are the parties' rights and obligations when a casualty occurs? The answers will depend on the terms of the casualty provision in the lease.

Casualty responsibilities arise on many fronts. Insurance coverage and responsibility, waivers and releases, and lease-related documents such as loan agreements can be connected and impact the parties' rights and obligations. Here, however, the focus is on the casualty provision itself rather than the interplay with related subjects.

The following is a sample provision addressing casualty rights and responsibilities. It is by no means a model provision. Instead, it serves as an example, raising numerous issues for the parties.

> Subject to the other provisions of this section, if the premises or the shopping center are damaged by fire or other perils, this lease shall remain in full force and effect, and landlord shall restore the premises to a state ready for restoration by tenant of tenant's improvements. Notwithstanding the foregoing, landlord will have no obligation to restore the premises when: (i) the landlord's lender elects not to permit use of insurance proceeds for reconstruction; (ii) the damage is not fully covered by landlord's insurance; (iii) the damage occurs during the last two years of the term of this lease; or (iv) 30% or more of the premises or the shopping center is damaged. In any such event, landlord may terminate this lease by so notifying tenant within 120 days after the date of the damage, which termination will be effective as of the date of the notice. Landlord shall not be required to make any repairs or replacement of any improvements, or any other property installed in or located on the premises by tenant. Tenant shall be entitled to an abatement in minimum annual rent during landlord's restoration in proportion to the portion of the premises that is rendered untenantable by such damage; provided, however, if the damage is occasioned by the acts or omissions of tenant or its employees, there shall be no abatement of rent. The abatement shall commence as of the date of that damage and shall terminate on the date landlord completes its restoration work.

---

18. *Id.* at 48.

19. This section was written by Thad Armstrong, of the Houston office of Thompson & Knight, based on his article *Anatomy of a Casualty Clause*, NZIB 33 (Spring 2006), *available at* http://www.nbizmag.com/magarticles/anatomyofacasualityclause.pdf.

[a]—Obligation to Restore the Premises

As in most leases, the preceding sample provision obligates the landlord to rebuild the premises, with only limited exceptions. The landlord does not have to restore the premises if its lender will not permit the insurance proceeds to be used for the restoration. Without the right to use the proceeds to restore, the landlord can face extraordinary costs that outweigh the benefits of rebuilding. This type of exception is typical and reasonable. And, according to Thad Armstrong,

> It is also important to landlords because most loan documents allow the lender to choose whether the insurance proceeds will be used for restoration or applied to the debt. In other words, the landlord, likely, is not in control of its insurance proceeds; thus, it would be a disaster if the landlord found itself contractually obligated to rebuild a multimillion dollar building when no insurance proceeds were available to cover the cost involved.[20]

[b]—Timing of the Casualty

When one is drafting the provision, thought should be given to obligations at various times during the lease term. There are numerous costs involved for a tenant and landlord during the time when the tenant cannot use the premises. For example, the tenant has business interruptions costs, possible relocation and associated costs, and design and many other costs. If the casualty is not too great and occurs early in the lease term, the tenant may find it worth waiting for the premises to be restored. However, if the lease will end within months or a short time after restoration, the parties are probably better off allowing the tenant to terminate the lease. In any event, tenants should ask for a mutual right to terminate the lease especially in the case of a casualty that occurs near the end of the term.

Note that the sample provision above states that the landlord does not have to restore if the casualty occurs during the last two years of the term. This is a common exception sought, since it may not be economically feasible for a landlord to restore the premises of a tenant whose lease will terminate within months after the restoration is complete.[21] The point is that the timeframe set here should reflect the fact that little time remains on the lease. It should not be an option exercisable early in the lease when the landlord may simply wish to rid itself of an unfavorable lease or tenant.[22]

---

20. *Id.*
21. *Id.*
22. *Id.*

A landlord may also want to add another exception to its obligation to rebuild if the time required to restore the premises is estimated to exceed a specified period. This, too, is a common, reasonable exception. Drafters should be cautious, however, as

> long periods of restoration correspondingly create a business interruption issue for the tenant; therefore, a tenant should ask for a right of termination if restoration is estimated to take longer than it would be willing to wait under the circumstances.[23]

The rationale for a tenant's right of termination stems from the possibility that an extended wait time can cause serious business interruption issues for the tenant.[24]

Often leases will allow the landlord to terminate if a significant portion of the building (e.g., 30 percent) is damaged. Again, this is a common exception that should not raise concerns for either party. However, the tenant should be sure that the percentage set is not unreasonably low, allowing the landlord to use it as an excuse to rid itself of an undesirable tenant or unfavorable lease. A tenant in a strong bargaining position should require a provision stating that its lease cannot be terminated in this instance unless the landlord also terminates all other leases at the property. Again, a tenant does not want its landlord to take advantage of the situation in a high-cost leasing market or to use a small casualty to simply get rid of the tenant.

As further protection, the tenant should require the landlord to obtain property insurance on an "all risks" basis (correctly termed "causes of loss—special form") in an amount equal to the full replacement value of the building.[25]

Finally, the example provides that the landlord's obligation to rebuild does not include those improvements for which it was not originally responsible. This makes sense. If the tenant paid for and installed certain improvements, the tenant should look to its own insurance proceeds to pay for those restorations.[26]

The sample provision above lacks some clarity here. It would be improved by stating,

> (1) requiring the landlord to restore the premises to the condition they were in on the day prior to the casualty, except for those improvements, fixtures, and other items of personal property paid for and installed by the tenant, and (2) requiring the tenant to restore the improvements, fixtures, and other items of personal property paid for and installed by it.[27]

23. *Id.*
24. *Id.*
25. *Id.*
26. *Id.*
27. *Id.*

[c]—Landlord's Notice to Tenant Regarding Restoration

The notice period for the landlord to decide whether to restore should be reasonable for the tenant, since every day the tenant is left without a decision is added time away from its business. Also, the tenant knows when to search for new premises without the fear that it will have to go back to its original premises. A period of 120 days for the landlord to notify the tenant is not uncommon in many leases, and the sample provision above allows such a 120-day period. But a 120-day period can place a great strain on the tenant to have to wait that long for the landlord to make up its mind whether to rebuild or terminate while the tenant remains obligated under the lease. On the one hand, the landlord needs a reasonable amount of time in which to assess the damage, coordinate the insurance adjustment, and engage architects and contractors. On the other hand, the tenant should not have to wait an unreasonably long period of time for the landlord to decide whether to rebuild or terminate. During the lease negotiation process, the parties need to recognize each other's needs and strike an appropriate balance.

[d]—Abatement during Restoration

The COVID-19 pandemic has brought to the forefront the importance of defining a party's rights when it cannot access its premises to do business with the public or open its offices for its employees due to a pandemic or government shutdown orders. It is not uncommon for a casualty clause to include a rent abatement, although it has to be negotiated and is usually not implied as a tenant's right. The preceding sample provision grants to the tenant an abatement of rent during any period of restoration. However, the clause does not provide for such an abatement during a pandemic, governmental shutdown, or other untypical event. The author's own experience extended to a bomb at the World Trade Center and the 9/11 plane attack on the same buildings, neither of which a drafter could have reasonably predicted. A challenge for all of us drafting in this area is figuring out what will be the next unusual events for which we need to anticipate assuring that we capture all such casualties and force majeure events with which we will need to provide solutions for the affected parties. We later look at these issues in greater detail in Chapter 3 when we discuss force majeure events and concepts. An abatement should continue until the landlord's restoration is complete. Landlords often create an exception to the abatement right if the tenant has caused the casualty. This exception raises a number of issues. First, it could be argued that the landlord should have rental insurance, which the tenant should expect the landlord to rely on; after all, tenants pay for the landlord's insurance anyway through operating expenses.[28] Second, landlords are almost certainly better off granting an

---

28. *Id.*

unlimited abatement. Otherwise, the tenant's loss of business coupled with an ongoing obligation to pay rent may force the tenant out of business altogether, leaving the landlord with a likely uncollectible claim against an insolvent tenant.[29] The landlord should look to its rental insurance during the restoration period while the tenant should look to its business interruption policy during the same time.[30] This leaves the parties in as good a position when the restoration is complete as they were before the casualty. Leases often contain a free-rent period at the beginning of the term in order for the tenant to outfit the space with its equipment, inventory, and furnishings. A tenant should ask for a similar free-rent period after a casualty to ensure that it has sufficient time without the pressure of rent payments to fit up its space after the building has been restored and the abatement period is over.

Parties to a lease transaction generally focus on what they consider to be the material deal terms—rent, lease term, build-out responsibilities, and any other bargained-for rights that they consider to be fundamental to their transaction. All too often, casualty provisions are overlooked because the parties consider them to be mere "boilerplate." Many parties simply dismiss the importance of the casualty clause, thinking that the problems it addresses will not ever arise.

While casualties are not common, the costs involved when they occur can be extraordinary. The time to address the potential problems, concerns, and parties' responsibilities is during the lease negotiation, not after the casualty has occurred. In this way, the parties know their rights and obligations and the disaster can be handled in a more efficient, effective, and calm manner.

29. *Id.*
30. *Id.* at 35.

Chapter 2
Modern Liability Theory

[1]—Generally

Tenants usually assume considerable casualty and liability risk when they enter into a commercial lease. Both the common law and more modern theories place a lot of risk for casualties on a tenant, which typically is not fully realized until a disaster occurs. In the few instances where state statutes even address casualties, those states differ greatly from one another in apportioning responsibility to the landlord and tenant for a casualty loss.

Case law has not done much to clarify the liability of each party. The risks are illustrated in several fire damage cases.[1] The holdings in those cases even vary with respect to the theories of liability that should be applied. The practitioner should be familiar with the current law in each state where his or her client has commercial leases and must find methods of limiting casualty liability that are acceptable in those jurisdictions.

A tenant may incur liability to its landlord for casualty damage to the premises or structure under four theories: (1) tort, (2) contract or lease covenant, (3) application of indemnification, or (4) vicarious liability.

[2]—Tort

A tenant's liability will arise under tort principles if its negligence or that of its agents or employees causes the casualty or damage.[2] Tort liability arises apart from any lease

1. For an extensive citation of authority on this point, see Milton R. Friedman, Friedman on Leases at 525–28 (3d ed. 1990). *See also* Eugene L. Grant, Subrogation, Indemnification and Exculpation in the Context of Commercial Leases, from Enforceability of Subrogation and Indemnity Clauses, Chair, Di Sciullo, American Bar Association program (Aug. 12, 1991).

2. As for injuries to invitees on the premises, a business establishment owes an invitee on its premises the duty of "ordinary care to maintain its premises in a reasonably safe condition and to warn [the invitee] of any hidden dangers." Amos v. NationsBank, 256 Va. 344, 504 S.E.2d 365, 1998 Va. LEXIS 108 (1998) (bank had no duty to an invitee who slipped on its premises during an ice storm), citing Wynne v. Spainhour, 215 Va. 16, 17, 205 S.E.2d 634, 635 (1974). However, the court held that "a business

covenant or other written agreement whereby the tenant assumes this liability. Several cases have held that this liability is not necessarily excused by the landlord's covenant to repair fire damage[3] nor by the owner's or landlord's receipt of insurance proceeds obtained at that party's own cost.[4] The theory applied in these cases is that a tenant's liability is excusable only if (1) the landlord is contributorily negligent, (2) the landlord has agreed in writing or by actions to insure the premises and building on behalf of both the landlord and tenant, or (3) the tenant is able to prove that a substantial portion of the landlord's insurance premiums has been paid for by the tenant or is attributable to payments in operating expenses and other rents made by the tenant.[5]

As an example, a plaintiff who sued both his employer and the owner of the office building in which he worked for damages claiming permanent physical injuries because of his exposure to mold in the workplace recovered $1.6 million from the building owner under a negligence theory with respect to the premises.[6] The court held that there was sufficient evidence that the plaintiff's injuries were proximately caused by his exposure to mold.[7]

[3]—Contract or Lease Covenant

Contractual liability arises quite apart from tort liability but may originate from the same events. The tenant's responsibility for fire and other casualty damage may arise from a lease covenant to surrender or "yield up" possession of the premises in good condition. The covenant may also provide an obligation for the tenant to repair the premises at lease expiration or termination. The covenant is obviously breached if the premises or building are destroyed and cannot be restored in a timely manner.[8]

The parties can allocate the risk of damage and injury and clarify their responsibilities for obtaining insurance to cover the risks. The following provision is an

---

establishment, landlord, common carrier or other inviter may wait until the end of a storm and a reasonable time thereafter before removing ice and snow from an outdoor entrance, walk, platform or steps." *Id.*, citing Walker v. The Memorial Hospital, 187 Va. 5, 13, 45 S.E.2d 898, 902 (1948).

3. *See, e.g.*, Fourth Circuit: National Motels, Inc. v. Howard Johnson, Inc., 373 F.2d 375 (4th Cir. 1967); District of Columbia Circuit: Maiatico v. Hot Shoppes, Inc., 287 F.2d 349 (D.C. Cir. 1961).

4. *See, e.g.*, Precisionware, Inc. v. Madison County Tobacco Warehouse, Inc., 411 F.2d 42, 48 (5th Cir. 1969).

5. *Id. See also* Friedman, *supra* note 1, § 9.9 at 526.

6. Cameron v. Merisel Properties, Inc. and Brian Goldsworthy, No. 07-54 (N.C. App. Nov. 6, 2007) (unofficial).

7. *Id.*

8. Taylor v. ROA Motons, Inc., 114 Ga. App. 671, 152 S.E.2d 631 (1966).

example of one such provision that clearly allocates the risks and sets forth the insurance obligations of both the landlord and tenant.[9]

> The parties desire, to the extent permitted by law, to allocate certain risks of personal injury, bodily injury or property damage, and risks of loss of real or personal property by reason of fire, explosion or other casualty, and to provide for the responsibility for insuring those risks. It is the intent of the parties that, to the extent any event is insured for or required herein to be insured for, any loss, cost, damage or expense, arising from such event, including, without limitation, the expense of defense against claims or suits, be covered by insurance, without regard to the fault of Tenant, its officers, employees or agents ("Tenant Protected Parties"), and without regard to the fault of Landlord, its respective partners, shareholders, members, agents, directors, officers and employees ("Landlord Protected Parties"). As between Landlord Protected Parties and Tenant Protected Parties, such risks are allocated as follows:
>
> (a) Tenant shall bear the risk of bodily injury, personal injury or death, or damage to property, of third persons occasioned by any event(s) occurring on the Premises, provided such event is occasioned by the wrongful act or omission of Tenant Protected Parties.
>
> (b) Landlord shall bear the risk of bodily injury, personal injury, or death or damage to the property of third persons occasioned by any event(s) occurring on or about the Building (other than premises leased to tenants), provided such event is occasioned by the wrongful act or omission of any Landlord Protected Parties.
>
> (c) Tenant shall bear the risk of damage to Tenant's contents, trade fixtures, machinery, equipment, furniture, and furnishings in the demised premises arising out of loss by the events required to be insured against pursuant to this Article.
>
> (d) Landlord shall bear the risk of damage to the Building arising out of loss by events required to be insured against pursuant to this Article.
>
> (e) Landlord shall, at its own cost and expense, maintain insurance on the Building against fire and risks covered by "extended coverage" on an "replacement cost" basis or containing a "replacement cost" endorsement in an amount sufficient to prevent Landlord from becoming a co-insurer ("All Risk" coverage). Landlord's insurance shall cover all items of Landlord's Work. Landlord shall also maintain a commercial general liability insurance policy, including contractual liability coverage (or with contractual liability endorsement) on an occurrence basis in amounts not less than Five Million ($5,000,000) Dollars combined single limit per occurrence with respect to bodily injury or death and property damage, to

9. Excerpts from "no fault clause" by the late Sidney G. Saltz. Copyright 1995. Reprinted with permission of the late author.

any one person and not less than Five Million ($5,000,000) Dollars with respect to bodily injury or death to any number of persons in any one occurrence and with respect to property damage. Landlord shall name Tenant as an additional insured on such policies and shall deliver a Certificate of Insurance upon Tenant's request. Landlord shall also carry rental value insurance for a loss period of at least One (1) year in an amount equal to the aggregate of all rent and additional rent payable by any and all tenants in the Building. Landlord shall provide Tenant with no less than Thirty (30) days' written notice of any cancellation, nonrenewal or material change in coverage.

(f) Tenant shall, at its own cost and expense, maintain insurance on its own furniture, fixtures and equipment in the Premises against fire and the risks covered by "extended coverage" for their full insurable value ("All Risk coverage Special Forms"), minus any applicable deductible(s), but in no event shall Tenant be required to carry plate glass insurance. Tenant, at its own cost and expense, shall maintain a commercial general liability insurance policy, including fire damage legal liability insurance and contractual liability coverage (or with contractual liability endorsement) on an occurrence basis in the amount of not less than Five Million Dollars ($5,000,000) combined single limit per occurrence in respect of bodily injury or death.

[4]—Indemnification[10]

A landlord's or tenant's liability may similarly spring from an indemnification or exculpatory clause in the lease[11] requiring one party to hold the other harmless from casualties caused by the first party, its agents, employees, invitees, or third parties. The exculpatory clauses typically protect the landlord from liability to the tenant even for the landlord's own negligence.

The following provision limits the landlord's liability to the tenant for injuries and property damage negligently caused by cotenants and limits the landlord's liability for injury or damage resulting from landlord's own negligence or tortious acts or omissions and those of its agents, employees, and contractors. The provision requires the landlord to make sure that all tenants carry adequate insurance to cover injury and damage. And the landlord indemnifies the tenant for any "liabilities" caused by or relating to the negligent or tortious acts or omission of the landlord, its officers, employees, agents, or contractors.

---

10. For an excellent examination of insurance indemnification clauses and a survey of the laws of selected states, see M. Moore, *Indemnification Provisions in Leases: What We Ask For and What Really Matters*, Prop. & Probate, 33–40 (Sept./Oct. 2008).

11. See discussion of indemnification and exculpatory clauses in Chapter 6.

> Landlord shall not be liable to Tenant for any personal injury or property damage resulting from the negligence of a co-tenant or anyone else other than Landlord, or for any damage to person or property resulting from any condition of the Premises or other cause, except for such injury or damage that results from the negligent or otherwise tortious acts or omissions of Landlord or Landlord's agents, employees and contractors. However, Landlord shall require all other tenants in the building to carry reasonably adequate amounts of liability (including property damage) and fire and extended coverage insurance. Nothing herein, however, shall be construed to relieve Landlord of liability for the negligent or otherwise tortious acts or omissions of its officers, employees, agents and contractors, and Landlord shall hold harmless, indemnify, and defend Tenant from and against all claims, demands, suits, causes of action, judgments, damages, losses, costs and expenses (including reasonable attorneys' fees and disbursements) (collectively, "Liabilities"), caused by, arising from or related thereto.

[5]—Vicarious Liability

A tenant may be vicariously liable for any casualty or damage caused by the subtenant, licensee, or assignee whose performance the tenant guarantees. Liability has been found under the theory of res ipsa loquitur ("the thing speaks for itself"),[12] as well as under the theories of liability discussed above.

[6]—Fraud or Misrepresentation

Absent fraud or misrepresentation, both landlords and tenants have insurable interests in the premises and building structure. Without that insurable interest, a fire or casualty policy is void and invalid. Unless there is a subsequent waiver or estoppel, an insurer may elect to void a fraudulently obtained policy.

A landlord or tenant will be charged with any misrepresentations made by their agents as if those fraudulent statements were their own. Under these circumstances, the insured landlord or tenant is excused, and coverage restored only if (1) the insured can prove that the agent's statements were unauthorized and (2) the insured is able to defeat the prima facie case for avoiding a policy obtained by misrepresentation or fraud. To defeat a prima facie case, the insured must show the scienter of the party making the representation,[13] that the intent was to deceive the insurer, and that the insurer relied upon the false or misleading statements to its detriment.[14] This is an

12. See Friedman, *supra* note 1, § 9.9 at 527–28; Annot., Res Ipsa Loquitur *as a Cause of Liability for Real Property Fires*, 21 A.L.R.4th 929–1074 (1983).

13. The party must be shown to have made the representation knowingly.

14. 44 C.J.S. *Insurance*, §§ 179, 362.

exceptional situation. Generally, once an insurable interest has been established and there is no fraud or misrepresentation in obtaining the policy, either the landlord or tenant can obtain coverage.

[7]—Environmental Insurance

"Environmental insurance policies have their roots in liability insurance, but they also provide coverage for restoration expenses and business interruption, which are traditionally written in property policies."[15] The standard environmental policy would require some modification to assure coverage for damage and injury resulting from mold.[16] The definition of "pollutants" under the policy would, at a minimum, have to be expanded to cover "mold, fungus and microbial matter."[17]

Since 1986, most general liability insurance policies contain a so-called absolute pollution exclusion that results in little or no insurance protection provided to owners or operators of real property for environmental risks.[18] There are a number of types of so-called environmental insurance coverage available. Each is discussed in the next chapter.

---

15. D.J. Dybdahl & Steven J. Lemon, *The Risk Advisor's Survival Guide to Mold Exclusions*, Envtl. Claims J. 5 (Winter 2003).

16. For a discussion of mold, see Chapter 6 [2], *infra*.

17. Dybdahl & Lemon, *supra* note 15.

18. Jack Fersko & Ann M. Waeger, A Premium on the Future: Emerging Insurance Products Covering Commercial Properties and Activities, p. 1, Managing Environmental Risks Through Insurance program, American Bar Association Real Property Probate Section Spring Meeting (May 21, 1999).

Chapter 3
Insurance Coverage Types[1]

Generally, small- and medium-sized tenants are required to carry specific types of insurance and with clearly defined limits. However, there is usually little or nothing mentioned about the landlord's insurance obligations.

Nearly all landlords require that their tenants carry liability insurance. After the tragic events of September 11, 2001, tenants need to be concerned that landlords carry adequate insurance as well.

Coverage in the case of a disaster like the World Trade Center (WTC) tragedy can come from many types of insurance. Business interruption insurance[2] and rent insurance are just a couple. "Business interruption insurance is intended to compensate the tenant for revenue interrupted by an event and incremental increased costs of doing business incurred during such an interruption."[3] However, what will be covered, the extent of coverage, and the coverage period all depend of the language of the specific policy.[4] Businesses that cannot resume business because of government closures may be able to recover if they have civil interruption (civil authority coverage) insurance. "Rent insurance is intended to protect the property's rental stream in case of an event that allows tenants to stop paying rent or makes the orderly payment of rent impossible. This coverage is principally the concern of building mortgagees."[5] Again, the specific language of the policy will determine whether and to what extent the insured is covered.

Insurance costs are really borne by the tenant in the form of operating expenses or a combination of base rent and escalations and operating expense escalations.

1. For a good primer on insurance clauses in leases, see Wesch & Rowe, *What Every Leasing Attorney Needs to Know about Insurance: Ask for What You Want, Then Make Sure the Insurance Covers What You Need*, PROP. & PROBATE 40–44 (March/April 2008).

2. Reidy, Carter & Tuer, *Business Interruption Coverage: Issues to Consider When Disaster Strikes*, THE CORPORATE COUNSELLOR 9 (Law Journal Newsletters Oct. 2001).

3. *See id.* at 9.

4. *See id.* at 1–5.

5. Goodman & Thanhauser, *Commercial Lease Provisions Get New Focus after Attack*, N.Y. TIMES SPECIAL SECTION: IN THE AFTERMATH OF DISASTER: STRUGGLING WITH LEGAL ISSUES ARISING FROM WTC ATTACK, at 9 (Nov. 27, 2001).

Landlords argue that tenants should rely on business interruption insurance while the tenants argue that the landlords should rely on their rent insurance to cover displacements. However, neither type of insurance is paid forever. There are limits. For instance, after the WTC attack, certain types of insurance, such as the terrorist endorsements that many landmark buildings were required to have, had become very costly or unobtainable. At that time, some commentators were even suggesting that tenants might likely want to require that landlords provide usable space, not simply space to lease, although this concept did not seem to be adopted.[6] Financial losses arising out of the September 11, 2001, terrorist attack exceeded $100 billion.[7] A significant portion of that was paid by the insurance industry. In fact, losses sustained by the insurance industry were unprecedented in virtually every respect, producing catastrophic losses not only in terms of property coverage but also in the life insurance, disability, and workers' compensation lines. Aviation and liability insurers also suffered their largest losses stemming from a single event.[8]

The first major question involving 9/11 was whether the terrorist act constituted an "act of war," since most insurance policies exclude "acts of war" from coverage. Other types of claims included those against the building owners and managers based on "improper or inadequate evacuation plans and/or implementation."[9] Still other issues included the extent of business interruption coverage, the determination of how such losses should be calculated, and whether and to what extent such losses were covered.[10] Businesses in neighboring building that were not destroyed in the WTC tragedy also submitted claims based on losses resulting from business interruption. They claimed that services were impaired, including telephone and utilities, and access to the area was denied or restricted and so on. Civil authority coverage arguably covered losses caused by "government or police activity impeding access to the insured's building."[11] The securities industry claimed loss of income during the closure of the stock market. Service industries such as hotels and airports also claimed lost income.

When access is impeded, an ingress/egress policy may provide the necessary coverage. Service coverage comes into play when telephone, utilities, and so forth are unavailable, and contingent business interruption covers the insured for losses

6. *Id.*

7. G. Finnerty III & Eric S. Connuck, *Sept. 11: What Is the Impact on the Insurers*, N.Y. Law J. 1 (Nov. 26, 2001).

8. Robert P. Hartwig, *One Hundred Minutes of Terror that Changed the Global Insurance Industry Forever*, Insurance Information Institute.

9. Finnerty & Connuck, supra note 7, at 1, 6.

10. Reidy, Carter & Tuer, *supra* note 2.

11. Finnerty & Connuck, *supra* note 7, at 1, 9.

resulting when other businesses are unable to provide necessary services to the insured.[12] Coverage in each instance is dependent on the precise wording of the policy involved. There is no simple answer.

In the first World Trade Center attack in 1993, the court of appeals said that, in spite of a lower court jury finding that the Port Authority was negligent in failing to listen to the warnings from its security experts that the center's underground garages could be targets of terrorists' attacks, the agency was entitled to the protection of sovereign immunity and could not be treated as a private landlord that had failed its duty to meet security obligations to tenants. The court made it clear that the agency had good reasons to believe it had to concentrate its security efforts in other places in the center. The court noted that the agency had engaged in "informed, policy-based decision making that entitles a governmental agency to immunity "and that "governmental entities cannot be expected to be absolute guarantors of public safety."[13] The court reasoned that, "if the essential nature of the governmental agency's injury-causing acts or omissions was a failure to provide security involving police resources—i.e., police protection—then a governmental function was being performed. Any failure to secure the parking garage against terrorist attack predominately derives from a failed allocation of police resources."[14]

Although there are many specific types of insurance coverage, typical insurance in commercial leasing transactions involves two types of broad coverage: property and liability. The tenant may be responsible for procuring these and additional types of coverage or endorsements depending on the nature of the tenancy, such as a "net" or "triple net" lease.

[1]—Property Coverage

[a]—Direct Losses

[i]—Insurance Types

Property insurance for a commercial lease generally encompasses fire insurance, fire and extended coverage, and "all-risk" insurance. This insurance includes such specialized coverages as boiler and machinery insurance and electronic data processing (EDP) insurance.

---

12. *Id.*

13. *See High Court Rules Port Authority Isn't Liable in '93 Bombing*, N.Y. Times, Sept. 23, 2011, http://www.nytimes.com/2011/09/23/nyregion/high-court-rules-port-authority-isnt-liable-in-93-bombing.html.

14. *See* AP, *N.Y. Court Backs Port Authority in '93 World Trade Center Bombing Case*, NJ.com, Sept. 22, 2011, http://www.nj.com/news/index.ssf/2011/09/ny_court_backs_transit_agency.html.

Property insurance pays claims directly to the insured party. As such, it is "first-party" insurance. Property insurance coverage is narrowly defined. The policies pay for only named, covered perils and generally exclude flood, earthquakes and hazardous waste coverage. These perils can be insured for in special riders, but they are expensive to obtain.

A common form of property coverage carried by landlords is a fire insurance policy with "extended coverage endorsement" (ECE). ECE perils are "named perils," that is, risks specifically listed in the policy. Typical ECE named perils are fire, smoke, explosion, windstorm, civil commotion, or hail. High-risk events such as nuclear explosions, state-sponsored terrorist attacks, and steam boiler and pipe explosions are excluded.

A very popular form of coverage in recent years is "all-risk" property insurance. It would now be unusual for any insured to purchase an ECE or other specified perils policy if an all-risk policy were available. In an all-risk policy, insurers are covered against all perils except those that are expressly and specifically excluded.[15] However, would the insured be covered for business losses resulting when its employees working in the World Trade Center vicinity failed or refused to return to work because they were too traumatized to do so? It remains to be seen whether and to what extent recent disasters and events will have on tenants' recovery rights under an all-risk policy.

There are four common but troublesome exclusions to the typical all-risk policy. These exclusions are (1) the "ordinance or law" clause, which generally denies coverage for losses due to the "enforcement of any ordinance or law regulating the construction, repair, demolition or condemnation of any building or structure"; (2) the "flood or earthquake" hazards clause, which also covers damage from surface water overruns, sewer and drain backups, or damage caused by subsurface waters under hydrostatic pressures; (3) the "computer-related or electronic data processing" damages clause; and (4) the "boiler and machinery" clause.[16] When one or more of these clauses are in force, the following events may not be covered by an all-risk policy: electronic disturbances (except when attributable to a sudden event such as lightning), mechanical breakdown and damages caused by sudden temperature changes, and damages caused by atmospheric conditions or extremes, to name but a few.

An all-risk policy may cover damages differently depending upon the circumstances. For instance, in the World Trade Center bombing of 1993, all-risk coverage paid for the cleaning of soot, dust, and electromagnetic residue on thousands of computers from the explosion and smoke generated from the blast but did not cover

---

15. All-risk exclusions may be similar to those situations not covered in an ECE or other specified perils policies, but the premise of the types of coverage is the opposite.

16. *See* Ferrell, Property and Liability Insurance in Lease Transactions at 4 (1991).

any subsequent mechanical breakdown of the computers from the accumulated soot if left untreated.

Natural disasters and calamities—hurricanes, natural disasters, high winds, flooding, and fires—require that professionals draft their documents to deal properly with property damage coverage to allow rebuilding and recovery.[17]

The Insurance Service Office, Inc. (ISO) promulgates forms for its underwriter clients, and these forms show customary form coverages as opposed to what can be provided by a manuscript policy.[18] The first two sets of letters and numbers identify the type of form and are usually consistent through many years (e.g., CP 10 30 04 02). The last two sets of numbers identify the year and month in which the form was promulgated. Leasing professionals should be careful about the dated forms since they periodically change.

The ISO Form CP 00 10 04 02 Building and Personal Property Coverage Form describes what is insured and what is not insured with generally three types of commercial property.

Property coverage varies despite the existence of standardized ISO forms. Coverage also depends upon what the parties negotiate. Usually, the landlord will bargain for the tenant to carry a contents policy with the landlord reserving its rights to carry its property coverage under a blanket policy if it owns several properties. Where the landlord is an insurance company or large net worth entity, it may bargain to self-insure its risk. In that instance as a self-insurer, the landlord acts as its own insurance carrier for the property and may have to establish reserves for losses. Alternatively, and less risky, the landlord may carry insurance but maintain a large deductible equal to a set amount of loss per incident.

The ISO form defines "Covered Property" as the "Building (including additions, permanent and outdoor fixtures and personal property used to maintain and service the building), Business Personal Property located in or on the Building or within 100 feet of the Building and Personal Property of others in the insured's care, custody or control."[19] "Business Personal Property" is defined to include furniture and fixtures, "stock," machinery and equipment and all other materials, and labor or services furnished or arranged by the insured or other party's personal property. For a tenant, "Business Personal Property" may also cover the permanent improvements the tenant has made in the building. One commentator has warned, however, that personal property or contents coverage may not include these "tenant improvements."[20] Even

---

17. Osborne et al., *Water, Wind, Quake and Pestilence: Property Insurance for Calamity*, ABA Real Property and Probate Conference (Spring 2012).

18. *Id.* at 1.

19. I.S.O. *Building and Personal Property Coverage Form*, § A.1.a.

20. *See* FERRELL, *supra* note 16.

if these improvements are included, coverage may be for an inadequate amount or reimbursed only for their unamortized or depreciated value rather than replacement value.[21]

Even though "Covered Property" has a broad meaning and most policies, as such, broadly describe covered personal property, the standard ISO policy may specifically exclude either a particular coverage or the amount of recovery elsewhere in the policy. An example would be boiler and machinery "objects" and perils that will typically be excluded under most policies and will need to be covered under a separate policy and a specialized type of coverage.

[ii]—Typical Policy Exclusions

A complete reading of the policy is necessary to know what is included or excluded and the amount of recovery that will be obtained in a loss.

As firms and companies become increasingly dependent upon computers and computer media for record retention and data processing, an insured should exercise a great degree of care in insuring for these losses in the event of a casualty at its premises. While "Covered Property" typically includes "valuable papers and records and computer equipment and media," there are coverage limitations with each. "Valuable papers and records coverage" will typically insure for the cost of replacing computer disks, CDs, and microfilm in blank form. However, it will not cover the expenses of reproducing the lost data on the microfilm, disk, or CD, a far more expensive process than the cost of replacing blank materials. Similarly, computer equipment and media will be covered, but with the several limitations of coverage attributable to the "specified perils" discussed elsewhere.

[b]—Indirect Losses

[i]—Usual Coverage

Loss coverage is usually only for direct losses under the general insuring agreement. There is no coverage for consequential or indirect losses. Thus, unless there is specific coverage for earnings losses, extra expenses, or the costs of replacing a favorable lease that is terminated as a result of a direct loss, there is no coverage for these costs and expenses.

There is another problem associated with indirect losses. Under most standard property policies, a covered direct loss must first trigger any indirect loss coverage a party may have. Direct damage coverage, however, is usually limited to property that the insured owns at the scheduled premises. If the circumstances that trigger indirect

21. *Id.*

loss originate from an incident that occurs off the insured's premises or from property not owned by the insured, the insured will not be able to recover for the indirect losses. For example, a fire in an adjoining anchor store in a shopping mall may result in an insured tenant losing a substantial amount of customer traffic leading to a substantial loss of resulting revenues. The insured, however, will not recover lost revenues unless it has contingent business interruption coverage.[22]

In some instances, indirect damages may not trigger coverage for business interruption or extra expense coverage. An example of this problem may arise when a business suffers damage to its computer system. The largest extent of damage attributable to a computer-related peril generally falls into the category of indirect damages—that is, damages to the data stored within the memory of the physical equipment itself. However, because the insured may not be able to collect on its direct damages, the business interruption or extra expense coverage that would constitute the overwhelming portion of an insured's loss due to a computer-related disaster may not be triggered. To avoid such consequences, the insured may negotiate to delete the applicable exclusions, particularly with respect to the EDP-related losses or the insured may obtain a separate EDP policy specifically addressing these scenarios.[23]

[ii]—Miscellaneous Alternative Coverages

Several types of contingent or indirect loss coverages are tied into lease transactions. Each covers an insured for revenue losses from a disruption of business from a casualty, be it an interruption in the rent stream or in other sources of income. "Business interruption coverage" is similar to "rents coverage," but the former is often more speculative than the latter. Landlords and tenants often negotiate over which party will carry the rent coverage or rent interruption insurance. The relative ease of collecting on a rent's coverage claim compared to submitting a business interruption claim is part of the reason for trying to obtain rents coverage.

Tenants will look to "extra expense" coverage to compensate them for additional rental expenses if temporary premises are necessary while the leased premises are being renovated or restored following a casualty. The extra expense coverage will reimburse the tenant only for the duplicative rents incurred as a result of the loss. These reimbursements will be offset by any rent abatements the tenant has negotiated at the original premises.

In drawing upon extra expense coverage, both landlord and tenant should consider all the factors that constitute "rent." In the typical gross lease found in most

22. *Id.*
23. *Id.* at 11.

commercial buildings, the insurer's definition of "rent" excludes the tenant's portion of taxes, operating expenses, common area expenses, and amortized work allowances.

"Leasehold interest insurance" would fill this gap and cover the instances where the tenant suffers the loss of a favorable lease when the landlord elects its cancellation rights under a damage and destruction clause of the lease. This coverage regards the leasehold as a valuable asset and reimburses the tenant for the difference in rent it would pay in replacement premises over the more favorable lease that was terminated. The calculation is for net extra rents—that is, it would include the expected (presumably favorable) costs in unexercised option periods in the original contract, while offsetting any favorable investment in a new lease (rent abatements, for example) that a tenant may negotiate in a new contract.

[2]—Property Endorsements

Endorsements cover the specific perils not usually covered in an all-risk or other inclusionary policy. Typical endorsements include:

- *Specific perils*—provides for specific inclusions in the coverage, such as the EDP records coverage.
- *Rental income insurance*—provides coverage in a business policy for the loss of rents due to a covered loss.
- *Plate glass insurance*—covers damage to the glass described in the policy schedule and to the lettering and ornamentation separately described in the endorsement from covered perils. This type of endorsement is very expensive to obtain. Even though it usually applies only to a retail lease, office tenants are still required to carry it.
- *Vandalism endorsement*—covers willful and malicious damages to the insured's property. It may be necessary due to the relief from liability that landlords typically want in the event of theft at the premises. Most tenants do not realize that they have assumed the risk for property losses from theft or vandalism since the exculpatory clause is usually buried in the rules and regulations section rather than in the main body of the lease.
- *Agreed amount endorsement*—works like a "friendly" liquidated damages provision. The insurance company agrees to pay an undisputed stated amount in the event of a loss. The difficulty occurs in ascertaining the amount at the time the endorsement is obtained, especially taking into consideration the replacement value of the lost property at the time of the occurrence of a possible loss.
- *Inflation or replacement value endorsement*—may be the possible solution to the problem in the previous endorsements in determining the value of a loss at

time of occurrence. This endorsement will automatically increase the amount of property loss coverage to reflect the increased replacement cost of the building or premises.

- *Changed conditions endorsement*—covers perils not usually insured in an all-risk policy, including the expenses that an insured may incur due to building code regulations enacted after the original construction and to which the insured must comply if it does any additional alterations.
- *Contractual liability*—covers the insured for any indemnity obligations to which it has agreed in the lease. It assures the indemnified party that it will receive the contracted protection to which the insured has obligated itself under a lease indemnification provision. This endorsement is more typical of a liability rather than a property policy.
- *Rent or business interruption*—serves two purposes. First, it covers a landlord for the interruption of its rental income stream due to a casualty loss and, conversely, covers a tenant for any resulting business losses from the same event. Second, if correctly drafted, it avoids the problems associated with such losses being uncovered indirect losses, although this coverage may vary from policy to policy.

[3]—Liability Coverage

[a]—In General

Liability insurance, also known as commercial general liability (CGL), public liability, and comprehensive general liability insurance, pays claims to the injured party and not the insured. Due to this feature, it is known as third-party insurance. Both landlord and tenant will insist that the other carry a CGL policy with, quite possibly, the other party being listed as an insured on the other's policy.

Coverage is more extensive under a liability policy than under the previously described property policies since a liability policy insures for both the third party's bodily injuries and property losses. Under the 1986 ISO CGL policy currently in use today, "bodily injury" refers to sickness, disease, or death, as well as physical injury. "Property damage" refers to physical injury to tangible property, including the loss of use of property that is either physically damaged or still intact but unusable due to the injury or casualty.

[b]—Claims-Made Coverage

CGL coverage insures against losses that occur while the policy is in place, even if the event or action that triggers the loss occurs prior to the effective date of the coverage.

Because coverage is determined based on whether the liability policy is in effect when the claim is made, it is known as a "claims-made policy."[24]

Under claims-made coverage, the insured and claimant avoid the exercise of going back in time to identify the policy in effect at the time of the injury. The insurer, on the other hand, incurs the risk that it will have to pay out on claims submitted during the coverage period that occurred years before the policy began. The injured party may not know it has a loss until sometime after the event or may not know the full extent of its losses until months or even years after the incident. Moreover, even after the claim has been identified and losses reasonably ascertained, the insured and injured party may spend a considerable period negotiating the loss before it is presented to an insurance carrier.[25]

Usually, a CGL policy includes contractual liability coverage. Contractual liability coverage is broad, and a leased premises may fall under one of the covered insured contracts. But contractual liability coverage is also typically complicated and should be examined for its exclusions. This coverage may also create various defenses, raise enforcement issues, and exceed policy limits, thereby limiting the coverage anticipated when the lease was negotiated. Because of these complexities, most parties negotiate to have the other named as an insured or other beneficiary under its liability policy.[26]

[c]—Common Beneficiary Designation

[i]—Named Insured

The "named insured" is the party who pays the premiums and is specifically designated by name as the insured in the policy. If a landlord bargains for this designation in a tenant's policy, the insurer can hold the landlord jointly responsible with the tenant for the payment of premiums.

---

24. The claims-made policy is to be distinguished from the occurrence policy. Under an occurrence policy, the injury or damage must have happened during the period in which the coverage was in effect. In an occurrence policy, the parties will look to the policy in effect at the time of injury or damage when the claim is later brought, even if that policy has subsequently lapsed.

25. This is one of the main reasons why the occurrence basis policy still predominates over claims-made coverage even though there are instances such as directors and officers and errors and omissions liability where claims-made policies predominate.

26. Landlord and tenant may negotiate to have the right to access the other party's liability policy. This can be done in two ways, the first being under the CGL contractual liability coverage and the second by including the other as an insured or other beneficiary under its liability policy.

[ii]—Additional Insured

Alternately, the landlord may wish to be named an "additional insured" under the policy. An additional insured has less protection than a named insured but has no obligations under the policy and is not responsible for paying premiums.[27]

Named insured and additional named insured status for a stranger to the policy will result in an adjustment of premiums since the insurer is effectively writing two policies. The insurer will want to include the risk record of the landlord or tenant requesting such designation in evaluating the policy. The premiums will most likely increase.

An additional insured endorsement specifies its coverage and is subject to the limits of the named insured's policy. It results in the named insured's insurance carrier providing the additional insured a defense to claims by injured parties due to injuries arising out of the covered aspects of the relationship between the named insured and additional insured. It works to shift to the named insured the risk of loss due to injuries caused wholly or partially by the named insured's operations, ownership, or use of the premises.[28] The intent for naming a party as an additional insured is the perceived fairness of making the named insured's carrier responsible for the increased exposure of the additional insured due to then named insured's operations.

[iii]—Loss Payee

The last common designation is the "loss payee." The loss payee is the party to whom payment is made. A loss payee receives neither the benefits nor the responsibilities that a named, additional, or additional named insured incurs, but is simply the recipient of payments from a claim or loss.

[4]—Additional Insured

[a]—In General

Increasingly, landlords are requiring that they be added as additional insureds on their tenants' liability insurance coverage relating to the tenants' premises and operations or activities on the premises. However, the value of the coverage clearly depends on the insurance policy language. A careful review of the policy before losses occur is important to assure that the coverage desired is in fact provided for. All too often, a party is merely added as an additional insured. The party added fails to review the policy. Then, when a claim arises, it is discovered that coverage is inadequate

27. Together with "hold harmless clause" protection in the lease, additional insured status is a powerful contractual protection from lease liability. Each works hand in hand with the other since additional insured status alone is responsive only to limits and extent of the CGL policy accessed.

28. Bill Locke, Jr., *The Most Common yet Most Misunderstood Risk Management Tool—The Additional Insured Endorsement*, 26(2) ACREL News 8–11 (May 2008).

or subject to an exclusion or limitation. Thus, care should be taken when a tenant is obligated to name a landlord as an additional insured since the provision may be unenforceable if it is a veiled attempt to relieve the landlord from liability for damages caused by the landlord where a statute voids a landlord's attempt to exempt itself from its own negligence.[29]

There is a hierarchy to additional beneficiary status. Each has its own benefits and responsibilities. Insurers will frequently require that a party be designated as an "additional named insured." The additional named insured frequently is treated as a named insured for policy exclusions but may not be accorded the same benefits as an additional insured. CGL policies usually have exclusions that apply only to named insureds but not to an additional insured. Thus, the latter may actually have more protection under the policy than the party that takes out the policy and is paying the premiums. Moreover, underwriters typically are less likely to include a party as an additional named insured, making the inclusion of the party more difficult from the onset.[30]

With that in mind, no one should simply rely on a certificate of insurance stating that he or she is an additional insured under the relevant policy. Instead, it is important to review the policy itself to assure coverage adequacy and to reveal exclusions, conditions, or endorsements that may significantly impact the additional insured's coverage rights and entitlements.[31]

Changes in the industry endorsements forms for additional insureds may have the effect of limiting coverage to the additional insured. Changes in 2013 resulted in modifications to the additional insured endorsement form that limit the coverage provided to additional insureds.[32] The limits of the additional insured's coverage will not exceed the limit of the insurance coverage that the tenant or contractor is required to maintain in the lease or construction contract, and the naming of a party as an additional insured in a tenant's or contractor's policy may not be enough to give a landlord or property owner comfort in being adequately protected as an additional insured. The landlord or property owner must require that its contract or lease require the tenant or contractor keep CGL insurance with sufficiently high enough limits and coverage types to completely cover what the additional insured endorsement is intended to protect.[33]

---

29. Radius v. Newhouse, 624 N.Y.S.2d 227 (App. Div. 1995), referring to N.Y. Gen. Oblig. Law § 5-321.

30. Ferrell, *supra* note 16, at 25.

31. Gregory J. May, *Don't Let Your Additional Insured Coverage Be a Mystery*, Law 360 (Apr. 12, 2013).

32. The current versions of the additional insured forms are included below, in this section. For an excellent summary of the 2013 changes, see Marie A. Moore, *New Insurance Forms Have Impact on Additional Insureds*, Retail Law Strategist—The Problem-Solving Tool for Retail Law (Spring 2014).

33. *Id.* at 1.

By way of background, the additional insured endorsement form used to protect lessors has changed over the past decades. In 1985, for example, the ISO CG 20 10 11 85, the additional insured endorsement used for construction contracts, stated that the party named in the endorsement was also considered to be an insured under the insured's policy regarding liability arising out of activities of the named insured or on the named insured's behalf.[34] By 2004, this protection was limited and covered only the additional insured for liability caused in whole or in part by the named insured's actions or omissions or by those acting on the named insured's behalf. Note that the owner's own sole negligence and the sole negligence of other contractors were no longer covered by the contractor's insurance.[35] The endorsement forms for lessors have also changed with limitations put into effect in 1996. These changes cover the additional insured for liability and now exclude occurrences taking place after the named insured ceases being a tenant in the premises and structural alterations, new construction, or demolition operations performed by or on behalf of the additional insured or manager.[36]

The additional insured forms promulgated in 2013 continue this limitation of protection provided to the additional insured and include the following forms: Additional Insured—Designated Person or Organization Endorsement,[37] Additional Insured—Managers or Lessors of Premises,[38] Additional Insured—Owners, Lessees or Contractors—Scheduled Person or Organization,[39] and Additional Insured—Owners, Lessees or Contractors—Automatic Status When Required In Construction Agreement.[40] These forms amend in each instance who is an insured in Section II and limit such coverage to "liability for bodily injury, property or personal and advertising injury caused in whole or part by the acts or omissions of those acting on behalf of the Insured and is limited by (i) permitted by law; and (ii) the amount of contractual coverage required to be provided to the additional insured."[41] In the CG 20 11 04 13 endorsement, insurance does not apply to any occurrence taking place after the insured ceases to be a tenant in the premises or structural alterations, new construction, or demolition activities performed by or on behalf of the additional insured.

---

34. *Id.*
35. *Id.*
36. *Id.* at 2. ISO CG 20 11 01 96.
37. ISO CG 20 26 04 13.
38. ISO CG 20 11 04 13.
39. ISO CG 20 01 04 13.
40. ISO CG 20 33 04 13.
41. These forms are copyrighted by and proprietary to Insurance Services Office, Inc. ("ISO Material") and are included in this publication. Use of the ISO Material is limited to ISO Participating Insurers and their Authorized Representatives. Use by ISO Participating Insurers is limitedto use in those jurisdictions for which the insurer has an appropriate participation with ISO.Use of the ISO Material by Authorized Representatives is limited to use solely on behalf of one or more ISO Participating Insurers.

POLICY NUMBER:

COMMERCIAL GENERAL LIABILITY
CG 20 10 04 13

THIS ENDORSEMENT CHANGES THE POLICY. PLEASE READ IT CAREFULLY.

ADDITIONAL INSURED – OWNERS, LESSEES OR CONTRACTORS – SCHEDULED PERSON OR ORGANIZATION

This endorsement modifies insurance provided under the following:

COMMERCIAL GENERAL LIABILITY COVERAGE PART

SCHEDULE

Name Of Additional Insured Person(s) Or Organization(s)	Location(s) Of Covered Operations
Information required to complete this Schedule, if not shown above, will be shown in the Declarations.	

A. Section II – Who Is An Insured is amended to include as an additional insured the person(s) or organization(s) shown in the Schedule, but only with respect to liability for "bodily injury", "property damage" or "personal and advertising injury" caused, in whole or in part, by:

1. Your acts or omissions; or

2. The acts or omissions of those acting on your behalf;

in the performance of your ongoing operations for the additional insured(s) at the location(s) designated above.

However:

1. The insurance afforded to such additional insured only applies to the extent permitted by law; and

2. If coverage provided to the additional insured is required by a contract or agreement, the insurance afforded to such additional insured will not be broader than that which you are required by the contract or agreement to provide for such additional insured.

B. With respect to the insurance afforded to these additional insureds, the following additional exclusions apply:

This insurance does not apply to "bodily injury" or "property damage" occurring after:

1. All work, including materials, parts or equipment furnished in connection with such work, on the project (other than service, maintenance or repairs) to be performed by or on behalf of the additional insured(s) at the location of the covered operations has been completed; or

2. That portion of "your work" out of which the injury or damage arises has been put to its intended use by any person or organization other than another contractor or subcontractor engaged in performing operations for a principal as a part of the same project.

POLICY NUMBER:

COMMERCIAL GENERAL LIABILITY
CG 20 10 04 13

THIS ENDORSEMENT CHANGES THE POLICY. PLEASE READ IT CAREFULLY.

ADDITIONAL INSURED – OWNERS, LESSEES OR CONTRACTORS – SCHEDULED PERSON OR ORGANIZATION

This endorsement modifies insurance provided under the following:

COMMERCIAL GENERAL LIABILITY COVERAGE PART

SCHEDULE

Name Of Additional Insured Person(s) Or Organization(s)	Location(s) Of Covered Operations
Information required to complete this Schedule, if not shown above, will be shown in the Declarations.	

A. **Section II – Who Is An Insured** is amended to include as an additional insured the person(s) or organization(s) shown in the Schedule, but only with respect to liability for "bodily injury", "property damage" or "personal and advertising injury" caused, in whole or in part, by:

1. Your acts or omissions; or
2. The acts or omissions of those acting on your behalf;

in the performance of your ongoing operations for the additional insured(s) at the location(s) designated above.

However:

1. The insurance afforded to such additional insured only applies to the extent permitted by law; and
2. If coverage provided to the additional insured is required by a contract or agreement, the insurance afforded to such additional insured will not be broader than that which you are required by the contract or agreement to provide for such additional insured.

B. With respect to the insurance afforded to these additional insureds, the following additional exclusions apply:

This insurance does not apply to "bodily injury" or "property damage" occurring after:

1. All work, including materials, parts or equipment furnished in connection with such work, on the project (other than service, maintenance or repairs) to be performed by or on behalf of the additional insured(s) at the location of the covered operations has been completed; or
2. That portion of "your work" out of which the injury or damage arises has been put to its intended use by any person or organization other than another contractor or subcontractor engaged in performing operations for a principal as a part of the same project.

POLICY NUMBER: XXX 1111111 00

COMMERCIAL GENERAL LIABILITY
CG 20 26 04 13

THIS ENDORSEMENT CHANGES THE POLICY. PLEASE READ IT CAREFULLY.

ADDITIONAL INSURED – DESIGNATED PERSON OR ORGANIZATION

This endorsement modifies insurance provided under the following:

COMMERCIAL GENERAL LIABILITY COVERAGE PART

SCHEDULE

Name Of Additional Insured Person(s) Or Organization(s):
Unigroup, Inc. c/o Ebix BPO P.O. Box 881639, San Diego, CA 92168-1639
Information required to complete this Schedule, if not shown above, will be shown in the Declarations.

A. **Section II – Who Is An Insured** is amended to include as an additional insured the person(s) or organization(s) shown in the Schedule, but only with respect to liability for "bodily injury", "property damage" or "personal and advertising injury" caused, in whole or in part, by your acts or omissions or the acts or omissions of those acting on your behalf:

1. In the performance of your ongoing operations; or
2. In connection with your premises owned by or rented to you.

However:

1. The insurance afforded to such additional insured only applies to the extent permitted by law; and
2. If coverage provided to the additional insured is required by a contract or agreement, the insurance afforded to such additional insured will not be broader than that which you are required by the contract or agreement to provide for such additional insured.

B. With respect to the insurance afforded to these additional insureds, the following is added to **Section III – Limits Of Insurance:**

If coverage provided to the additional insured is required by a contract or agreement, the most we will pay on behalf of the additional insured is the amount of insurance:

1. Required by the contract or agreement; or
2. Available under the applicable Limits of Insurance shown in the Declarations;

whichever is less.

This endorsement shall not increase the applicable Limits of Insurance shown in the Declaration.

The most common error, though, is for the additional insured to not specify the coverage terms that need to be contained in the additional insured endorsement. The typical wording of an insurance clause and ultimate scope of coverage are left to the named insured's insurance carrier.[42] When an additional insured fails to specify more than a generic "additional insured" coverage, the named insured's insurer has the option of picking between the available ISO forms or issuing a manuscripted form that effectively can eliminate or condition the coverage for the additional insured.[43] The most frequently used ISO endorsement forms are ISO Form CG 20 10 Additional Insured—Owners, Lessees or Contractors—Scheduled Person or Organization and ISO Form CG 20 11 Additional Insured—Managers or Lessors of Premises. These forms specify coverage occurrences and certain exclusions from coverage.

As another example, an AIG manuscripted additional language endorsement covers additional insureds but excludes "any negligent acts committed by such additional insured." The exclusion effectively eliminates all liabilities from coverage that the additional insured would expect or want as an additional insured.[44] Where the premises are not within the exclusive use of one party or are maintained by another (e.g., common area facilities), it makes sense to tailor the additional insured endorsement to exclude common facilities maintained by others.

These examples illustrate the peril in resorting to a "one size fits all" approach and the additional insured concept is not fully understood by the parties. Parties may list others as additional insureds that would better rely on their own CGL insurance than be listed as additional insureds on another's policy.[45]

[b]—Policy Limits

Policy limits provide another constraint on coverage. Even if a landlord or tenant obtains preferred status on the other party's policy, claims will be subject to whatever policy limits the insured contracted for with the carrier.

The 1986 CGL policy added a policy aggregate for insured incidences. Like its predecessors, the 1986 CGL contains "per occurrence" limits. Unlike the prior policies, the new CGL pays out claims subject to a total policy limit called the "general aggregate." For the landlord who is an additional insured under the policy of its tenant or any other party, its ability to collect under a liability policy is subject to the

42. Moore, *supra* note 32.

43. *Id.*

44. *Id.* at 10.

45. *Id.* at 11. For a more extensive examination of this topic, see Locke, Jr., *Additional Insured Endorsements to Liability Policies: Typical Defects and Solutions*, submitted to American College of Real Estate Lawyers, 2008 Mid-year Meeting (March 2008).

remaining coverage under the CGL's limits. Umbrella (or excess layer) policies will cover liability losses that exceed the insured party's primary CGL's liability policy's aggregate limits. Coverage under the umbrella policy is triggered after the primary or precedent policy's aggregate coverage is exceeded.

Umbrella policies serve to reduce premium costs. As insurance coverage becomes more expensive and difficult to obtain and there exists a good probability that an insured will not be covered for a significant portion of an expected or actual loss, landlords and tenants frequently work with one another to obtain two or more policies to assure their reimbursement from casualty losses. The umbrella policies kick in after the primary insurance limits have been reached. These excess policies provide the same coverage as primary policies but increase the primary policies' limits at lower premium costs. Surplus insurance is also available to cover high and substandard risks, such as flood and earthquake losses, not normally insured for in the usual property or liability policies.

[5]—Self-Insurance/Captive Insurance Companies

In the typical commercial lease, the landlord will require that the tenant carries a minimum amount of general liability insurance (e.g., per occurrence and general aggregate) and that the insurance carrier meets certain minimum standards, "such as a minimum policyholder rating and financial size (as rated by an agency such as AM Best)."[46] Although most tenants obtain insurance from a commercial insurance company, some tenants will request the right to "self-insure"[47] or to insure through the use of a "captive insurance company."

[a]—Self-Insurance

Typically, the "most predictable losses of the risk are retained and self-insured, forming a first or 'working' layer of cover, and a stop-loss or stop-gap policy is purchased from a commercial insurance company."[48] In such instances, the commercial insurance company pays for losses above the specified self-insurance limit per loss, serving as a "stop-gap," limiting the insured's costs.

---

46. Levin, *The Use of a Captive Insurance Company by a Commercial Tenant*, Commercial Leasing Law & Strategy 1 (Law Journal Newsletters Dec. 2010).

47. See § 11.02[1][c] Negotiating and Drafting Commercial Leases (hereafter "Commercial Leases").

48. Levin, *supra* note 46, at 1, 5.

[b]—Captive Insurance Companies

In general, a captive insurance company is a "wholly owned subsidiary that insures or reinsures only the risks of its parent company and its affiliates,[49] although a captive insurance company sometimes insures risks of the group's customers as well."[50] Captive insurance is a risk management technique under which a company "forms its own insurance company subsidiary to finance its retained losses in a formal structure."[51] A "single-parent captive" insures the risks of its noninsurance parent or affiliates. Whichever form it takes, a captive insurance company essentially provides a form of self-insurance and offers the owner "an opportunity to stabilize premium payments, address policyholder needs and address cost-prohibitive, or unavailability of, insurance coverage."[52] Captive arrangements also enable business owners to exercise control over claims and provide other advantages as compared to other types of coverage. These include underwriting and investment income and tax planning, asset protection, and estate planning benefits.[53]

Frequently, when a captive is set up, a "fronting agreement" (also known as a reinsurance agreement) will also be put into place.[54] A fronting agreement is an "agreement between the captive and a commercial insurance company, licensed in the state where the risk to be insured is located, under which the insurance company agrees to issue a policy to the insured."[55] Via the fronting agreement, the risk is transferred from the fronting company to the captive. "The end result is that the risk of coverage lies with the captive, but the insurance policy is issued on the paper of the commercial insurance company."[56] Essentially, the captive covers claims against the insured, and the fronting company acts as a backstop to cover amounts, up to the policy limit, in excess of what the captive can cover.[57] If no fronting agreement exists, the captive issues the policies and certificates in its own name as the insurer.[58]

---

49. Mark Koogler, *Can you afford the risk of not having a captive insurance company?*, Federal Securities Law Source (June 5, 2014).
50. Levin, supra note 46, at 1, 5.
51. *Id.*
52. Koogler, *supra* note 49.
53. *Id.*
54. *Id.*
55. *Id.*
56. *Id.*
57. *Id.*
58. *Id.* at 6.

[c]—Landlord's Concerns and Protections

While using a self-insurance plan (SIP) or a captive can be advantageous for a tenant in terms of lower premiums, more control over its insurance program, and more efficient claims management, it can raise certain concerns for a landlord.[59]

The landlord's major concern is the financial risk undertaken by the tenant (and guarantor, if any), especially when the tenant does not obtain a commercial insurance policy. Since insurance from a third-party carrier typically has a deductible associated with the policy, the deductible is the maximum amount that the insured will have to pay in on any covered claims. That means that the insured's financial risk is clearly delineated and limited.

For example, landlords like to limit the financial risk assumed by a tenant that self-insures or insures through a captive. "If a tenant self-insures without a stop-gap policy, or sets up a captive without a reinsurance agreement, the tenant (or its parent company) is essentially self-funding the entire insurance amount and thus is at risk for the entire amount of any claims, not just the amount of the deductible or self-insured retention."[60] In those instances, "the landlord should be especially concerned about, and carefully review the financial strength of the tenant and the entity funding the captive . . . [to determine] whether or not the SIP or captive is sufficiently funded to cover any potential claims brought against the insured."[61]

A landlord should also require a fronting arrangement if a large number of claims can be filed against the tenant in any one year that could drain the captive of its assets.[62] Such is unlikely to happen when coverage is obtained through a third-party carrier.

If the tenant obtains its liability coverage through use of a SIP and has a stop-gap policy in place, "the landlord should require a limit on the insured's self-insured retention. For example, if the landlord requires the tenant to carry $3 million of general liability insurance, the landlord may limit the self-insured retention to $1 million," capping the tenant's exposure at $1 million with the third-party carrier covering the balance of the claims up to any policy limit.[63] The landlord should also require the right to review SIP documentation from time to time to make sure that the SIP is sufficiently funded.[64]

"If the tenant obtains its liability coverage through the use of a captive and a fronting agreement exists when the lease is signed, the insurance provisions of the

59. *Id.*
60. *Id.*
61. *Id.*
62. *Id.*
63. *Id.*
64. *Id.*

lease should require that the fronting agreement remain in place throughout the term of the lease and that the certificates of insurance identify the commercial insurance carrier as the insurer."[65] If the fronting agreement is terminated or expires during the lease term, the tenant should be required to obtain its coverage from a carrier that meets the criteria set forth in the lease.[66]

If the tenant chooses "to self-insure and does not carry a stop-gap policy or if the captive does not have an agreement with a fronting company and will not agree to enter into such an agreement, the insurance provisions of the lease must be modified accordingly. One solution is to set a minimum net worth (or minimum capital and surplus) for the tenant (in the case of a SIP) or the captive, and a minimum net worth for the party that funds the captive."[67] The landlord should make the determination as to the appropriate net worth after reviewing the financial statements of all relevant parties. The landlord will need the right to receive and review financial statements for the tenant, the captive, and the party funding the captive throughout the term of the lease in order to confirm that the net worth/capital and surplus test(s) are being met.[68]

All of these and other issues should be discussed with the landlord's risk manager or insurance adviser.

[d]—Sample Lease Provision

The following is a sample lease provision under which the lease guarantor funds the captive:

> Tenant shall have the right to maintain the commercial general liability coverage required above through an affiliated entity, a captive insurance company, XYZ, Inc., a corporation ('XYZ'); provided that: (i) XYZ at all times maintains at least ________________________Dollars ($) in total capital and surplus; and (ii) Guarantor at all times maintains a tangible net worth of at least _________________Dollars ($). In the event that: (i) Tenant no longer obtains the commercial general liability insurance required above through XYZ or (ii) XYZ fails to meet the aforementioned capital and surplus test; or (iii) Guarantor fails to meet the aforementioned net worth test, Tenant shall obtain such coverage through an insurer with a policyholder rating of at least A– and a financial size category of at least Class VIII as rated in the most recent edition of 'Best's Key Rating Guide' for insurance companies. Within fifteen (15) days after delivery of written request from Landlord, Tenant will furnish XYZ's most recent audited financial statements

65. *Id.*
66. *Id.*
67. *Id.*
68. *Id.*

(including any notes to them) to Landlord or, if no such audited statements have been prepared, such other financial statements (and notes to them) as may have been prepared by an independent certified public accountant or, failing those, XYZ's internally prepared financial statements certified by an authorized officer of XYZ. Tenant and XYZ will also discuss XYZ's financial statements with Landlord, or Landlord's representative, as reasonably necessary.[69]

[e]—Conclusion

The landlord can generally be comfortable that the tenant will maintain the required coverage throughout the term of the lease if a tenant obtains its liability insurance from a third-party carrier, particularly one that meets the landlord's rating and size requirements, assuming the tenant pays its premiums.[70] "If a tenant requests or requires the right to self-insure its liability coverage, particularly the right to do so through a captive insurance company, a landlord must do its due diligence to understand the implications of allowing the tenant to do so rather than procuring such insurance through a traditional third-party insurance carrier."[71] A proper due diligence investigation should include "a thorough review of the financial statements for the tenant, the captive and the entity that funds the captive."[72] Additionally, the landlord should consult its insurance broker and/or risk manager as early as possible so that any concerns or problems can be resolved.

[6]—Post 9/11 Changes

[a]—Generally

There has been a considerable change in policy types since 9/11. Basically, the WTC tragedy has resulted in a revamping of the insurance industry. Policies are viewed with a new perspective. Premiums have risen dramatically. Insurers more carefully consider whom they want to insure and who is too great a risk. They also offer more limited coverage in terms of scope and payment amount.

Reinsurers have refused coverage for risks associated with future terrorism activities in the United States. Primary insurers have followed suit. Many reinsurance treaties expired at the end of 2001. As a result, President George W. Bush signed into law the Terrorism Risk Insurance Act of 2002 (TRIA) on November 26, 2002.[73] The

69. *Id.* at 6–7.
70. *Id.* at 7.
71. *Id.* at 8.
72. *Id.*
73. Pub. L. No. 107-297, 116 Stat. 2322. See this chapter [7] *infra* for a discussion of the Act.

Act, originally expiring on December 31, 2005, was extended for two years by the Terrorism Risk Insurance Extension Act of 2005 (TRIEA),[74] and extended again on December 26, 2007. The current law, the Terrorism Risk Insurance Program Reauthorization Act, expired on December 31, 2014.

With increased premiums and decreased coverage, landlords and tenants will have to consider alternative means to protect their interests. Additionally, clear wording of the insurance coverage requirements in the lease will be key in determining responsibility. Courts will not read into the lease a requirement that is not there, especially such a costly requirement as obtaining terrorism insurance.[75]

[b]—Policies and Coverage

Before 9/11, the best policy a commercial insured could purchase was the "all-risk" policy. There are now three types of policies that the ISO has promulgated: the basic form (CP 10 10), broad form (CP 10 20), and special form (CP 10 30). The ISO policy form is the standard used in the insurance industry. Each policy form has certain exclusions, and additional coverage can be obtained through endorsements.[76] Manuscript policies, which are individualized policies created for a particular client, may be developed by an agent or broker representing an insurance company and may be broader than the standard ISO form.

The basic form (CP 10 10) is sometimes called "fire and extended coverage" and provides direct damage coverage for the repair and replacement of property damaged by a specific covered cause of loss.[77] It includes the tenant's use interest in improvements and betterments that the tenant paid to make a part for the building it occu-

---

74. Terrorism Risk Insurance Extension Act of 2005, S. 467, 109th Cong., 1st Sess. (2005). See this chapter [7] *infra* for a discussion of TRIA and TRIEA.

75. In a New York case, *TAG 380 LLC v. ComMet 380, Inc.*, New York Law Journal, p. 22, col. 1 (N.Y.. App. Div. Feb. 20, 2007), the court refused to extend the lease's insurance coverage provision to require terrorism insurance. The New York Appellate Division reversed a lower court finding and held that 1989 lease that required the tenant to acquire insurance covering "fire, explosion and physical contact of an aircraft" with the property did not extend to require coverage for damage resulting from acts of terrorism. The court reasoned that an insurance policy "should not be extended beyond its plain meaning to include perils not specifically covered by its provisions." *Id.* The fact that damage due to one cause of terrorism would be covered does not mean that all acts of terrorism will be covered. Physical contact with an aircraft could be due to the aircraft's malfunction, pilot error or an act of terrorism, or perhaps some other cause. The lease provision requiring insurance covered an event (contact of an aircraft) without regard to the cause. Terrorism, specifically, was not covered by the provision, and the court refused to extend the required coverage to terrorist acts, which would be beyond the requirements of the lease.

76. Remarks of Stephen C. Mixter, Esq., Jones Day at American Bar Association's Spring Meeting, Apr. 3, 2003, and CoreNet Global Summit, Oct. 13, 2003.

77. Arthur E. Pape, *Selected Insurance Issues Affecting Leases of Real Property Insurance Basics/McCreary's Real Estate Review*, NEGOTIATING COMMERCIAL LEASES (2007).

pies and cannot remove legally.[78] The basic form only covers losses from 14 specified causes: fire, lighting, explosion, smoke, windstorm, hail, riot, civil commotion, aircraft, vehicles, vandalism, sprinkler leakage, sinkhole collapse, and volcanic eruption.[79] This form specifically excludes coverage for loses attributable to ordinance or law, earth movement, governmental action, nuclear hazard, loss of utility services, war and military action, and water.[80]

The next more comprehensive policy, the ISO Form CP 10 20 Causes of Loss—Broad Form, provides named perils coverage for the perils insured under the basic form plus five additional causes:[81] glass breakage; falling objects; weight of snow, ice, or sleet; water damages (sudden incidents); and collapse from certain specified causes. The exclusions under the broad form are the same as under the basic form.

The Special Form ISO Form CP 10 30 Causes of Loss—Special Form replaces the former all-risk coverage. It is the most commonly issued policy and provides coverage for losses from all causes that are not specifically excluded. This form is also referred to as special extended coverage. The form clarifies the misconception that had been associated with all-risk coverage and provides coverage for "direct damage from [covered perils] . . . except as otherwise excluded."[82] The excluded perils are the same as under the basic form, and an insured can obtain additional coverage by specific endorsements. Specifically excluded from coverage are the following perils: (1) ordinance or law, (2) earth movement, (3) governmental action, (4) nuclear hazard, (5) utility services, (6) war and military action, and (7) water. The damage that results from a fire or explosion is covered for some of the excluded perils.[83] This would include earth movement resulting from a fire and explosion or a nuclear hazard, which may occur following a fire. Floods, surface water, mudslides, sewerage backups, waves, and tides are examples of sources for which the water exclusion would apply.[84]

Policyholders can expand their coverage with several endorsements. Some important endorsements under the CP 10 30 include business income, extra expense, extended period of indemnity coverage, leasehold interest (which covers losses by a tenant due to cancellation of a favorable lease due to damage to the leased premises caused by a covered cause of loss),[85] service interruption, ordinance or law (under

78. *Id.*
79. *Id.* at 5; Mixter, *supra* note 76.
80. Mixter, *supra* note 76.
81. Pape, *supra* note 77, at 5.
82. *Id.* at 6.
83. *Id.*
84. *Id.*
85. *Id.* at 8.

ISO CP 04 05, which provides coverage for losses caused by the enforcement of ordinances or laws regulating the construction and repair of damaged buildings), prevention of ingress and egress and act of civil authority, contingent business interruption, and debris removal.

Regardless of the policy or the loss, so-called NBC (nuclear, biological, or chemical) events are not covered.[86] Before 9/11, policies did not have a specific exclusion for terrorist acts.[87] As these pre-9/11 policies expire or come up for renewal, almost all of the new policies issued will exclude at least certain terrorist acts.

"Terrorism" is defined by the ISO as "activities against persons, organizations, or property of any nature that involves the following: Use or threat of force or violence; or commission or threat of a dangerous act; or commission or threat of an act that interferes with or disrupts an electronic, communication, information or mechanical system; and when one or both of the following apply: (a) The effect is to intimidate or coerce a government or the civilian population or any segment thereof; or to disrupt any segment of the economy; or (b) it appears that the intent is to intimidate or coerce a government or to further political, ideological, religious, social or economic objectives or to express (or express opposition to) a philosophy or ideology."[88]

[7]—The Terrorism Risk Insurance Act of 2002 (TRIA) and Subsequent Extensions and Acts

In response to the wider-spread exclusion of the risk of "terrorist acts," Congress passed TRIA in November 2002, ensuring that businesses would be provided with terrorism insurance at reasonable rates. "TRIA created a federal program that provided a system of public and private compensation for certain insured losses that resulted from a certified act of terrorism. The Secretary of Treasurer is responsible for program administration with the assistance of the Federal Insurance Office. Under TRIA, insurance agreements that contain exclusionary clauses for terrorist attacks are void for the duration of the federal program."[89] TRIA voided any insurance policies' exceptions for coverage of foreign terrorist acts occurring in the United States that met specified conditions and were certified as such.[90] The Act prohibited insurance

86. Mixter, *supra* note 76.

87. *Id.*

88. *Id.*

89. Bock & Steiner, *A Primer on Terrorism Insurance*, Commercial Leasing Law & Strategy 7 (LJN Dec. 2005).

90. Remarks of Jo-Ann Marzullo at the American Bar Association Spring Meeting, Apr. 2003, and CoreNet Global Summit, Oct. 13, 2003.

companies from offering only a sublimit for such terrorism coverage.[91] TRIA did not cover wars (except for workers' compensation claims) or acts resulting in property and casualty losses not exceeding $5 million, in the aggregate, from being certified as an act of terrorism.[92] The Act established a temporary program under which the federal government would share the risk of insured losses from certified acts of terrorism with commercial property and casualty insurers until the program expired on December 31, 2005. However, TRIEA extended the Act through 2007, with some changes.[93]

The 2005 extension legislation "focused primarily on reducing the government's upfront financial exposure under the act by increasing the program trigger, increasing the insurer deductible, reducing the government's share of losses, and increasing the post-event mandatory recoupment of federal share."[94] TRIA, as extended by TRIEA, required all commercial property and insurance companies to offer foreign terrorism coverage and provides federally funded protection for insurers if losses exceed certain amounts. TRIA went into effect on November 26, 2002, and, as such, did not cover losses from 9/11.[95] It covers all losses certified by the Secretary of the Treasury resulting from terrorist activities that are dangerous to "human life, property or infrastructure in the United States, on U.S. air carriers, vessels, missions, committed by an individual or individuals acting on behalf of any foreign person or as part of an effort to coerce the civilian population of the United States, or to influence the political conduct of the U.S. Government by coercion" and that result in at least $5 million in insured losses (not during an act of declared war except for workers' compensation).[96] Such acts constitute certified acts of terrorism and are covered by the terms of TRIA. The Act did not, however, cover domestic terrorism defined as a terrorist act committed on behalf of any U.S. person or interest.

Under TRIA, "commercial property insurers are required to offer terrorism insurance on the same terms that apply to their coverage of other types of losses. However, the U.S. Treasury would reimburse 90% of certified insured losses (beyond a relatively small deductible amount) from acts of terrorism until total losses reach $100

---

91. Pub. L. No. 107-297, § 103, 116 Stat. 2322. The Terrorism Risk Insurance Extension Act of 2005 (TRIEA) extended the Act through 2007, with some changes. Terrorism Risk Insurance Extension Act of 2005, S. 467, 109th Cong., 1st Sess. (2005).

92. *Id.*

93. Terrorism Risk Insurance Extension Act of 2005, S. 467, 109th Cong., 1st Sess. (2005).

94. Coleman, Gorrell & Dinh, *Congress Agrees on Six-year Reauthorization of Terrorism Risk Insurance Act (TRIA)*, Government Relations Alert (Jan. 8, 2015), ***available at*** http://ehoganlovells.com/rv / ff001ca03fe26425500464d6864db7abbbeb94eb.

95. Pub. L. No. 107-297, § 103, 116 Stat. 2322.

96. *Id.*

billion in a year and to take responsibility for the entire amount of losses beyond that threshold."[97] In effect, the government has become the "world's largest reinsurer."[98]

TRIA also excluded reimbursement to insurers for a portion of a certified loss over $100 billion. The definition of terrorism in Section 102 was narrow, and only losses attributable to a terrorist event are recoverable under the Act. The Act was intended to ensure the continued availability of commercial property and casualty insurance for terrorism risk and to allow the markets to stabilize after 9/11. NBC events were excluded from general coverage under TRIA, and where states still required coverage regardless of cause, this mandatory coverage applied despite exclusions or sublimits for terrorist acts.[99] Final Treasury Regulations were issued during 2003 and 2004.[100] New York took the position like several other states that sublimits should be only for special events and not required to be offered to all property owners. New York's classifications for the use and amount of sublimits included building characteristics, occupancy, and measures used by the insured to mitigate its terrorist exposure.[101] According to one commentator, Georgia has advised its insurers that "[Georgia] will waive its requirements for supporting documentation for rates for certified losses for filings that do not increase the premium charges for any policyholder by more than 1.5%."[102]

TRIA did not deal with domestic terrorism and left open how to deal with destruction of major buildings in the largest cities, which exceeds the maximum amount of federal backstop.[103] TRIA left to the states whether the premiums are excessive, which is still an issue with the highest risk properties.[104] The Act required insurers increasingly to carry the risk going from 7 percent to 10 percent and finally 15 percent of premiums received until the program expired on December 31, 2005.[105] Under TRIEA, that amount increased to 17.5 percent in 2006 and 20 percent in 2007. However, the annual program cap of $100 billion (combined federal and industry shared insured losses) that existed under TRIA remained the same. Some other notable changes included the following:

---

97. Robert Higgs, *Terrorism Risk Insurance Act to Be Extended, of Course*, INDEPENDENT INSTITUTE (Dec. 9, 2005), *available at* http://www.independent.org/newsroom/article.asp?id=1635.

98. *Id.* (citing a 2004 comment by the General Accounting Office).

99. *Id.*

100. *See* 69 Fed. Reg. 39296 (June 29, 2004); 68 Fed. Reg. 59715 (Oct. 17, 2003); 68 Fed. Reg. 48280 (Aug. 12, 2003); 68 Fed. Reg. 41250 (July 11, 2003).

101. *See* 69 Fed. Reg. 39296 (June 29, 2004); 68 Fed. Reg. 59715 (Oct. 17, 2003); 68 Fed. Reg. 48280 (Aug. 12, 2003); 68 Fed. Reg. 41250 (July 11, 2003).

102. *See* Ga. Bulletin 02-Ex-3 (Dec. 19, 2002).

103. Marzullo, *supra* note 90. *See* N.Y. Circular Letter No. 25 (2002).

104. *Id.*

105. *Id.*

- There is a more limited range of coverage. For example, commercial automobile, professional liability (except director and officer liability), surety, burglary and theft, and farm-owners multi-peril are no longer covered under TRIEA.
- A trigger amount is imposed—$50 million in 2006 and $100 million in 2007. Under TRIA there was no loss trigger requirement.
- The federal share of insured losses excluding a deductible had been 90 percent under TRIA. Under TRIEA, the amount remained 90 percent for 2006, but decreased to 85 percent in 2007.
- The mandatory post-event recoupment of the federal share under TRIA was the difference between $15 billion and the aggregate insurer retention. Under TRIEA, the $15 billion figure is raised to $25 billion for 2006 and $27.5 billion for 2007.[106]

The bottom line when it comes to post-9/11 coverage is that an insured could be subject to extensive federal and state regulation.

Whether a party to the lease would be required to obtain terrorism insurance depended in large part on the specific language of the parties' agreement and what they contemplated when they signed the agreement. Many leases required the maintaining of all-risk insurance. However, since 9/11, all-risk policies had been excluding terrorism from coverage. Separate policies, often quite expensive, did cover terrorism. The question arises of whether the tenant would be required to obtain the additional insurance. All-risk—or causes of loss, as they are now known—policies change over time as new or different risks are recognized. Language could require the tenant to maintain insurance at industry standard, which would obligate the tenant to do what is commonly done in the industry.[107] The lease can state that the coverage must continue to the extent it exists when the lease is signed, and then the court would look to the policy requirements and coverage at the time the lease was signed. Later exclusions would have to be covered under a new policy.[108]

Note that there has been a recognized distinction between a cause and the resulting effect of a loss.[109] If a specific peril is covered, then the resulting loss would be covered as well. However, the same loss will not be covered if the cause of that loss is specifically excluded. In other words, if a fire results from an electrical malfunction, an enumerated cause in the lease, the damage caused by the electrical fire will be covered. However, if the lease specifically excludes terrorist acts, the fire caused by

106. *See* Congressional Budget Office Cost Estimate, S. 467 Terrorism Risk Insurance Extension Act of 2005 as passed by the Senate on Nov. 18, 2005 (Dec. 14, 2005).

107. Schafler & Landrey, *Terrorism Insurance: Pact Language Rules Duty to Buy*, N.Y. LAW J. 4, 7 (Aug. 29, 2007).

108. *Id.*

109. See *id.* for a detailed discussion of the cause-and-effect concept.

terrorists will not be covered. It is the cause that must be clearly set forth as a covered event. If a specific cause is covered, then the effect or resulting damage will be covered.

[8]—Terrorism Risk Insurance Program Reauthorization Act of 2007

On December 26, 2007, then-President George W. Bush signed the Terrorism Risk Insurance Program Reauthorization Act of 2007 (the 2007 Act), making some significant changes to the initial Terrorism Risk Insurance Act. The 2007 Act "essentially maintained the prior TRIA program, but it made several significant changes. The legislation accelerated the post-event mandatory recoupment of federal share and expanded the program to cover losses from domestic acts of terrorism in addition to foreign acts of terrorism."[110] The 2007 Act extended the temporary federal program providing for a transparent system of shared public and private compensation for insured losses that result from acts of terrorism. Changes to the initial Act include

- revision of the definition of a "certified act of terrorism," eliminating the requirement that the individual(s) act on behalf of any foreign person or foreign interest;
- extension of the program through December 31, 2014;
- requirement of a clear and conspicuous notice to policyholders of a $100 billion cap;
- imposition of a fixed insurer deductible based on 20 percent of an insurer's direct earned premium, and a reduction of the federal share of compensation to 85 percent of insured losses exceeding the insurer's deductibles;
- imposition of a program trigger fixed at $100 million for all additional program years;
- requirement that the U.S. Treasury promulgate regulations for determining pro rata shares of insured losses under the program when insured losses are in excess of $100 billion;
- requirement that the Comptroller General study and report on the availability and affordability of insurance coverage for losses caused by terrorist attacks involving nuclear, biological, chemical, or radiological materials no later than one year after the enactment of the Terrorism Risk Insurance Program Reauthorization Act of 2007;
- requirement that the Comptroller General determine and report within 180 days of the enactment of the 2007 Act on whether there are specific U.S.

110. Coleman, Gorrell & Dinh, *supra* note 94.

markets in which there are unique capacity constraints on the amount of terrorism insurance available;
- requirement that the President's Working Group on Financial Markets to conduct ongoing study of the long-term availability and affordability of terrorism risk insurance; and
- an acceleration of the timing of the mandatory recoupment of the federal share through policyholders' surcharges.[111]

The U.S. Department of the Treasury also implemented the program and provided updated information on its website about the program, including announcements of all rulemakings, interpretive guidance, and requests for public comments.[112]

Under the terms of the 2007 Extension Act, an eligible insurer is: "any entity or affiliate that:

- "Is a recipient of direct earned premiums for any type of commercial property and casualty insurance coverage.
- "Is licensed (or admitted) to provide insurance in any State, approved for the purpose of offering property and casualty insurance by a Federal agency in connection with maritime, energy, or aviation activity, or is a State residual market insurance entity or State workers' compensation fund
- "And meets any other criteria that the Secretary may reasonably prescribe."[113]

The program was triggered following the occurrence of an event determined by Secretary of the Treasury to be an act of terrorism.[114] Losses had to exceed $50 million in 2006 and $100 million in 2007, and the trigger or deductible for an individual company would be 17.5 percent of premiums in 2006 and 20 percent in 2007.[115]

Under the terms of the Act, the industry as a whole had to cover $15 billion in 2005, $25 billion in 2006, and $27.5 billion in 2007 of the losses before any federal assistance was available.[116] Such federal assistance is capped at $100 billion per year. The difference between this amount and the aggregate amount that insurers must pay (e.g., deductibles and copayments) can be recouped from commercial policyholders.[117]

When the program was triggered, the federal government would pay 90 percent of the insured terrorism losses that exceed individual insurer trigger/deductibles and the insurer would be responsible for the remaining 10 percent.[118] In 2007, the

111. *See* http://www.govtrack.us/congress/bill.xpd?bill=h110-2761&tab=summary.
112. *Id.*
113. *See* http://en.wikipedia.org/wiki/Terrorism_Risk_Insurance_Act.
114. *Id.*
115. *Id.*
116. *Id.*
117. *Id.*
118. *Id.*

insureds contribution increased to 15 percent, and the government remained responsible for the reduced amount of 85 percent.[119]

Further, under the 2007 Act, recoupment of assistance was subject to a surcharge of up to 3 percent of annual premiums on all policyholders.[120] However, the Secretary of the Treasury has discretion to recoup additional amounts.[121] Insurers had to offer terrorism insurance in all commercial policies for the first two years, and such coverage had to be available on the same terms and in the same amounts and with the same coverage limitations applicable to losses incurred from events other than acts of terrorism.[122] Under the 2007 Act, insurers were required to disclose terrorism insurance premiums and the existence of the federal backstop.[123]

Punitive damages did not constitute insured losses under the terms of the 2007 Act and thus are not the subject of federal participation.[124] Civil monetary penalties of $100 million could be imposed against insurers for failing to pay assessments or surcharges, for providing erroneous data, or for violation of regulations.[125]

[9]—TRIA's Program Reauthorization through 2027

On January 8, 2015, the House of Representatives passed H.R. 26, the Terrorism Risk Insurance Program Reauthorization Act of 2015, by a vote of 416–5, and on January 9, 2015, the Senate passed H.R. 26 by a 93–4 vote. President Barack Obama signed the law on January 12, 2015, reauthorizing TRIA until December 31, 2020.[126]

That law "incrementally raise[d] the trigger for reinsurance coverage under the program from $100 million to $200 million beginning in 2016, along as increasing insurers' co-pays from 15 to 20 percent and raising the federal government's mandatory recoupment from $27.5 billion to $37.5 billion. The reauthorization also required additional reporting from the insurance industry beginning in 2016, concerning the market for terrorism coverage, including premiums earned, location of exposures, and the market for private reinsurance for terrorism coverage. Likewise, in 2016 the Secretary of the Treasury was required to report to Congress on the overall effectiveness of the program."[127] "In addition to renewing the insurance program, the law provided for the creation of the National Association of Registered Agents

119. *Id.*
120. *Id.*
121. *Id.*
122. *Id.*
123. *Id.*
124. *Id.*
125. *Id.*
126. Coleman, Gorrell & Dinh, *supra* note 94.
127. Joshua D. Davey & Alec Covington, *President Signs TRIA Reauthorization into Law* (Jan. 13, 2015), available at https://www.mondaq.com/unitedstates/reinsurance/368372/president-signs-tria-reauthorization-into-law.

and Brokers (NARAB), which was made up of state insurance commissioners and insurance market representatives. NARAB was intended to streamline the licensing process for registered insurance agents and brokers, and help insurance agents and brokers operate on a multistate basis."[128]

TRIA was extended for a fourth time under the Terrorism Risk Insurance Program Reauthorization Act of 2019 (TRIPRA of 2019) and is scheduled to expire on December 31, 2027. This bill reauthorizes the Terrorism Risk Insurance Program within the Department of the Treasury through 2027. Among the additions to the program, the Government Accountability Office (GAO) is required to report on insurance coverage of cyberterrorism.

[10]—Evidencing That Coverage Exists

The most common method of evidencing insurance coverage is through a certificate of liability or property coverage. The standard forms of certificates are published by ACORD, a not-for-profit insurance association. The ACORD 25-5 contains a number of disclaimers that do not create contractual obligations or rights.[129] The holder of the certificate has no rights against a carrier.

The ACORD 27 and 28 forms are designed to cover property insurance only, with no prohibitions existing against modifying the forms to include liability coverage. The ACORD 28 form, effective January 2004, like the ACORD 27 for, contains an area on the form for types and amounts of property coverage protecting the insured and any other additional interests but is more comprehensive than the ACORD 27 in its descriptions and categories and also contains areas for business income and rental value coverage, blanket equipment breakdown, ordinance of law, earth movement, flood, and wind/hail coverage (which are normally excluded from traditional all-risk type coverages) and enumerates terrorism insurance and mold coverage. It is a much more detailed and comprehensive version of prior forms.

The ACORD 27 and 28 forms once contained representations that there was "evidence that insurance as identified below has been issued, and conveys all the rights and privileges afforded under the policy," but now contain the disclaimer that "This evidence of commercial property insurance is issued as matter of information only and confers no rights upon the additional interest named below. This evidence does not affirmatively or negatively amend, extend or alter the coverage afforded by the policies below."

---

128. *Id.*

129. Alfred S. Joseph III & Arthur E. Pape, *Certificates of Insurance: The Illusion of Protection*, Probate & Property (Jan./Feb. 1995).

The ACORD 28 has had a somewhat tortured history. Successor to the ACORD 24 "Certificate of Property Insurance," the ACORD 28 revised in 2003 in collaboration with the Mortgage Bankers Association was short lived and revised on July 28, 2006. It mirrored the ACORD 27's language that "conveys all the rights and privileges afforded under the policy" and requires issuers to give written notice before canceling the policy. The insurance industry was concerned that the 2003 form potentially expanded the insurer's obligations beyond the policy's terms. However, when the form was revised in 2006, the new form substantially limited the ACORD 28's usefulness by stating it was "issued as a matter of information only and confer[ed] no rights upon the additional insured named below." Thus, while the 2003 ACORD 28 could be seen as evidence of insurance and could potentially bind the insurer for the information contained on the certificate, the revised ACORD 28 in 2006 did not convey that status on the certificate and, for all intents, bringing it back to the old ACORD 24.[130]

The current version of the ACORD 28 is of little value to mortgagees. On its face, it confers no rights and courts have generally held that this disclaimer is enforceable. A majority of states have enacted statutes or issued administrative bulletins to the effect that ACORD certificates cannot be modified, and generally courts have enforced disclaimers in certificates of insurance.[131] Freddie Mac has refused to accept the 2006 language since the form conflicts with the standard mortgagee loss payment endorsement requiring notice to the lender in case of policy cancellation.[132] Insurers argue that a policy can be changed only by an endorsement and not by a certificate. Furthermore, they claim a certificate cannot impose any further obligations upon the insurer and the statement on the ACORD that it is "for informational purposes only" is correct.[133] The new form that had previously been used by brokers and their insureds to provide "evidence" that the insured had insurance coverage identified by the form in effect now contains the statement that it is issued "as a matter of convenience only" and "confers no rights upon the additional insured named below" and "does not amend, extend or alter the coverage afforded by the policies" identified in the completed form.[134]

---

130. W. Rodney Clement, Jr., *Is a Certificate of Commercial Property Insurance a Worthless Document?*, Probate & Property 46–49 (May/June 2010). This publication incorporates licensed copyrighted or other proprietary material of ACORD Corporation. All rights reserved. Used with permission of ACORD Corporation. The name ACORD and the ACORD logo are registered marks of ACORD Corporation. This document and any opinions it may contain are solely the product of its author(s) and are neither endorsed, nor warranted, by ACORD

131. *Id.* at 48.

132. *Id.*

133. *Id.*

134. *See* Arthur E. Pape, *A Hot Tip and a Soup Sandwich*, Negotiating Commercial Leases: How Owners & Corporate Occupants Can Avoid Costly Errors, Vol. 2, pp. 83–118 (Spring 2009).

ACORD®

CERTIFICATE OF LIABILITY INSURANCE

DATE (MM/DD/YYYY)

THIS CERTIFICATE IS ISSUED AS A MATTER OF INFORMATION ONLY AND CONFERS NO RIGHTS UPON THE CERTIFICATE HOLDER. THIS CERTIFICATE DOES NOT AFFIRMATIVELY OR NEGATIVELY AMEND, EXTEND OR ALTER THE COVERAGE AFFORDED BY THE POLICIES BELOW. THIS CERTIFICATE OF INSURANCE DOES NOT CONSTITUTE A CONTRACT BETWEEN THE ISSUING INSURER(S), AUTHORIZED REPRESENTATIVE OR PRODUCER, AND THE CERTIFICATE HOLDER.

IMPORTANT: If the certificate holder is an ADDITIONAL INSURED, the policy(ies) must have ADDITIONAL INSURED provisions or be endorsed. If SUBROGATION IS WAIVED, subject to the terms and conditions of the policy, certain policies may require an endorsement. A statement on this certificate does not confer rights to the certificate holder in lieu of such endorsement(s).

PRODUCER	CONTACT NAME:	
	PHONE (A/C, No, Ext):	FAX (A/C, No):
	E-MAIL ADDRESS:	
	INSURER(S) AFFORDING COVERAGE	NAIC #
	INSURER A :	
INSURED	INSURER B :	
	INSURER C :	
	INSURER D :	
	INSURER E :	
	INSURER F :	

COVERAGES **CERTIFICATE NUMBER:** **REVISION NUMBER:**

THIS IS TO CERTIFY THAT THE POLICIES OF INSURANCE LISTED BELOW HAVE BEEN ISSUED TO THE INSURED NAMED ABOVE FOR THE POLICY PERIOD INDICATED. NOTWITHSTANDING ANY REQUIREMENT, TERM OR CONDITION OF ANY CONTRACT OR OTHER DOCUMENT WITH RESPECT TO WHICH THIS CERTIFICATE MAY BE ISSUED OR MAY PERTAIN, THE INSURANCE AFFORDED BY THE POLICIES DESCRIBED HEREIN IS SUBJECT TO ALL THE TERMS, EXCLUSIONS AND CONDITIONS OF SUCH POLICIES. LIMITS SHOWN MAY HAVE BEEN REDUCED BY PAID CLAIMS.

INSR LTR	TYPE OF INSURANCE	ADDL INSD	SUBR WVD	POLICY NUMBER	POLICY EFF (MM/DD/YYYY)	POLICY EXP (MM/DD/YYYY)	LIMITS	
	COMMERCIAL GENERAL LIABILITY						EACH OCCURRENCE	$
	CLAIMS-MADE / OCCUR						DAMAGE TO RENTED PREMISES (Ea occurrence)	$
							MED EXP (Any one person)	$
							PERSONAL & ADV INJURY	$
	GEN'L AGGREGATE LIMIT APPLIES PER:						GENERAL AGGREGATE	$
	POLICY / PRO-JECT / LOC						PRODUCTS - COMP/OP AGG	$
	OTHER:							$
	AUTOMOBILE LIABILITY						COMBINED SINGLE LIMIT (Ea accident)	$
	ANY AUTO						BODILY INJURY (Per person)	$
	OWNED AUTOS ONLY / SCHEDULED AUTOS						BODILY INJURY (Per accident)	$
	HIRED AUTOS ONLY / NON-OWNED AUTOS ONLY						PROPERTY DAMAGE (Per accident)	$
								$
	UMBRELLA LIAB / OCCUR						EACH OCCURRENCE	$
	EXCESS LIAB / CLAIMS-MADE						AGGREGATE	$
	DED / RETENTION $							$
	WORKERS COMPENSATION AND EMPLOYERS' LIABILITY Y / N						PER STATUTE / OTH-ER	
	ANYPROPRIETOR/PARTNER/EXECUTIVE OFFICER/MEMBER EXCLUDED? (Mandatory in NH)	N / A					E.L. EACH ACCIDENT	$
	If yes, describe under DESCRIPTION OF OPERATIONS below						E.L. DISEASE - EA EMPLOYEE	$
							E.L. DISEASE - POLICY LIMIT	$

SAMPLE

DESCRIPTION OF OPERATIONS / LOCATIONS / VEHICLES (ACORD 101, Additional Remarks Schedule, may be attached if more space is required)

CERTIFICATE HOLDER	CANCELLATION
	SHOULD ANY OF THE ABOVE DESCRIBED POLICIES BE CANCELLED BEFORE THE EXPIRATION DATE THEREOF, NOTICE WILL BE DELIVERED IN ACCORDANCE WITH THE POLICY PROVISIONS.
	AUTHORIZED REPRESENTATIVE

ACORD 25 (2016/03)

ACORD®

EVIDENCE OF PROPERTY INSURANCE

DATE (MM/DD/YYYY)

THIS EVIDENCE OF PROPERTY INSURANCE IS ISSUED AS A MATTER OF INFORMATION ONLY AND CONFERS NO RIGHTS UPON THE ADDITIONAL INTEREST NAMED BELOW. THIS EVIDENCE DOES NOT AFFIRMATIVELY OR NEGATIVELY AMEND, EXTEND OR ALTER THE COVERAGE AFFORDED BY THE POLICIES BELOW. THIS EVIDENCE OF INSURANCE DOES NOT CONSTITUTE A CONTRACT BETWEEN THE ISSUING INSURER(S), AUTHORIZED REPRESENTATIVE OR PRODUCER, AND THE ADDITIONAL INTEREST.

AGENCY	PHONE (A/C, No, Ext):	COMPANY	
FAX (A/C, No):	E-MAIL ADDRESS:		
CODE:	SUB CODE:		
AGENCY CUSTOMER ID #:			
INSURED		LOAN NUMBER	POLICY NUMBER
		EFFECTIVE DATE / EXPIRATION DATE	CONTINUED UNTIL TERMINATED IF CHECKED
		THIS REPLACES PRIOR EVIDENCE DATED:	

PROPERTY INFORMATION

LOCATION/DESCRIPTION

THE POLICIES OF INSURANCE LISTED BELOW HAVE BEEN ISSUED TO THE INSURED NAMED ABOVE FOR THE POLICY PERIOD INDICATED. NOTWITHSTANDING ANY REQUIREMENT, TERM OR CONDITION OF ANY CONTRACT OR OTHER DOCUMENT WITH RESPECT TO WHICH THIS EVIDENCE OF PROPERTY INSURANCE MAY BE ISSUED OR MAY PERTAIN, THE INSURANCE AFFORDED BY THE POLICIES DESCRIBED HEREIN IS SUBJECT TO ALL THE TERMS, EXCLUSIONS AND CONDITIONS OF SUCH POLICIES. LIMITS SHOWN MAY HAVE BEEN REDUCED BY PAID CLAIMS.

COVERAGE INFORMATION PERILS INSURED BASIC BROAD SPECIAL

COVERAGE / PERILS / FORMS	AMOUNT OF INSURANCE	DEDUCTIBLE

REMARKS (Including Special Conditions)

CANCELLATION

SHOULD ANY OF THE ABOVE DESCRIBED POLICIES BE CANCELLED BEFORE THE EXPIRATION DATE THEREOF, NOTICE WILL BE DELIVERED IN ACCORDANCE WITH THE POLICY PROVISIONS.

ADDITIONAL INTEREST

NAME AND ADDRESS	ADDITIONAL INSURED	LENDER'S LOSS PAYABLE	LOSS PAYEE
	MORTGAGEE		
	LOAN #		
	AUTHORIZED REPRESENTATIVE		

ACORD 27 (2016/03)

ACORD®

EVIDENCE OF COMMERCIAL PROPERTY INSURANCE

DATE (MM/DD/YYYY)

THIS EVIDENCE OF COMMERCIAL PROPERTY INSURANCE IS ISSUED AS A MATTER OF INFORMATION ONLY AND CONFERS NO RIGHTS UPON THE ADDITIONAL INTEREST NAMED BELOW. THIS EVIDENCE DOES NOT AFFIRMATIVELY OR NEGATIVELY AMEND, EXTEND OR ALTER THE COVERAGE AFFORDED BY THE POLICIES BELOW. THIS EVIDENCE OF INSURANCE DOES NOT CONSTITUTE A CONTRACT BETWEEN THE ISSUING INSURER(S), AUTHORIZED REPRESENTATIVE OR PRODUCER, AND THE ADDITIONAL INTEREST.

PRODUCER NAME, CONTACT PERSON AND ADDRESS — PHONE (A/C, No, Ext):	COMPANY NAME AND ADDRESS — NAIC NO:
FAX (A/C, No): — E-MAIL ADDRESS:	IF MULTIPLE COMPANIES, COMPLETE SEPARATE FORM FOR EACH
CODE: — SUB CODE:	POLICY TYPE
AGENCY CUSTOMER ID #:	
NAMED INSURED AND ADDRESS	LOAN NUMBER — POLICY NUMBER
	EFFECTIVE DATE — EXPIRATION DATE — ☐ CONTINUED UNTIL TERMINATED IF CHECKED
ADDITIONAL NAMED INSURED(S)	THIS REPLACES PRIOR EVIDENCE DATED:

PROPERTY INFORMATION (ACORD 101 may be attached if more space is required) ☐ BUILDING OR ☐ BUSINESS PERSONAL PROPERTY

LOCATION / DESCRIPTION

THE POLICIES OF INSURANCE LISTED BELOW HAVE BEEN ISSUED TO THE INSURED NAMED ABOVE FOR THE POLICY PERIOD INDICATED. NOTWITHSTANDING ANY REQUIREMENT, TERM OR CONDITION OF ANY CONTRACT OR OTHER DOCUMENT WITH RESPECT TO WHICH THIS EVIDENCE OF PROPERTY INSURANCE MAY BE ISSUED OR MAY PERTAIN, THE INSURANCE AFFORDED BY THE POLICIES DESCRIBED HEREIN IS SUBJECT TO ALL THE TERMS, EXCLUSIONS AND CONDITIONS OF SUCH POLICIES. LIMITS SHOWN MAY HAVE BEEN REDUCED BY PAID CLAIMS.

COVERAGE INFORMATION PERILS INSURED ☐ BASIC ☐ BROAD ☐ SPECIAL

COMMERCIAL PROPERTY COVERAGE AMOUNT OF INSURANCE: $	YES	NO	N/A	DED:
☐ BUSINESS INCOME ☐ RENTAL VALUE				If YES, LIMIT: — Actual Loss Sustained; # of months:
BLANKET COVERAGE				If YES, indicate value(s) reported on property identified above: $
TERRORISM COVERAGE				Attach Disclosure Notice / DEC
IS THERE A TERRORISM-SPECIFIC EXCLUSION?				
IS DOMESTIC TERRORISM EXCLUDED?				
LIMITED FUNGUS COVERAGE				If YES, LIMIT: — DED:
FUNGUS EXCLUSION (If "YES", specify organization's form used)				
REPLACEMENT COST				
AGREED VALUE				
COINSURANCE				If YES, %
EQUIPMENT BREAKDOWN (If Applicable)				If YES, LIMIT: — DED:
ORDINANCE OR LAW - Coverage for loss to undamaged portion of bldg				If YES, LIMIT: — DED:
- Demolition Costs				If YES, LIMIT: — DED:
- Incr. Cost of Construction				If YES, LIMIT: — DED:
EARTH MOVEMENT (If Applicable)				If YES, LIMIT: — DED:
FLOOD (If Applicable)				If YES, LIMIT: — DED:
WIND / HAIL INCL ☐ YES ☐ NO Subject to Different Provisions:				If YES, LIMIT: — DED:
NAMED STORM INCL ☐ YES ☐ NO Subject to Different Provisions:				If YES, LIMIT: — DED:
PERMISSION TO WAIVE SUBROGATION IN FAVOR OF MORTGAGE HOLDER PRIOR TO LOSS				

CANCELLATION

SHOULD ANY OF THE ABOVE DESCRIBED POLICIES BE CANCELLED BEFORE THE EXPIRATION DATE THEREOF, NOTICE WILL BE DELIVERED IN ACCORDANCE WITH THE POLICY PROVISIONS.

ADDITIONAL INTEREST

☐ CONTRACT OF SALE ☐ LENDER'S LOSS PAYABLE ☐ LOSS PAYEE ☐ MORTGAGEE	LENDER SERVICING AGENT NAME AND ADDRESS
NAME AND ADDRESS	AUTHORIZED REPRESENTATIVE

SAMPLE

ACORD 28 (2016/03)

Recent ISO forms were adopted in 2012, making significant changes to provisions in the Commercial Property (CP) and Commercial General Liability (CGL) forms and endorsements. The CP 00 10 10 12 Building and Personal Property Coverage Form provides direct damage coverage for the repair or replacement of property damaged by a covered cause of loss. Like its predecessors, the form defines what is covered under building, business personal property, personal property of others, and property not covered.[135]

[a]—Business Personal Property Form (CP 00 10)

The Business Personal Property Form (CP 00 10) includes the tenant's use interest in improvements and betterments that the tenant paid to make a part of the building he or she occupies and cannot legally remove. The coverage also defines the extent coverage will apply to newly acquired property, property of premises, valuable papers and records, and property of others' outdoor property. Replacement cost coverage is indicated by a check box on the declarations page. The value of this coverage—if damaged tenant improvements are not repaired or replaced—is determined by the proportion of the tenant's original cost adjusted by the amount of time until the lease expiration or renewal.

135. Pape, *supra* note 77, at 2.

COMMERCIAL PROPERTY
CP 00 10 10 12

BUILDING AND PERSONAL PROPERTY COVERAGE FORM

Various provisions in this policy restrict coverage. Read the entire policy carefully to determine rights, duties and what is and is not covered.

Throughout this policy, the words "you" and "your" refer to the Named Insured shown in the Declarations. The words "we", "us" and "our" refer to the company providing this insurance.

Other words and phrases that appear in quotation marks have special meaning. Refer to Section **H.** Definitions.

A. Coverage

We will pay for direct physical loss of or damage to Covered Property at the premises described in the Declarations caused by or resulting from any Covered Cause of Loss.

1. Covered Property

Covered Property, as used in this Coverage Part, means the type of property described in this section, **A.1.**, and limited in **A.2.** Property Not Covered, if a Limit Of Insurance is shown in the Declarations for that type of property.

a. Building, meaning the building or structure described in the Declarations, including:

(1) Completed additions;

(2) Fixtures, including outdoor fixtures;

(3) Permanently installed:

(a) Machinery; and

(b) Equipment;

(4) Personal property owned by you that is used to maintain or service the building or structure or its premises, including:

(a) Fire-extinguishing equipment;

(b) Outdoor furniture;

(c) Floor coverings; and

(d) Appliances used for refrigerating, ventilating, cooking, dishwashing or laundering;

(5) If not covered by other insurance:

(a) Additions under construction, alterations and repairs to the building or structure;

(b) Materials, equipment, supplies and temporary structures, on or within 100 feet of the described premises, used for making additions, alterations or repairs to the building or structure.

b. Your Business Personal Property consists of the following property located in or on the building or structure described in the Declarations or in the open (or in a vehicle) within 100 feet of the building or structure or within 100 feet of the premises described in the Declarations, whichever distance is greater:

(1) Furniture and fixtures;

(2) Machinery and equipment;

(3) "Stock";

(4) All other personal property owned by you and used in your business;

(5) Labor, materials or services furnished or arranged by you on personal property of others;

(6) Your use interest as tenant in improvements and betterments. Improvements and betterments are fixtures, alterations, installations or additions:

(a) Made a part of the building or structure you occupy but do not own; and

(b) You acquired or made at your expense but cannot legally remove;

(7) Leased personal property for which you have a contractual responsibility to insure, unless otherwise provided for under Personal Property Of Others.

c. Personal Property Of Others that is:

(1) In your care, custody or control; and

(2) Located in or on the building or structure described in the Declarations or in the open (or in a vehicle) within 100 feet of the building or structure or within 100 feet of the premises described in the Declarations, whichever distance is greater.

From Selected Insurance Issues Affecting Leases of Real Property Insurance Basics/ McCreary's Real Estate Review at p. 2. Submitted by Pape, for Practising Law Institute's Negotiating Commercial Leases, Spring 2004 Program.

COMMERCIAL PROPERTY
CP 10 10 10 12

CAUSES OF LOSS – BASIC FORM

Words and phrases that appear in quotation marks have special meaning. Refer to Section **E.** Definitions.

A. Covered Causes Of Loss

When Basic is shown in the Declarations, Covered Causes of Loss means the following:

1. Fire.

2. Lightning.

3. Explosion, including the explosion of gases or fuel within the furnace of any fired vessel or within the flues or passages through which the gases of combustion pass. This cause of loss does not include loss or damage by:

a. Rupture, bursting or operation of pressure-relief devices; or

b. Rupture or bursting due to expansion or swelling of the contents of any building or structure, caused by or resulting from water.

4. Windstorm or Hail, but not including:

a. Frost or cold weather;

b. Ice (other than hail), snow or sleet, whether driven by wind or not;

c. Loss or damage to the interior of any building or structure, or the property inside the building or structure, caused by rain, snow, sand or dust, whether driven by wind or not, unless the building or structure first sustains wind or hail damage to its roof or walls through which the rain, snow, sand or dust enters; or

d. Loss or damage by hail to lawns, trees, shrubs or plants which are part of a vegetated roof.

5. Smoke causing sudden and accidental loss or damage. This cause of loss does not include smoke from agricultural smudging or industrial operations.

6. Aircraft or Vehicles, meaning only physical contact of an aircraft, a spacecraft, a self-propelled missile, a vehicle or an object thrown up by a vehicle with the described property or with the building or structure containing the described property. This cause of loss includes loss or damage by objects falling from aircraft.

We will not pay for loss or damage caused by or resulting from vehicles you own or which are operated in the course of your business.

7. Riot or Civil Commotion, including:

a. Acts of striking employees while occupying the described premises; and

b. Looting occurring at the time and place of a riot or civil commotion.

8. Vandalism, meaning willful and malicious damage to, or destruction of, the described property.

We will not pay for loss or damage caused by or resulting from theft, except for building damage caused by the breaking in or exiting of burglars.

9. Sprinkler Leakage, meaning leakage or discharge of any substance from an Automatic Sprinkler System, including collapse of a tank that is part of the system.

If the building or structure containing the Automatic Sprinkler System is Covered Property, we will also pay the cost to:

a. Repair or replace damaged parts of the Automatic Sprinkler System if the damage:

(1) Results in sprinkler leakage; or

(2) Is directly caused by freezing.

b. Tear out and replace any part of the building or structure to repair damage to the Automatic Sprinkler System that has resulted in sprinkler leakage.

Automatic Sprinkler System means:

(1) Any automatic fire-protective or extinguishing system, including connected:

(a) Sprinklers and discharge nozzles;

(b) Ducts, pipes, valves and fittings;

(c) Tanks, their component parts and supports; and

(d) Pumps and private fire protection mains.

(2) When supplied from an automatic fire-protective system:

(a) Non-automatic fire-protective systems; and

(b) Hydrants, standpipes and outlets.

From Selected Insurance Issues Affecting Leases of Real Property Insurance Basics/ McCreary's Real Estate Review at p. 2. Submitted by Pape, for Practising Law Institute's Negotiating Commercial Leases, Spring 2004 Program.

COMMERCIAL PROPERTY
CP 10 20 10 12

CAUSES OF LOSS – BROAD FORM

Words and phrases that appear in quotation marks have special meaning. Refer to Section **F.** Definitions.

A. Covered Causes Of Loss

When Broad is shown in the Declarations, Covered Causes of Loss means the following:

1. Fire.

2. Lightning.

3. Explosion, including the explosion of gases or fuel within the furnace of any fired vessel or within the flues or passages through which the gases of combustion pass. This cause of loss does not include loss or damage by:

a. Rupture, bursting or operation of pressure-relief devices; or

b. Rupture or bursting due to expansion or swelling of the contents of any building or structure, caused by or resulting from water.

4. Windstorm or Hail, but not including:

a. Frost or cold weather;

b. Ice (other than hail), snow or sleet, whether driven by wind or not;

c. Loss or damage to the interior of any building or structure, or the property inside the building or structure, caused by rain, snow, sand or dust, whether driven by wind or not, unless the building or structure first sustains wind or hail damage to its roof or walls through which the rain, snow, sand or dust enters; or

d. Loss or damage by hail to lawns, trees, shrubs or plants which are part of a vegetated roof.

5. Smoke causing sudden and accidental loss or damage. This cause of loss does not include smoke from agricultural smudging or industrial operations.

6. Aircraft or Vehicles, meaning only physical contact of an aircraft, a spacecraft, a self-propelled missile, a vehicle or an object thrown up by a vehicle with the described property or with the building or structure containing the described property. This cause of loss includes loss or damage by objects falling from aircraft.

We will not pay for loss or damage caused by or resulting from vehicles you own or which are operated in the course of your business.

7. Riot or Civil Commotion, including:

a. Acts of striking employees while occupying the described premises; and

b. Looting occurring at the time and place of a riot or civil commotion.

8. Vandalism, meaning willful and malicious damage to, or destruction of, the described property.

We will not pay for loss or damage caused by or resulting from theft, except for building damage caused by the breaking in or exiting of burglars.

9. Sprinkler Leakage, meaning leakage or discharge of any substance from an Automatic Sprinkler System, including collapse of a tank that is part of the system.

If the building or structure containing the Automatic Sprinkler System is Covered Property, we will also pay the cost to:

a. Repair or replace damaged parts of the Automatic Sprinkler System if the damage:

(1) Results in sprinkler leakage; or

(2) Is directly caused by freezing.

b. Tear out and replace any part of the building or structure to repair damage to the Automatic Sprinkler System that has resulted in sprinkler leakage.

Automatic Sprinkler System means:

(1) Any automatic fire-protective or extinguishing system, including connected:

(a) Sprinklers and discharge nozzles;

(b) Ducts, pipes, valves and fittings;

(c) Tanks, their component parts and supports; and

(d) Pumps and private fire protection mains.

(2) When supplied from an automatic fire-protective system:

(a) Non-automatic fire-protective systems; and

(b) Hydrants, standpipes and outlets.

From Selected Insurance Issues Affecting Leases of Real Property Insurance Basics/ McCreary's Real Estate Review at p. 2. Submitted by Pape, for Practising Law Institute's Negotiating Commercial Leases, Spring 2004 Program.

COMMERCIAL PROPERTY
CP 10 30 10 12

CAUSES OF LOSS – SPECIAL FORM

Words and phrases that appear in quotation marks have special meaning. Refer to Section **G.** Definitions.

A. Covered Causes Of Loss

When Special is shown in the Declarations, Covered Causes of Loss means direct physical loss unless the loss is excluded or limited in this policy.

B. Exclusions

1. We will not pay for loss or damage caused directly or indirectly by any of the following. Such loss or damage is excluded regardless of any other cause or event that contributes concurrently or in any sequence to the loss.

   a. Ordinance Or Law

   The enforcement of or compliance with any ordinance or law:

   (1) Regulating the construction, use or repair of any property; or

   (2) Requiring the tearing down of any property, including the cost of removing its debris.

   This exclusion, Ordinance Or Law, applies whether the loss results from:

   (a) An ordinance or law that is enforced even if the property has not been damaged; or

   (b) The increased costs incurred to comply with an ordinance or law in the course of construction, repair, renovation, remodeling or demolition of property, or removal of its debris, following a physical loss to that property.

   b. Earth Movement

   (1) Earthquake, including tremors and aftershocks and any earth sinking, rising or shifting related to such event;

   (2) Landslide, including any earth sinking, rising or shifting related to such event;

   (3) Mine subsidence, meaning subsidence of a man-made mine, whether or not mining activity has ceased;

   (4) Earth sinking (other than sinkhole collapse), rising or shifting including soil conditions which cause settling, cracking or other disarrangement of foundations or other parts of realty. Soil conditions include contraction, expansion, freezing, thawing, erosion, improperly compacted soil and the action of water under the ground surface.

   But if Earth Movement, as described in **b.(1)** through **(4)** above, results in fire or explosion, we will pay for the loss or damage caused by that fire or explosion.

   (5) Volcanic eruption, explosion or effusion. But if volcanic eruption, explosion or effusion results in fire, building glass breakage or Volcanic Action, we will pay for the loss or damage caused by that fire, building glass breakage or Volcanic Action.

   Volcanic Action means direct loss or damage resulting from the eruption of a volcano when the loss or damage is caused by:

   (a) Airborne volcanic blast or airborne shock waves;

   (b) Ash, dust or particulate matter; or

   (c) Lava flow.

   With respect to coverage for Volcanic Action as set forth in **(5)(a)**, **(5)(b)** and **(5)(c)**, all volcanic eruptions that occur within any 168-hour period will constitute a single occurrence.

   Volcanic Action does not include the cost to remove ash, dust or particulate matter that does not cause direct physical loss or damage to the described property.

   This exclusion applies regardless of whether any of the above, in Paragraphs **(1)** through **(5)**, is caused by an act of nature or is otherwise caused.

From Selected Insurance Issues Affecting Leases of Real Property Insurance Basics/ McCreary's Real Estate Review at p. 2. Submitted by Pape, for Practising Law Institute's Negotiating Commercial Leases, Spring 2004 Program.

[i]—Analysis of the Current Versions of the Form

The language in the Commercial Property Basic, Broad and Special forms now states:

b. Your Business Personal Property consists of the following property located in or on the building described in the Declarations or in the open (or in a vehicle) within 100 feet of the building or structure or within 100 feet of the premises described in the Declarations, whichever distance is greater.

c. Personal Property of Others that is "(1) In your care, custody or control; and
(2) Located in or on the building *or structure* described in the declarations or in the open (or in a vehicle) within 100 feet of the *building or structure or within 100 feet of the premises described in the declaration, which- ever distance is greater*. (Italics added for emphasis.)

[A]—Property Not Covered

Among the items excluded from coverage are accounts, bills, currency, food stamps, or other evidence of debt; automobiles held for sale; foundations of buildings, structures, machinery, or boilers if the foundations are below the lowest basement floor or surface of the ground if there is no basement; land; and electronic data except as provided under the Additional Coverage, Electronic Data definition. Electronic data refers to information, facts, or computer programs stored as or on, created or used on, or transmissions to or from computer software (including systems and appliances software), on hard or floppy disks, CD-ROMs, tapes, drives, cells data processing devices, or any other repositories of computer software that are used with electronically controlled equipment. Coverage also excludes the cost to replace or restore the information on valuable papers and records, including those that exist as electronic data, as well as most vehicles or self-propelled machines, such as aircraft or watercraft.

[B]—Covered Causes of Loss

The 2012 revisions slightly modify both the Causes of Loss—Basic Form and Causes of Loss—Broad Form from their prior 2007 versions. In Covered Causes, Windstorm or Hail coverage excludes loss or damage by hail to lawns, trees, shrubs, or plants that are part of a vegetated roof. In Covered Volcanic Action, the 2012 forms tie coverage to all volcanic action, defined as airborne volcanic blast or airborne shock waves, ash, dust, or particulate matter or lava flow to a 168-hour period constituting a "single occurrence."

In the Causes of Loss—Broad Form alone (since Weight of Snow, Ice, or Sleet is not a covered event in the Basic Form), Weight of Snow, Ice, or Sleet Coverage now excludes loss or damage to lawns, trees, shrubs, or plants that are part of a vegetated roof.

The Earth Movement Exclusion carried over from the 2007 forms for both Basic and Broad coverage has language that states that the exclusion applies to the listed categories regardless of whether any of the listed items are caused by an act of nature or are "otherwise caused." The Exclusion for Water damage adds a fifth category that also excludes from coverage any waterborne material carried or moved by mudslide or mudflow.

[C]—Causes of Loss Changes

The new CP 10 30 10 12 has reworked the form to delete the word "risk" and simply states that the policy's meaning of "covered cause of loss" is "direct physical loss unless the loss is excluded or limited in this policy." The 2007 form defined coverage as "Risks of Direct Physical Loss unless the loss was specifically excluded in the Exclusions section or limited in the Limitations section of the policy." Effectively, there is no change in coverage, but this may be an attempt to avoid over-extension of coverage by the courts. The new language in the Basic and Broad forms appears in the Causes of Loss, where applicable.

Prior to 1983, ISO used the term "all risks" to indicate the cause of loss form we have today, but courts said that the all-risk aspect was that all risks were covered. In the 1983 edition of the form, "all" was deleted, and the industry began using the term "risk of physical loss."

There is no change in the ordinance or law exclusion. The new wording just states that the exclusion applies to the enforcement of "or compliance with" (new wording) any ordinance or law. The term "compliance" indicates that the insured is voluntarily complying with the current law or ordinance so punitive "enforcement" is not required for the exclusion to apply.

A second change relating to ordinance or law is found in the increased cost of construction wording under Additional Coverage. The phrase "enforcement of" is replaced with "the minimum standards of." The provision recognizes the voluntary nature of complying with a jurisdiction's building codes. There is no change in coverage or intent.

Four types of property subject to sublimits now have an option for increasing the limit of coverage. Previously, the only way to increase coverage was by entry on the declarations page. These property types are:

- Electronic data ($2,500 basic aggregate limit)
- Newly acquired locations (for Business Income Coverage) ($100,000 per location basis limit)
- Interruption of computer operations (in Business Income forms) ($2,500 basis aggregate limit)
- Limitations for theft (allow an increase for all theft sublimits in the form)

Both the Causes of Loss—Basic Form (CP 10 10) and Causes of Loss—Broad Form (CP 10 20) add wording below the form title stating that words and phrases appearing in quotation marks have special meaning, and the forms refer the reader to the definitions section to read the definitions of the new terms.

Because of the growing trend in green building methods, ISO revised "Property Not Covered" to make exceptions for lawns, shrubs, and plants that are part of vegetated roofs. However, there are limits. For example, CP 10 13 specifies that there is no coverage for loss of vegetation caused by dampness or dryness of atmosphere or soil, extremes of temperatures, disease, frost, hail, rain, snow, ice, or sleet.[136]

The revised earth movement exclusion does not alter the breadth of coverage, but the reworded exclusion simply strengthens the intent to reinforce that earth movement is excluded regardless of the cause of the earth movement. Earthquake is also refined to include tremors and aftershocks.

The current wording in CP 10 32 Water Exclusion is included in the Causes of Loss Form. The change makes CP 10 32 unnecessary, and the endorsement should be withdrawn. There is no change in coverage with inclusion of the endorsement's wording into the Causes of Loss Form. The new wording differs in that water from tidal waves, tsunamis, and storm surge is specifically excluded. Damage from any water discharged from sewer, drain, sump pump, or related equipment is excluded. Damage from waterborne material carried in any way or moved by water or mudslide/mudflow is excluded, and the exclusion applies regardless of water source by nature or "otherwise."

ISO broadened coverage for entrusted property in the Causes of Loss Form (CP 10 13). The current wording excludes loss caused by anyone to whom the insured entrusts property and could be interpreted to exclude loss caused by tenants and bailees. The new wording differentiates between those persons who are part of the insured's business (managers, officers, employees, etc.) and "others" not part of the business (e.g., tenants and bailees). With the "others" the exclusion is limited to loss caused by theft, and the exception to the exclusion is revised to extend coverage to damage caused by authorized representatives (although theft is still excluded).

ISO broadened coverage for the wear and tear exclusion on the special form by redefining water damage within the defined phrase "specified causes of loss" found in CP 10 13. The wording adds coverage for accidental discharge of water as the direct result of the breaking or cracking of a municipal water or sewer system off the described premises. The breaking or cracking must be by wear and tear. The form clearly states that this broadened coverage does not extend to include losses excluded in the form's water exclusion.

In the Commercial Property program, there were 16 major policy form changes and 27 endorsement changes including new and revised endorsements.[137]

These include the following:

---

136. *See* Christopher J. Boggs, *ISO Commercial Property Changes Coming to a Carrier Near You—Parts 1 and 2* (Mar. 20, 2013).

137. *See Ask Mike #2103-02 ISO's New Commercial Property and CGL Changes.*

(1) Earth Movement Exclusion,
(2) Debris Removal,
(3) Fire Department Service Charge Coverage,
(4) Business Personal Property in Described Structures,
(5) Extended Business Income, Extended Period of Indemnification,
(6) Coverage Radius (broadens applicability of 100-feet limitation),
(7) Water Exclusion,
(8) Property in Storage Units,
(9) Entrusted Property,
(10) Vegetative Roofs,
(11) Electronic Data in Building Equipment,
(12) Newly Acquired Property,
(13) Ordinance or Law Exclusion,
(14) Wear and Tear Exclusion—Special form,
(15) Covered Causes of Loss in CP 10 30 "All Risks," and
(16) Options for Increasing Specified Limits.

Item 6 broadens coverage for commercial tenants by amending the 100-feet limitation to certain personal property. In the prior CP 00 10 06 07 form, coverage for Business Personal Property and Personal Property of others only applied to such property "in or on the building described in the declarations or in the open (or in a vehicle) within 100 feet of the described premises.[138] There has been considerable debate, especially for commercial tenants in multioccupancy buildings, about from where ("described premises") the 100-feet limitation is to be measured—that is, from the building they occupy or from their particular portion of the building? The ISO revision applies the 100-feet radius to the greater of either the distance from the building where the insured-commercial tenant is located or from the insured's specific premises. This broadens coverage for commercial tenants in strip malls and high-rises.[139]

[b]—Business Income and Extra Expense Form (CP 00 30) and Other Time Element Forms

The Business Income and Extra Expense Form (CP 00 30) is the most frequently used form.[140] The other time element forms for direct damage include the CP 00 32 Business Income Coverage Form Without Extra Expense, the CP 00 50 Extra

138. *Id.*
139. *Id.*
140. Pape, *supra* note 77, at 2.

Expense Form, and the CP 00 60 Leasehold Interest Coverage Form. These forms are considered to be "time element" because dollar amount of loss depends on how long it takes to repair or replace damaged property.[141]

The scope of coverage in the CP 00 30 follows the Causes of Loss Form insuring buildings or personal property that was damaged. Both forms cover the loss of income suffered by a business because of not being able to use property damaged by a covered cause of loss during the time required to repair or replace it.

Extra expense insurance covers expenses in excess of normal operating expenses that are incurred to continue after a direct damage loss. Another type of coverage, rental value insurance, protects the landlord and is included in the Business Income Form by selecting the appropriate coverage choice on the declarations page.

A tenant's coverage under CP 00 30 is triggered by damage to the portion of the premises that the tenant occupies or any area within the building or at the site that services or is used to gain access to an insured's space. Coverage is usually written for six or twelve months and can be for a longer period.[142]

[c]—Important Exclusions

There are several very important exclusions to bear in mind. Both mold and terrorism are now commonly excluded from coverage, although insureds can purchase coverage for terrorism (ISO endorsements IL 09 41 or IL 09 40 Exclusion of War Military Action and Terrorism) for use with commercial property policies) and IL 09 42 for use with boiler and machinery policies have been adopted by 38 states as of January 1, 2002.[143]

While there are no ISO-approved endorsements, some companies are attaching exclusions for damage from mold or fungus attack.[144] Frequently, exclusions for water damage from leakage or seepage extending beyond 14 days eliminate coverage for mold damage to a building. Some types of fungi can appear within 48 hours of water release and may make it necessary to remove significant portions of the building.[145] Insureds should be aware that the usual exclusion for water damage that extends from leakage and seepage continuing beyond 14 days will typically eliminate mold damage coverage.[146]

---

141. *Id.*

142. *Id.*

143. See sections 10.04[4][e] and 25.02[8] *supra* for discussions of insurance coverage for mold; see Chapter 3[4] and [5] Commercial Leases *supra* for a discussion of terrorism coverage.

144. *Id.*

145. Pape, *supra* note 77, at 2.

146. *Id.*

[d]—Commercial General Liability Coverage

COMMERCIAL GENERAL LIABILITY
CG 00 01 04 13

COMMERCIAL GENERAL LIABILITY COVERAGE FORM

Various provisions in this policy restrict coverage. Read the entire policy carefully to determine rights, duties and what is and is not covered.

Throughout this policy the words "you" and "your" refer to the Named Insured shown in the Declarations, and any other person or organization qualifying as a Named Insured under this policy. The words "we", "us" and "our" refer to the company providing this insurance.

The word "insured" means any person or organization qualifying as such under Section **II** – Who Is An Insured.

Other words and phrases that appear in quotation marks have special meaning. Refer to Section **V** – Definitions.

SECTION I – COVERAGES

COVERAGE A – BODILY INJURY AND PROPERTY DAMAGE LIABILITY

1. Insuring Agreement

a. We will pay those sums that the insured becomes legally obligated to pay as damages because of "bodily injury" or "property damage" to which this insurance applies. We will have the right and duty to defend the insured against any "suit" seeking those damages. However, we will have no duty to defend the insured against any "suit" seeking damages for "bodily injury" or "property damage" to which this insurance does not apply. We may, at our discretion, investigate any "occurrence" and settle any claim or "suit" that may result. But:

(1) The amount we will pay for damages is limited as described in Section **III** – Limits Of Insurance; and

(2) Our right and duty to defend ends when we have used up the applicable limit of insurance in the payment of judgments or settlements under Coverages **A** or **B** or medical expenses under Coverage **C**.

No other obligation or liability to pay sums or perform acts or services is covered unless explicitly provided for under Supplementary Payments – Coverages **A** and **B**.

b. This insurance applies to "bodily injury" and "property damage" only if:

(1) The "bodily injury" or "property damage" is caused by an "occurrence" that takes place in the "coverage territory";

(2) The "bodily injury" or "property damage" occurs during the policy period; and

(3) Prior to the policy period, no insured listed under Paragraph **1.** of Section **II** – Who Is An Insured and no "employee" authorized by you to give or receive notice of an "occurrence" or claim, knew that the "bodily injury" or "property damage" had occurred, in whole or in part. If such a listed insured or authorized "employee" knew, prior to the policy period, that the "bodily injury" or "property damage" occurred, then any continuation, change or resumption of such "bodily injury" or "property damage" during or after the policy period will be deemed to have been known prior to the policy period.

c. "Bodily injury" or "property damage" which occurs during the policy period and was not, prior to the policy period, known to have occurred by any insured listed under Paragraph **1.** of Section **II** – Who Is An Insured or any "employee" authorized by you to give or receive notice of an "occurrence" or claim, includes any continuation, change or resumption of that "bodily injury" or "property damage" after the end of the policy period.

d. "Bodily injury" or "property damage" will be deemed to have been known to have occurred at the earliest time when any insured listed under Paragraph **1.** of Section **II** – Who Is An Insured or any "employee" authorized by you to give or receive notice of an "occurrence" or claim:

(1) Reports all, or any part, of the "bodily injury" or "property damage" to us or any other insurer;

(2) Receives a written or verbal demand or claim for damages because of the "bodily injury" or "property damage"; or

(3) Becomes aware by any other means that "bodily injury" or "property damage" has occurred or has begun to occur.

e. Damages because of "bodily injury" include damages claimed by any person or organization for care, loss of services or death resulting at any time from the "bodily injury".

Commercial General Liability coverage is primary coverage against liability claims for a variety of matters. ISO Form CG 00 01 04 13 is the current CGL form.

[i]—What Is Covered

Under the CGL form, the insurer agrees to pay sums that the insured is legally obligated for, such as damages arising from "bodily injury" or "property damage", and has the right and duty to defend the insured against any suit seeking damages. The policy limit on damages is described in the section on limits of insurance, and the duty to defend ends when the insurer has used up the applicable limit of insurance in payments of judgments, settlements, or medical expenses, as these are defined in the policy.

This is liability insurance covering third-party claims for property damage or bodily injury on the tenant's premises or resulting from the tenant's business operations. This form covers liability claims for bodily injury and property damage arising from damage or interference with the premises and the tenant's business, bodily injury and property damage arising on the premises or from the insured's operations, products and completed operations, advertising, and personal injury, including false arrest.

Coverage for damages from bodily injury or property damage is limited to occurrences in the "coverage territory," during the policy period ("occurrence basis"), and where the insured had no prior knowledge of an "occurrence" or claim before the policy period began. Coverage territory is defined to mean the United States (including its territories and possessions), Puerto Rico, and Canada, and international waters or airspace, but only if the injury or damage occurs during travel or transportation between the aforementioned places. Coverage will also accrue for injuries or damages in other parts of the world if the same relate to goods or products made or sold by the insured in the coverage territories, the activities of a person whose home is in the aforesaid territory but is away for a short period of time, or personal and advertising injury offenses taking place through the Internet or similar electronic means of communication.

Damages for bodily injury also include damages that a person or organization may incur for care, loss of services, or death resulting from such bodily injury.

[ii]—What Is Excluded

The CGL form has a significant list of exclusions from coverage for bodily injury. This list of exclusions includes expected or intended injury (except for reasonable force to protect persons or property); contractual liability in most instances; liquor liability; workers' compensation and similar laws; employer's liability; pollution; most aircraft, autos, or watercraft; mobile equipment; war; most property damage; damage to product or work; impaired property; recall products; personal and advertising injury (however, see coverage below); electronic data; and recording and distribution of material or information in violation of law.

Although the CGL form does cover judgments or settlements for personal and advertising injury caused by an offense arising out of the insured's business, it provides coverage only if the offense was committed in the coverage territory during the policy period.

Here again, there is a significant list of exclusions that include knowing violations of rights or others, material published with knowledge of falsity, criminal acts, contractual liability, breach of contract, failure to conform to statements as to the quality or performance of goods, wrong description of prices, copyright and patent trademark infringements, insureds whose business is media and Internet-type businesses, electronic chat rooms or bulletin boards, unauthorized use of another's name or product, pollution and other pollution-related causes, war, and recording and distribution of material or information in violation of law.

While the policy will pay medical expenses for bodily injury caused by an accident on a premises the insured owns or rents, on ways next to the premises owed or rented by the insured, or because of the insured's operations, here again, there is a significant list of exclusions that includes payment for expenses of the insureds (except "volunteer workers"); hired persons; injuries on normally occupied premises, that is, a person injured on that part of the insured's premises that the injured person normally occupies; workers' compensation; athletic injuries; and expenses usually included within a "products-completed operations hazard."

Defense costs are covered outside of the policy limits.

On April 1, 2013, revisions to the ISO's CGL coverage forms became effective.[147] The purpose of the changes was to provide clarity regarding certain issues that were frequently resulting in coverage disputes, as well as to provide additional underwriting options.[148] "The revised forms and new endorsements afford casualty insurers the ability to more clearly define policy rights and obligations and meet policyholders' particular insurance needs."[149] Among the revisions made and endorsements included are the following:

- "Revised forms providing more broadly defined exclusions for claims based on conduct prohibited by federal statutes such as the Telephone Consumer Protection Act, Fair Credit Reporting Act and Fair and Accurate Credit Transactions Act

147. *Id.* at 11.

148. Kozloff & Pickles, Insurance Services Office Revises Commercial General Liability Coverage Forms (Apr. 11, 2013).

149. *Id.* "Revised professional services exclusions clarifying that claims for negligent supervision, hiring, employment, training or monitoring fall within the exclusion if the event causing injury or damage involved the rendering or failure to render professional services."

- "An endorsement removing rights of privacy violation claims from the CGL policy's coverage for 'personal and advertising injury' liability
- "An endorsement eliminating the need for contractual privity between a policyholder and proposed additional insured
- "Numerous provisions harmonizing additional insured coverage with a policyholder's contractual obligations to the proposed additional insured
- "New language limiting additional insured coverage to the extent permitted by state anti-indemnity statutes or common law
- "An endorsement modifying the 'other insurance' clause to clarify that coverage granted to an additional insured shall be the sole primary coverage for the loss if a contract between the parties so provides professional services exclusions clarifying that claims for negligent supervision, hiring, employment, training or monitoring fall within the exclusion if the event causing injury or damage involved the rendering or failure to render professional services."[150]

[e]—Various Other Types of Coverage

Among the other types of coverage available are insured contract insurance, claims-made coverage, nose coverage, and tail coverage. Each of these is discussed in turn below.

- *Insured contract insurance.* An insured contract includes a contract for the lease of premises. Coverage is triggered by any incident that occurs while the policy is in force regardless of when the claim arising from the incident is filed. It covers occurrence basis claims and provides coverage for the incidents that occur during any previous period during the time the policy was in effect.
- *Claims-made coverage.* Claims-made coverage is triggered by claims made (reported or filed) during the year the policy is in force for any incidents occurring during the year or during any previous period during which the insured was covered under a claims-made contract.
- *Nose coverage.* Nose coverage provides coverage under a claims-made policy back to a date prior to the policy's inception. The retroactive date is established by the underwriter to restrict how far back claims made will apply.
- *Tail coverage.* Tail coverage provides an extended period of time under a claims-made policy for claims occurring during the policy period but that were not reported until after the policy period.

These policies imply that there is a waiver of subrogation so long as the waiver is negotiated prior to the loss. While the insurer will not subrogate against an additional

150. *Id.*

insured, the additional insured may have some limitations. Therefore, it is recommended that the waiver of subrogation also be obtained.

Note further that personal property endorsements customarily written separately from the commercial property policy include the electronic data processing endorsement to cover hardware and software including electronic media. Damage to electronic data from an insured's Internet activity is not a covered property damage claim.

The definition of property damage excludes "electronic data as tangible property."[151]

[11]—Insurance Coverage for Tenant Improvements

A number of factors can impact ownership interests and insurance obligations for tenant improvements, furniture, fixtures and equipment, as well as other "personal property" within leased premises.[152] If such property is damaged or destroyed, landlords, tenants, and their property insurers must take into account the obligations of the landlord and the tenant under any lease in effect at the time of a loss, as well as the landlord and tenant's insurance policy coverage.[153] Often the terms of the applicable contracts as well as their interpretation will conflict, and disputes will arise over who bears responsibility for the damaged or destroyed property.

The first place to look is at the lease language, to determine which insurance policy or policies of the landlord or the tenant provide coverage.[154]

For example, a lease may provide that once affixed to the premises, all improvements and betterments become the sole property of the landlord. The lease may alternatively provide that furniture and equipment are the tenant's sole property.[155] Another possibility is that the lease provides for ownership of certain fixtures and improvements based on whether they were installed by the landlord or by the tenant or based on the items' precise nature.[156]

When a loss occurs, the lease will have to be carefully reviewed to determine (1) which party owns the item of property within the leased premises that has been damaged or destroyed, (2) whether the landlord is required to replace or repair any damaged or destroyed property within the leased premises, and (3) which party was obligated.

---

151. Pape, supra note 77, at 17.

152. *See* Millean & Geyen, *Insurance Coverage for Tenant Improvements*, INSURANCE LAW 360 (Jan. 6, 2011).

153. *Id.*

154. *Id.*

155. *Id.*

156. *Id.*

In the event of a fire, explosion, or other catastrophic loss, it can be extremely difficult to determine which items of property were (1) part of the building's core and shell, (2) part of the improvements and betterments and the like owned by the landlord under the terms of the lease, or (3) part of the property owned by the tenant under the terms of the lease. In addition to the question of ownership over those items, the lease language may specify whether the landlord is contractually required to pay for the replacement of any damaged or destroyed property.[157]

The lease should also address which party is responsible for insuring against the loss or damage to improvements, fixtures, and betterments. Regardless of which party owns the property and how that property is defined or designated under the lease, the parties should affirmatively decide between themselves who will insure which property, be it their own or that of the other party. It should be clear in the lease. For example, a lease may require the tenant to insure all of the property on the premises owned by the tenant, or it may require only that the tenant insure furniture, equipment, and other personal property. Still another alternative is for the lease to require the tenant to insure only those improvements and betterments or other personal property installed by the tenant. The lease should also address the landlord's responsibilities with respect to insurance, including what is covered, under what circumstances, and to what extent.[158] Clearly the best time to consider the rights and obligations of the parties is when the lease is negotiated. It is important that the language be consistent and clear, otherwise complications will surely arise when attempting to sort through the parties' respective rights and responsibilities in the event of a loss.

[a]—The Policy Terms

In the event of a loss involving the property within the leased premises, the landlord's and tenant's property insurance policies will come into play. Inconsistencies within and between the various contracts (the lease and the tenant and landlord insurance policies) can create considerable uncertainty regarding which party is economically responsible for the damage or destruction of property within leased premises.[159]

The practitioners are advised to review both their policies and the lease in context with one another. As frequently repeated throughout this book, it is best that the attorney has his or her risk manager or insurance broker review the insurance and indemnifications provisions of the lease and craft the insurance policy from this or vice versa if the lease overreaches what an insurance policy can cover. The author refers the reader to a sample "no fault" clause later in Chapter 7[2] as an

157. *Id.*
158. *Id.*
159. *Id.*

example where parties have clearly delineated their respective physical and legal areas of responsibility, indemnification, and waivers to effect a form of risk allocation that insurers have generally accepted as part of a no fault indemnification arrangement discussed in greater detail in that chapter. In a tenant's insurance policy, the scope of coverage for tenant improvements will typically be addressed by the general definition of "personal property" and any specific provisions that relate to coverage for tenant improvements and betterments, furniture, fixtures, equipment, and the like. For example, a tenant's policy may explicitly state that personal property includes improvements and betterments installed in any premises owned, leased, or occupied by the insured. Absent such an explicit provision, a general definition of personal property may refer to property owned by or in the possession of the insured.

If a tenant's lease states that "all improvements and betterments are solely owned by the landlord," the tenant may not be able to establish any ownership interest in the property and the insurer may take the position that the property is not covered. The tenant will then try to argue that it was in possession of the property and had an insurable "use interest," so that the property was insured despite the lack of its ownership.[160] Case law in some jurisdictions may support that argument. For instance, "under New York law, an insurable interest in property typically includes 'any lawful and substantial economic interest in the safety or preservation of property from loss, destruction, or pecuniary damage.'"[161] This argument is even stronger under New York law in instances when the tenant agreed in its lease to insure the premises.[162]

In a policy issued to a landlord, "the definition of 'personal property' may explicitly include tenant improvements and betterments and the like within premises owned by the landlord and leased to others," or the policy may explicitly state that the only improvements and betterments that are covered are those located within property occupied by the landlord."[163] In that case, the insurer may try to argue that "even if a lease between the landlord and the tenant states that the landlord owns the improvements and betterments, those items are not covered property since they are located in premises not occupied by the insured landlord."[164]

[b]—The "Other Insurance" Provision

A further complication arises when one or more other insurance policies at issue contain an "other insurance" provision. Such a provision makes coverage contingent

160. *Id.*

161. *See id.* citing Sigola Manufacturing, Inc. v. Dairyland Insurance Co., 124 A.D.2d 654, 654 (N.Y. App. Div. 1986).

162. *Id.*

163. *Id.*

164. *Id.*

on the availability of other insurance. These provisions are "designed to establish a requirement that in the event of a loss, any other applicable policy must respond first."[165] The idea is to limit the insurance company's obligation only to the extent that the "other insurance" is insufficient to cover the entire loss.[166] The case law in the specific jurisdiction will be significant in determining how to resolve competing "other insurance" clauses.[167]

[12]—Casualty and Insurance Issues Related to Green Leases[168]

[a]—In General

A number of unique casualty and insurance issues affect green buildings, so carefully drafted casualty and insurance provisions in green leases help protect the significant investments that property owners and tenants incur in "going green."[169]

Important terms include the time frame for rebuilding after a casualty event, the rebuilding costs involved and their allocation, and whether reconstruction will require restoration of the property in accordance with specific green standards (e.g., LEED, Green Globes, etc.).[170]

Reconstruction or restoration in accordance with green building standards will often take longer than conventional reconstruction or restoration. Time must be allowed for recertification of the building to the applicable green standard and obtaining green building materials.[171] Additionally, customized or upgraded building system equipment may take longer to replace.[172]

[b]—The Tenant's Perspective

Casualty provisions in a green lease should clearly address responsibility for building recertification costs, especially when the casualty was not the tenant's fault.[173] From a

165. *Id.*

166. *Id.*

167. *Id.* "For example, in Texas, when the 'other insurance' provisions conflict, both the tenant's insurer and the landlord's insurer must share the costs." *Id.*, citing Travelers Lloyds Insurance Co. v. Pacific Employers Insurance Co., 602 F.3d 677 (5th Cir. 2010).

168. See Chapter 13A Commercial Leases *supra* for a detailed discussion of green leases.

169. Michael P. Nicholson, ed., *Casualty and Insurance Considerations in the Context of Green Leases* (Dec. 6, 2010).

170. *Id.*

171. *Id.*

172. *Id.*

173. *Id.*

tenant's perspective, the landlord should carry sufficient insurance to cover the costs of restoring the building to a particular green certification standard. For some tenants, being in a green building is an important aspect of their identity. Such tenants will consider it important that the landlord be required to rebuild in accordance with at least the existing green certification standards. The tenant should try to include remedies in the lease in case the landlord fails to fulfill its restoration obligations. These may include self-help, a rent abatement, or the right to terminate the lease.

[c]—The Landlord's Perspective

Landlords may not want to be required to rebuild in accordance with a specific green standard. Standards may, and do, change over time so that obtaining certification may become more difficult in the future. Furthermore, "there are no guaranties that a building, once rebuilt, will ultimately receive the green certification that the landlord intended or promised to deliver in the casualty provisions of the lease."[174] Therefore, the landlord should try to limit its obligation to restore by limiting its obligation to using "commercially reasonable efforts" to restore the building to its original green certification standard.[175]

[d]—Insurance Coverage as Investment Protection

Property owners invest a great deal of their time, money, and peoplepower when going green. They should therefore make it a priority to protect their investments with adequate insurance coverage. In fact, "an increasing number of insurance providers have started offering innovative and customized insurance policies and endorsements to cover potential losses in green buildings."[176]

Not all insurers address risk assessment for green buildings in the same way. Some insurers believe that green buildings provide less exposure to loss. "They believe that new state-of-the-art equipment being used for building systems, coupled with the thorough review of HVAC, electrical, plumbing, and roofing systems performed during the LEED certification process, will ultimately lead to fewer incidents of loss."[177] These insurers tend to offer discounted pricing and reduced premiums for building owners who commit to going green.[178]

"Other insurers, due to a lack of historical precedent of risk and loss data, have expressed concern over calculating green building replacement values, as well as

174. *Id.*
175. *Id.*
176. *Id.*
177. *Id.*
178. *Id.*

accounting for the increase in time and cost that can be associated with constructing green certified buildings."[179] These insurers are concerned about green building sustainability concepts, designs, and products and may tend to view new and cutting-edge technology cautiously.[180]

[e]—Insurance Coverage Factors to Consider

"An insurance policy for a green building should provide coverage for recertification costs that may be incurred if a building sustains substantial damage," specifically addressing the "applicable level of green certification in question" and should "account for costs involved with engaging accredited green consultants, architects and engineers to assist in green design and reconstruction."[181] Additionally, the policy should not only "cover debris removal after a casualty, but should include specific coverage for the extra expenses of separating debris and having it sent to certified building material recycling facilities (as opposed to being deposited at a landfill)."[182] Additionally, it is important to have adequate business interruption insurance in a green building policy to protect against longer reconstruction time frames and for recovering lost rental income and losses resulting from onsite energy production that is sold back to local utility companies.[183]

Premiums for green coverage can be higher than those associated with non-green building casualty insurance coverage. "If a landlord is passing its insurance costs through to a tenant as part of building operating expenses, the lease should make it clear that the tenant is responsible for paying for the special, green-related insurance coverages required to restore and re-certify the building." If tenants are committed to going green, they should carry insurance on their personal property and "improvements that covers restoration costs for sustainable features and replacement costs for upgraded energy efficient equipment and trade fixtures."[184]

[13]—The Effect of COVID-19 on Lease Negotiations[185]

Coronavirus disease 19 (COVID-19) has sealed its place in American history as a disease along the lines of the Spanish flu of 1918 or the smallpox epidemic of 1775–1792 and in the annals of world history like the bubonic plague in the Middle Ages in

---

179. *Id.*
180. *Id.*
181. *Id.*
182. *Id.*
183. *Id.*
184. *Id.*
185. The author thanks George Bernhardt for his generous sharing of his notes for his presentation for the American College of Real Estate Lawyers (ACREL) on *The Impacts of the Coronavirus Pandemic*

Europe. What is striking in this age of 21st-century technology and advanced medicine is that we are still at its mercy and are adapting daily to its spread using, in part, steps and precautions that border on primitive common sense.

What is unique about this pandemic has been its effect on leasing practices and payments and the snowball effect this has had on real estate relations among tenants, landlords, lenders, and the economy generally.[186]

Since the beginning of 2020, when COVID-19 cases were first being identified in the United States, there has been a varying course of action by various states in shutting down, reopening, and then shutting down again as a first wave of the virus took hold in the country with fears of a second wave coming again in the fall. Even in the states such as New York, New Jersey, Connecticut, Vermont, and a few others where the virus has seemingly been brought under control and there has been an easing of shelter-in-place restrictions, tenants are still looking for relief from their landlords, insurance companies, and state and bankruptcy courts. Landlords are being stretched thin or are at the end of their rope. Insurance companies are generally denying claims for business interruption losses as not stemming from damage to property.[187]

Due to the virus, various stay-at-home orders, and the drop in business generally, there has been a significant number of bankruptcy filings primarily in the retail and hospitality spaces, with, as of this writing, Brooks Brothers, Tailored Brands, 24 Hour Fitness, J Crew, J. C. Penney, Neiman Marcus, Hertz, Gold's Gym, and a number of other entities having filed petitions under chapter 11.[188] This wave may continue into 2023, especially since more commercial retail tenants and restaurants are unable to pay rent.[189] This snowball effect will most likely create another round of bankruptcy filings by landlords, mall owners, property management companies, contractors, vendors, and others.[190] While various state governors have imposed moratoria on residential and commercial evictions, as these moratoria end, there will be a rush in new

---

on Real Estate Contracts: Frustration of Purpose, Impossibility, Impracticability and Force Majeure (July 9, 2020) (hereinafter ACREL).

186. Konrad Putzier & Esther Fung, *Businesses Can't Pay Rent, That's a Threat to the $3 Trillion Commercial Mortgage Market*, Wall Street J. (Mar. 30, 2020).

187. *Force Majeure in the Wake of the Coronavirus?* (March 3, 2020) (updated Mar. 16, 2020); *Abandonment of Leases and Abatement of Rent During the Coronavirus Pandemic* (March 24, 2020); Updated Ackerman, *Bankruptcy Courts Continue to Accept Equitable Arguments for Deferring Rent Payments during the COVID-19 Pandemic* (June 2020), collectively referred to as the Paul Weiss memos.

188. *Wave of Bankruptcies May Swamp System, and Action Is Urged*, N.Y. Times, June 22, 2020 at B1, B9.

189. *See* Hagg, *New York Tenants Worry Eviction Cases Will Surge*, N.Y. Times, June 23, 2020; Zimmerman, *Coronavirus Pandemic Prompts Wave of "Business Interruption" Lawsuits by Restaurants*, ABA Journal (May 26, 2020).

190. Putzier & Fung, *supra* note 186.

eviction cases, as well as the continuation of the thousands of cases that have already been in process and were paused during this time.[191]

Since the pandemic took hold in the United States earlier this year, there has been a scurrying on handling rent payment issues as a result of lost revenues from space users due to either lower foot traffic or governmental mandated shutdowns or restrictions in order to tackle the effect of the virus. Retail and restaurant tenants have been especially hit hard, but office and medical tenants have also been affected. Nonpaying tenants have placed their landlords in jeopardy with their lenders who have outstanding loans on their property. Foreclosures and bankruptcies will be a part of our environment in the coming months and years. It is safe to say that once we emerge from this crisis, commercial real estate will have a different look than it had before this pandemic hit the United States.

Since the outbreak, there have been a host of issues arising in lease relations as tenants have difficulty in making payments and there is the possibility of triggering default clauses in their leases. Given the present circumstances with current tenants, landlords' reluctance to bring default actions against otherwise good-paying tenants, the lack of substitute users to step in the shoes of these tenants, governmental orders requiring limited openings and prohibiting landlords from bringing default and eviction actions, and the unusual and hopefully temporary circumstances under which these issues are occurring, tenants and landlords have been focusing on means such as work-outs, rather than exercising what would be black letter contractual remedies.[192]

As the impact of the COVID-19 pandemic magnifies, parties are increasingly looking to their contracts for potential excuses of nonperformance, such as force majeure, only to find their contracts conspicuously silent on the issue. Where this is the case, companies should begin to assess the applicability of alternative common law mechanisms for excuse of nonperformance.[193]

[a]—Force Majeure Claims

While courts will likely reject a force majeure claim if the parties' agreement does not contain a force majeure clause,[194] parties seeking to excuse nonperformance may still avail themselves of the common law doctrines of impossibility or, in some jurisdictions, impracticability. These doctrines may excuse nonperformance where a party establishes that (1) an unexpected intervening event occurred, (2) the parties' agree-

191. Hagg, *supra* note 189.

192. *See* Paul Weiss memos, *supra* note 187.

193. *Id.*

194. General Electric Co. v. Metals Resources Group Ltd., 293 A.D.2d 417, 741 N.Y.S.2d 218 (2002) ("The parties' integrated agreement contained no force majeure provision, much less one specifying the occurrence that defendant would now have treated as a force majeure, and, accordingly, there is no basis for a force majeure defense.") (cited from Paul Weiss memos, *supra* note 187).

ment assumed such an event would not occur, and (3) the unexpected event made contractual performance impossible or impracticable. A party's nonperformance will not be excused under these principles, where the event preventing performance was expected or was a foreseeable risk at the time of the contract's execution.[195] Even if the event was unforeseeable, courts may still assess the event under the Restatement (Second) of Contracts § 261 (1981), whether the "nonoccurrence" of the event at issue was a "basic assumption on which the contract was made."[196] According to the Restatement (Second) of Contracts, "extreme impracticability of performance may properly be regarded as having the same effect as strict impossibility of performance," and performance is impossible when "it can only be done at an excessive and unreasonable cost, for which the parties had not bargained."[197] Mere market shifts or financial inability to perform generally does not constitute unforeseen events, the nonoccurrence of which was a "basic assumption" of the contract.

However, generally "a *force majeure* clause might cover the COVID-19 crisis if the contractual definition of a force majeure event expressly includes an epidemic/pandemic, or the force majeure clause covers extraordinary events or circumstances beyond the reasonable control of the parties. Action by a government authority explicitly requiring a party to suspend operations is likely to constitute force majeure. In contrast, if a contracting party takes steps in response to government advice or can't fulfill its obligations because staff is in self-isolation or one of its suppliers cannot deliver, the assessment as to whether force majeure applies will be more complicated and uncertain.

The impact of force majeure will depend on the specific law and circumstances. Even if suspension is permitted, the tenant may still have to perform obligations other than those directly affected by the "force majeure" event.[198]

Any changes to the contract must be in writing. Do not rely on an oral promise.

[b]—Retailer Considerations in the Era of COVID-19

The following are five things retailers should consider in the COVID-19 era.

[i]—Force Majeure

Most obvious is the force majeure provision. Make sure the clause includes a list of specific force majeure events, typically defined as events or occurrences that the parties

195. Paul Weiss memos, *supra* note 187.

196. *See Restatement (Second) of Contracts* § 261 (Am. Law Inst. 1981) (addressing the impracticability of performance).

197. 17A Am. Jur. 2d *Contracts* § 643 (2020).

198. Reidy, Carter & Tuer, *Business Interruption Coverage: Issues to Consider when Disaster Strikes*, The Corporate Counsellor 9 (Law Journal Newsletters Oct. 2001).

do not control, along with language that can cover unexpected but similar events that would trigger a force majeure event and remedies. Parties need to use their imagination to foresee and include these events in their drafting. Before the severe acute respiratory syndrome (SARS) outbreak in 2002–2003 and COVID-19 in 2020, few force majeure clauses included pandemics, viral exposures, and related outbreaks as events that would result in the obligations of the parties being tolled. Unfortunately, these clauses are usually only reactive and cover only the last experienced events, such as the terrorist attacks in 2001. A force majeure provision that references "government-imposed restrictions" is likely broad enough to include "shelter-in-place" and "safer-in-place" types of orders that require businesses to close, but it may be prudent to specifically reference such orders.

Notice provisions are important to a landlord and should require tenants to notify the landlord that they are making a claim under the force majeure provision to allow the landlord to cap the amount of time that such force majeure tolling is effective. Landlords will possibly want to require that, under all circumstances, the tenants continue to be obligated to pay rent (including triple net charges), even during a force majeure event like a pandemic.

Landlords will also want to make sure that any cotenancy provisions in their leases contain carve-outs for tenants who are forced to close or operate at a reduced capacity due to such orders. With the experience during the COVID-19 pandemic of parties being affected by governmental office closures, the force majeure definition should also address these closures.

[ii]—Use of Common Areas and Caps on Common Area Maintenance Expenses

Landlords should be sure that the control of common area language is broad enough for the landlord to be able to respond and adapt to pandemics and similar emergencies. This would include the ability to install items to improve health and safety conditions (e.g., upgrading HVAC systems and providing for monitoring customers and employees coming into the center and premises). Similarly, tenants may need the right to use portions of the common area (such as sidewalks) for customers to form lines outside the stores due to social distancing and store-capacity issues. As such, landlords should be willing to allow tenants to use the common area for customers waiting to enter the store but with the right to require the tenant to give the landlord prior written notice of the issue and the expected duration, peak times, and specific area the tenant wants to use. Landlords may also want to require that the tenant clean up the area used for queuing on a regular (not less than daily) basis. Even in a lease that provides the tenant with a cap on increases in common area maintenance (CAM) costs, the cap usually does not apply to "uncontrollable" costs. Following COVID-19, landlords should consider expanding the list of uncontrollable costs to include items such as hand sanitizing stations, automatic door upgrades, and personnel administering cleaning, and assurance that customers comply with social distancing requirements and be exempt from any cap on CAM costs.

Finally, if the "base year" for setting the stop price for CAM costs happens during a year when the common areas are used less because of a pandemic or related outbreak, the tenant should require the landlord to "gross up" its base CAM costs to a number that is more reflective of what these would have been but for the pandemic.

[iii]—Alterations

With the uncertainties following COVID-19, landlords should make sure that their leases require tenants, at their own expense, to make any and all alterations required by law, including those resulting from force majeure events. For example, the cost of any barriers within a premises needed to keep customers to "social distance" should be the tenant's responsibility. The usual requirements for the tenant obtaining the landlord's prior approval for these alternations should also apply.

[iv]—Rules and Regulations

The landlord may want to be able to enforce rules to protect against the potential spread of COVID-19 or similar future diseases and require the tenant and its employees and customers to comply with relevant governmental (i.e., Centers for Disease Control and Prevention [CDC] or World Health Organization [WHO]) requirements and recommendations. For example, landlords may want to be able to eject or remove people from the center who refuse to comply with the rules and regulations or relevant government requirements, such as if they refuse to wear a mask in the center's common areas.

[v]—Insurance and Rent Continuation

Another of the lessons of the COVID-19 pandemic has been that tenants have looked for rent abatement or moratoria on paying their rent and expenses, often failing in this regard because the lease did not provide for such abatement or its insurance would not cover its losses under a Business Interruption (BI) policy due to either the lack of "physical damage" necessary to trigger coverage or a specific exclusion in their policy for losses due to a "virus, bacterium or microorganism resulting in physical distress, illness or disease." Insurers were prone to add such exclusions in their standard BI policies and contingent BI policies after the SARS outbreak in 2002–2003. As a result, insurers have taken the position that communicable diseases not expressly defined in the policy at issue are not covered. Both landlords and tenants should closely examine their policies to see if such an exclusion is in the policy and make some effort to either have it eliminated or consider obtaining an endorsement to have these diseases covered. The situation brought on by COVID-19 in which tenants have been withholding or refusing to pay rent or being denied BI coverage has had a "snowball" effect on landlords' cash flow and their ability to meet their own operational expenses and their financial obligations to lenders or mortgagees.

[c]—Other Common Law Remedies

There are several common law remedies that have been in play along with the contractual theory of force majeure. Common law remedies include frustration of purpose, impossibility, impracticability, and, rarely, quiet enjoyment. These may be pleaded separately or together and in conjunction with force majeure, if the lease language in the force majeure clause did not limit remedies to the contract and preclude the common law remedies.[199] Another common alternative in the absence of a force majeure clause is the doctrine of frustration of purpose. This principal functions similarly to impracticability and impossibility but focuses on whether the event at issue has obviated the purpose of the contract, rather than whether it has made a party's contractual performance unviable. Frustration of purpose requires substantial frustration without fault of either party. It focuses on whether the event at issue has obviated the purpose of the contract, rather than whether it has made a party's contractual performance unviable.[200]

[i]—Frustration of Purpose

Frustration of purpose requires many of the same elements as the principles of impossibility or impracticability but does not require a supervening event that impedes a party's performance. A supervening event that impedes a party's performance would be (1) an event that substantially frustrates a party's principal purpose, (2) the nonoccurrence of the event was a basic assumption of the contract, and (3) the event was not the fault of the party asserting the defense. The overarching question with respect to frustration of purpose is whether the unforeseeable event has significantly altered the circumstances of an agreement such that performance would no longer fulfill any aspect of its original purpose. There are two primary obstacles to successfully invoking this defense. First, courts interpret a party's "purpose" broadly, and the mere fact that an event has prevented a party from taking advantage of the agreement in an expected manner may be insufficient. Second, frustration must be near total—it is not enough that a transaction was previously expected to be profitable but is now unprofitable.[201]

---

199. ACREL, *supra* note 185.
200. Paul Weiss memos, *supra* note 187.
201. *Id.*

The classic case about frustration of purpose is *Krell v. Henry*.[202] This case arose out of a contract to rent a London flat to view the coronation of King Edward VII. Henry contracted to rent a flat from Krell for two days to watch the coronation procession; however, the coronation was postponed due to the king's illness. Henry refused to pay the balance owed on the flat and Krell sued. The court determined that there was an implied condition and when that condition did not occur, the contract was voided. An analogy was made to an earlier case, *Taylor v. Caldwell*,[203] which relieved the parties from performance of a contract related to the rental of a concert hall after the concert hall burned down. Most likely, this doctrine will be successful in a short-term contract, rather than a lease for years. In terms of current circumstances, frustration of purpose would possibly be applied if state or local governments permanently shut down in-dining restaurants or movie theaters, rather than temporarily closing them down. Frustration of purpose applies when the parties entered a contract based on an assumed set of circumstances and something changes that frustrates the essential purpose of the contract.[204]

[ii]—Impossibility or Impracticability

As implied by the name, the doctrine of impossibility arose to excuse performance when it is made impossible due to an intervening occurrence not caused by the parties. Over time, this was softened by some courts to require only that performance becomes impractical, not impossible. outside of construction, force majeure and the common law doctrines of frustration and impracticability are not often applied to real estate contracts. When it is applied, impossibility must be an objective case of impossibility, notably (1) destruction of the property, such as in 2001 when the World Trade Center in New York was destroyed; (2) death of a party; (3) governmental action; or (4) natural causes beyond the control of the parties. The doctrine of impossibility provides that the parties are excused from performance of a contract when an unanticipated change in circumstances makes performance of the contract impossible. For example, the destruction of the concert hall in the *Taylor v. Caldwell* case made it impossible to hold a concert at the hall after it was destroyed. Modern courts more typically do not require strict impossibility, but rather have adopted the doctrine of impracticability rather than impossibility.[205] Impracticability may occur when performance is excessively burdensome and not caused by one of the parties. If a contractual obligation becomes excessively burdensome due to the occurrence

202. Krell v. Henry, 2 K.B. 740 (1903); notes from George Bernhardt, (hereinafter Bernhardt notes).
203. Taylor v. Caldwell, 122 Eng. Rep. 309 (1863).
204. Bernhardt notes, *supra* note 202.
205. *Id.*

of an unforeseen event not caused by one of the parties, the parties are excused from performing.[206]

[iii]—Quiet Enjoyment

Finally, quiet enjoyment may arise to a defensible theory in certain unusual circumstances. It involves balancing the circumstances when the objective performance is barred by interference or, more likely, landlord's interference. Note that it may have limited application, since quiet enjoyment usually is interpreted to assure the tenant freedom from challenges to the landlord's title to transfer possession of a property. It involves allowing a tenant to use the premises, despite the landlord's inability to transfer title to use the premises.

[d]—Proving Force Majeure

Force majeure has been at the forefront of almost all the reportable actions to date. Force majeure is a contractual and not a common law theory. To support a viable action, a lease must have a force majeure clause. In some instances, there is a requirement that there be physical damages to the premises and, in this instance, the attorney would need to look to the lease's casualty clause rather than the force majeure clause. Force majeure clauses are not frequently included in leases, and when they are present, such clauses tend to be landlord oriented and specifically exempt payment of rent from the clause. Other possible lease remedies that have been discussed in connection with the pandemic are implied warranties of habitability or suitability for a particular purpose. These warranties generally relate to the physical condition and repair of the premises, and typically they are focused on latent defects. With commercial tenancies, the standards are stricter than they are with residential leases and the defective condition must have existed at the time the lease was signed. Even if these doctrines are found to apply regarding contamination by COVID-19, it is unlikely that the tenant would have any rights beyond requiring the landlord to decontaminate the premises.[207] In *New York Majestic Hotel Co. v. Eyre*,[208] a tenant tried to cancel his residential lease due to the outbreak of scarlet fever, but since the implied warranty of habitability assumes a physical defect in the premises, the court held that the mere fear of contagion does not justify voluntarily abandoning the premises or does not excuse payment of rent. More recently, the Texas Supreme Court found in *Davidow v. Inwood North Professional Group*[209] that the implied warranty of fitness for a

---

206. *Id.*
207. *Id.*
208. Majestic Hotel Co. v. Eyre, 53 A.D. 273, 65 N.Y.S. 745 (1900).
209. Davidow v. Inwood North Professional Group, 747 S.W.2d 373 (Tex. 1988).

particular purpose "means that at the inception of the lease there are no latent defects in the facilities that are vital to the use of the premises for their intended commercial purpose and that these essential facilities will remain in a suitable condition."[210]

Force majeure clauses excuse a party's nonperformance under a contract when extraordinary events prevent a party from fulfilling its contractual obligations.[211] The applicability of a force majeure provision is contract specific, and there is a high bar for invocation of such a clause. Recent events, including the declaration of COVID-19 as a pandemic and the implementation of travel, movement, and large-gathering restrictions, have altered the force majeure landscape in a manner that may impact the availability of such provisions to nonperforming parties.[212]

In considering the applicability of force majeure, courts look to whether (1) the event qualifies as force majeure under the contract, (2) the risk of nonperformance was foreseeable and able to be mitigated, and (3) performance is truly impossible. The court's inquiry largely focuses on whether the event that gives rise to nonperformance is specifically listed as a qualifying force majeure in the clause at issue.[213] Even if a party can surmount this requirement, it cannot invoke force majeure if (1) it could have foreseen and mitigated the potential nonperformance and (2) performance is merely impracticable or economically difficult rather than truly impossible (unless the specific jurisdiction or contract at issue specifies a different standard). Recent COVID-19 developments may impact whether the outbreak and/or its effects constitute force majeure.[214]

The WHO's classification of COVID-19's as a pandemic can trigger a force majeure clause that expressly accounts for pandemics. That said, the declaration of pandemic standing alone—without a reference to pandemics in a force majeure clause—would not automatically constitute a force majeure, given the courts' focus on whether the event is specified within the contract language.[215] Clauses that are silent on pandemics, epidemics, or other viral outbreaks are likely to be insufficient for a force majeure defense due to COVID-19, unless, of course, courts liberalize the force majeure analysis to account for market realities. If a force majeure clause clearly covers COVID-19 as a qualifying event in light of the WHO's declaration, parties seeking to invoke the provision will not need to establish the event was unforeseeable, but will still need to show (1) that they took steps to mitigate the damage and (2) that performance is truly impossible (or meets any other standard the clause requires).[216]

---

210. *Id.*, from Bernhardt notes, *supra* note 202.
211. Paul Weiss memos, *supra* note 187.
212. *Id.*
213. *Id.*
214. *Id.*
215. *Id.*
216. *Id.*

Recent governmental regulations intended to contain the COVID-19 outbreak may similarly make it easier to invoke a force majeure clause not previously triggered by the virus. Expanding governmental restrictions on travel, movement, and large gatherings has resulted in significant business interruptions and widespread cancellation of events and travel. This has had a significant impact on the event, tourism, restaurant, airline, venue rental, and sports and entertainment sectors.[217] On March 15, 2020, New York City ordered the shutdown of thousands of public schools, restaurants, and bars in the largest shutdown in the country, and other cities and states instituted similar restrictive interventions. Businesses may be able to invoke force majeure provisions to excuse any contractual nonperformance resulting from these measures if the clauses at issue enumerate governmental orders or regulations that make performance impossible. As with clauses triggered by the WHO's pandemic declaration, the delineation of governmental regulations making performance impossible does not end the court's analysis, and parties seeking to avail themselves of force majeure must still establish inability to mitigate, along with impossibility of performance (or any other standard the clause requires).[218] As a result, companies should continue to closely monitor COVID-19 developments and their potential impact on contractual performance, and take and document all reasonable steps to mitigate, where possible, their effect on business operations.[219]

The lease needs to define what a force majeure event is and then to apply it to specific events for which relief is sought ("trigger") (e.g., war, pandemic, fire, flood, and so on) and then provide the specific relief being sought, such as rent abatement, rent postponement, or lease termination. Some force majeure clauses may be extremely broad, such as "any event neither caused by nor reasonably foreseeable by the parties," or may be an extremely specific list of events. Current force majeure clauses often do not cover a pandemic.

Terrorism was very uncommon in force majeure clauses before 9/11, and those involved in the legal and liability aftermath of that disaster looked more to the respective commercial all-risk property policies that, at that time, covered all events except for specifically excluded occurrences, of which terrorism was not one. Pandemics will probably be covered a lot more frequently in the future than they are now. Since the start of the COVID-19 pandemic, some national tenants have sent out blanket notices to all their landlords stating that they are not paying rent due to the "recent coronavirus force majeure event" or something similar. Because force majeure is purely contractual, a leaseholder cannot just send out a blanket notice without seeing

---

217. *Id.*
218. *Id.*
219. *Id.*

whether the lease even has a force majeure clause and if it does, reviewing it for applicability to the circumstances. Most force majeure clauses will specifically exclude payment of rent, and most do not cover pandemics. If there is a mandatory government order to shelter in place and the tenant is not an essential business, that is more likely to be covered, but you still need to review the lease language. Note that financial hardship alone is not a valid ground to avoid legal obligations.

Generally, a force majeure clause needs to define the specifically covered events, the so-called trigger, notice to the landlord, and the obligation to take reasonable steps to mitigate damages.[220] These mitigation steps may include, for example, a supplier using alternative manufacturing in a different location or maximizing online sales for a retailer that can be attributable to the premises or pick-up service for a restaurant.

In the current environment of COVID-19, for an actionable claim, a force majeure clause would most likely need specifically to define a pandemic such as COVID-19 as a covered event or to have such a board application that a court could excuse performance under the clauses' broad coverage. Language such as "acts of God" or "other causes beyond the control" of the parties who are without fault would be considered, and such a clause would trigger application of the remedies listed in the clause. Triggers under this broad application may include closures of nonessential businesses, government stay-at-home orders, virus outbreaks, and supply and labor shortages. In *Whole Foods Market Group, Inc. v. Wical Ltd. Partnership*,[221] the tenant retail grocer was excused from performance under a continuous operation clause due to rodent infestation in the building under a broad force majeure clause that included the language mentioned above. On the other hand, in *Kel Kim Corp. v. Central Markets, Inc.*,[222] the court stated that the triggering event needed to be like the listed events to provide coverage.[223]

In some instances where a lease contains a force majeure clause, that clause may preempt the tenant's ability to invoke common law remedies. If the lease does not contain a force majeure clause, the attorney might look to see if the forum state may have applicable state common law or statutory law. A few states such as California[224]

220. See *COVID-19: Force Majeure Event?*, Shearman & Sterling memo (Mar. 2020); Paul Weiss memos, *supra* note 187.

221. Whole Foods Market Group, Inc. v. Wical Ltd. Partnership, 2019 U.S. Dist. LEXIS 182086 (D.D.C. oct. 22, 2019).

222. Kel Kim Corp. v. Central Markets, Inc., 70 N.Y.2d 900, 519 N.E.2d 295, 524 N.Y.S.2d 384 (1987).

223. *Id.*; ACREL, *supra* note 185.

224. Cal. Civ. Code § 1511.

and Georgia[225] have statutory force majeure laws. Section 13-4-21 of the Georgia Code (acts of God) provides, "If performance of the terms of a contract becomes impossible because of an act of God, such impossibility shall excuse nonperformance, except where, by proper prudence, such impossibility might have been avoided by the promisor."[226] Elsewhere, the Georgia Code defines "act of God" to mean "an accident produced by physical causes which are irresistible or inevitable, such as lightning, storms, perils of the sea, earthquakes, inundations, sudden death, or illness. This expression excludes all idea of human agency."[227] The Georgia definition of acts of God focuses primarily on physical damage. While it does refer to "sudden death, or illness," it seems difficult to apply the statute to the COVID-19 pandemic, unless the party trying to be excused actually has contracted the virus, as performance must be made impossible because of the act of God. An argument might be made that closure due to government order issued due to the pandemic could qualify, although that seems to be a stretch.[228]

[e]—Guidance from Bankruptcy Court Decisions

Decisions in 2020 from bankruptcy courts in Illinois and Kansas offer points for consideration in navigating through these unprecedented times.[229] A recent case that has received considerable recognition is a bankruptcy case, *In re Hitz Restaurant Group*.[230] In this case, the bankruptcy court partially excused the restaurant tenant's ("Debtor") obligation to pay a full rent while Illinois Executive Order 2020-7 section 1 restricted the Debtor's ability to operate fully due to the COVID-19 virus.[231]

The case might give other businesses a road map for similar relief.[232] Hitz Restaurant Group operates a restaurant in Chicago, and on February 24, 2020, it filed a small business chapter 11 responding to receiving a five-day lease termination notice. Shortly after filing, the restaurant's landlord brought motions to (1) compel payment of post-petition rent under Bankruptcy Code section 365(d)(3) and (2) modify the automatic stay under section 362(d)(1). As rent payments were due on or before the

---

225. O.C.G.A § 13-4-21.

226. ACREL, *supra* note 185.

227. O.C.G.A. § 1-3-3.

228. ACREL, *supra* note 185.

229. Ackerman, *Bankruptcy Courts Continue to Accept Equitable Arguments for Deferring Rent Payments during the COVID-19 Pandemic* (June 11, 2020) (hereinafter Ackerman memo).

230. *In re* Hitz Restaurant Group, 2020 WL 2924523 (Bank. N.D. Ill. June 3, 2020).

231. Ackerman memo, *supra* note 229.

232. Joshua Stein, *Pandemic Closure Means an Illinois Restaurant Doesn't Have to Pay Full Rent, Court Says*, Forbes (June 18, 2020), *available at* https://www.forbes.com/sites/joshuastein/2020/06/18/pandemic-closure-means-an-illinois-restaurant-doesnt-have-to-pay-full-rent/?sh=311c69d02f51.

first of each month, the court deemed February rent as pre-petition and March and subsequent months post-petition.[233] As the court noted, the Bankruptcy Code usually requires "full payment of the March 2020 rent and all rental payments falling due thereafter." However, the lease contains the following force majeure clause that was different from a typical clause in that it said: "Lack of money shall not be grounds for Force Majeure":[234]

> Landlord and Tenant shall be excused from performing its obligations or undertakings provided in the Lease, in the event, but only so long as the performance of any of its obligations are prevented or delayed, retarded or hindered by . . . laws, governmental action or inaction, orders of government. . . . Lack of money shall not be grounds for Force Majeure.

At that time, in effect was an order issued on March 16, 2020, by Governor J. B. Pritzker that specifically pertained to restaurants, requiring their stopping service for on-premises consumption. However, the order allowed and encouraged restaurants to serve food and beverages via delivery, take out, and curbside pickup, so that they may be consumed off premises.[235]

The court analyzed whether the governor's order, like that in many other localities, triggered the force majeure clause. Initially, the court held that the lease's force majeure clause did not excuse payment of March rent because the order was enacted on the sixteenth and March rent was due on the first. Next, the court considered the application of the force majeure clause on rent for April, May, and June.

While the landlord advanced three primary arguments against application of the force majeure clause, the court dismissed all these arguments and found that the force majeure clause applied. It looked to Illinois law on contract interpretation and found that the clause had only limited application.[236] The court found that this order created a force majeure event under the lease and excused the tenant from having to pay 75 percent of its rent. The court rejected the landlord's argument that the debtor's inability to pay rent resulted from a "lack of money," which a force majeure provision generally excluded as a triggering event. Specifically, the court held that Hitz conceded that 25 percent of the restaurant's square footage, consisting of the kitchen, could have been used for carry out, curbside pickup, and delivery purposes. Thus, the court concluded that the debtor owed 25 percent of the rent amount under section 365(d)(3).[237] Lastly, the court required payment on or before June 16 of 25 percent of

233. Ackerman memo, *supra* note 229.
234. Stein, *supra* note 232.
235. Ackerman memo, *supra* note 229.
236. *Id.*
237. *Id.*

the rent, CAM, and property taxes for April, May, and June; otherwise "cause" would exist under section 362(d)(1) to lift the stay.[238]

Bankruptcy courts appear to be more lenient than law courts in agreeing to debtors' arguments for assistance in relief from COVID-19-economic hardship. While many landlords have been willing and able to offer to tenants rent deferral and even abatement, most concessions were limited to 90 days. Landlords are in similar straights with their lenders only for a limited period before the lender takes action to realize upon its collateral. Moreover, stays on eviction proceedings are expiring.[239]

Another case involved a group of debtor restaurants operating in the Kansas City area that had filed for chapter 11 in November 2019 because of a number of issues, including lower sales, increased debt load, and mounting pressure from landlords.[240]

According to the court, "[b]efore the coronavirus pandemic struck, Debtors demonstrated potential for a successful reorganization." On March 17, 2020, the debtors and all other area restaurants were ordered to cease operations. Approximately one month later, the debtors filed an emergency motion to suspend certain Bankruptcy Code requirements including, without limitation, the need to (1) pay post-petition rent to landlords and (2) assume or reject unexpired leases prior to the May 5 deadline. The debtors' landlords objected.[241]

The bankruptcy court cited to recent opinions in the *Pier 1 Imports, Inc.* and *Craftworks* cases,[242] stating that "no feasible alternative" exists and the relief sought offers "a short-term allocation of those scarce resources to meet immediate needs and preserve the value of the Debtors estates for all creditor constituencies."[243] Moreover, the court specifically cited to its equitable powers in overriding the black letter of the Code:

> These unprecedented circumstances require flexible application of the Bankruptcy Code and exercise of the Court's equitable powers under 11 U.S.C. § 105 to grant further relief, including extension of time to assume or reject the Debtors' nonresidential leases, notwithstanding the absence of written consent of the lessors under 11 U.S.C. § 365(d)(4)(B)(ii). Section 105(a) is understood as providing courts with discretion to accommodate the unique facts of a case consistent with the policies

---

238. *Id.*

239. *See* Hagg, *supra* note 189.

240. Ackerman memo, *supra* note 229.

241. *Id.*

242. *In re* Pier 1 Imports, Inc., 2020 Bankr. LEXIS 1242 (E.D. Va. May 10, 2020); *In re* Craftworks Parent LLC, Case No. 20-10475 (BLS) [Docket No. 535] (Bankr. D. Del. May 21, 2020). *See* Ackerman memo, *supra* note 230.

243. Ackerman memo, *supra* note 229.

or directives set by the other applicable substantive provisions of the Bankruptcy Code.[244]

Essentially, the bankruptcy court exercised its equitable power in overriding the landlord's statutory right to payment of post-petition rent in favor of maintaining (1) the debtors' perceived going-concern value and (2) prospects for recovery to all creditors, even though this case had been filed more than four months prior to entry of the shelter-in-place orders.[245] The *Hitz* and *Bread & Butter Concepts* decisions have opened the door for tenant-friendly court opinions and should be closely considered when engaging in lease-related negotiations.[246]

Another case worth noting is *Hart 353 North Clark LLC v. Jenner & Block LLP*.[247] Jenner & Block ("Jenner"), a large and prestigious law firm, stopped paying rent as of March 16, 2020, when it found that it could not use 89 percent of its premises. The landlord, successor in interest to the original landlord, 351 Mortgage Borrowers, LLC ("351 Mortgage"), who negotiated the original lease with Jenner & Block, sued the law firm for alleged past due rent. Jenner's response is interesting in that its answer claims that its rent abatement provision that it renegotiated with 351 Mortgage in 2005 allowed it to abate rent for "any event (Force Majeure or other) . . ." that covers all events, including the current pandemic. Jenner's answer includes an exhibit from Richard Stein, the chief negotiator for 351 Mortgage, that states that Jenner expressly negotiated for rent abatement for "any event" that "caused Jenner to reasonably determine that it could not use and occupy a material amount of its space as it intended in the normal course of business, regardless of whether that event was the Landlord's responsibility and regardless of whether that event caused physical damage to the building or space." Mr. Stein's statement also confirmed that COVID-19 is the kind of event from which the abatement provisions were designed to protect Jenner. The case was settled, and terms of the settlement have not been available..

[f]—Applicable Insurance Policy Provisions

Companies expecting potential business interruption should also review potentially applicable insurance policies and provisions, including business interruption and contingent business interruption insurance. Business interruption insurance is intended

244. *Id.*

245. *Id.*

246. *In re* Hitz Restaurant Group, 2020 WL 2924523 (Bank. N.D. Ill. June 3, 2020); *In re* Bread & Butter Concepts, LLC, Case No. 19-22400 (DLS) [Docket No. 219] (Bankr. D. Kan. May 16, 2019).

247. Hart 353 North Clark LLC v. Jenner & Block LLP, Case No. 2020-L-00576 (Cir. Ct. Cook County Ill., Law Div., filed June 22, 2020).

to cover losses resulting from direct interruptions to a business's operations and generally covers lost revenue, fixed expenses such as rent and utility, or expenses from operating from a temporary location.[248] Similarly, contingent business interruption insurance is intended to cover lost profits and costs that indirectly result from disruptions in a company's supply chain, including failures of suppliers or downstream customers.[249] While these policies frequently require physical property damage, businesses have been submitting claims for coverage of losses due to business interruptions resulting from COVID-19. The viability of these claims depends on the terms of the insurance policy at issue, but the historical trend, based on prior viral epidemics, has been against coverage for business interruptions related to a pandemic like COVID-19.[250]

In the wake of the SARS outbreak in 2002–2003, many insurers excluded viral or bacterial outbreaks from standard BI and contingent BI policies. Insurers have largely taken the position that communicable diseases not expressly defined in the policy at issue are not covered, although there may be some coverage in an environmental claim for cleanup of the building to allow tenants to safely enter and use the premises.[251] Some insurance policies already specifically disallow coverage for events such as the COVID-19 pandemic. The endorsement "Exclusion of Loss Due to Virus or Bacterium. CP 01 40 07 06" specifically does not pay for loss due to virus, bacterium, or other microorganism resulting in physical distress, illness, or disease. Its prohibitions apply to property damage to building or personal property, and it covers business interruption, extra expenses, or civil authority actions, although it excludes loss or damage due to fungus and wet or dry rot and has been amended to include coverage for losses from bacteria.

[g]—Other Potential Protections

The current situation has had a snowball effect, with tenants unable to operate and thus pay rent due to government actions taken due to the pandemic and property owners as borrowers unable to make scheduled mortgage payments.[252] The Coronavirus Aid, Relief and Economic Security Act (CARES Act), enacted March 27, 2020, included moratorium provisions protecting rights of these borrowers and tenants to remain in their dwelling without facing the immediate threat of foreclosure and eviction.[253]

248. Paul Weiss memos, *supra* note 187.
249. *Id.* Zimmerman, *supra* note 189.
250. *Id.*
251. Paul Weiss memos, *supra* note 187.
252. Orvin, *Eviction Moratoriums Under the CARES Act*, ACREL (April 20, 2020).
253. *Id.*

Section 4022 of the CARES Act provides a moratorium on residential foreclosures for borrowers with federally backed mortgage loans. Borrowers who affirm that they are experiencing COVID-19-related hardship can request forbearance from their loan service of up to 180 days, which can be extended for up to another 180-day period. Except for vacant or abandoned property, service providers cannot initiate a foreclosure, among other things, for a 60-day period from March 18, 2020.[254]

Under section 4023 of the CARES Act, borrowers with a federally backed multifamily mortgage loan may request a forbearance for up to 30 days, with two 30-day extensions. A tenant renting a dwelling unit within such a property cannot be evicted for nonpayment of rent or charged with late fees, penalties, or other charges during the forbearance.[255]

Section 4024 of the CARES Act provides eviction protection for residential tenants occupying a covered property, which is defined as any property that participates in a covered housing program as defined in section 41411(a) or the rural housing voucher program under section 542 of the Housing Act of 1949 or has a federally backed mortgage loan or a federally backed multifamily mortgage loan. During the moratorium period, landlords cannot charge fees, penalties, or other charges for nonpayment of rent; after the moratorium period expires, the landlord cannot evict a tenant without at least 30 days' notice. This does not affect eviction proceedings already filed.[256]

[h]—Conclusion

As a result of the pandemic, those of us in the commercial real estate industry have been finding ourselves faced with a unique set of cases with rarely used theories to try to resolve the issues in these cases. Hopefully, science will be able to discover a remedy to kill this deadly virus while we wrestle with the issues in interpreting these leases, including how to address rent defaults and the rolling effect of the nonpayments on tenant businesses, landlords as borrowers, lenders, and the economy in general. These cases will make precedent for future judges and case studies for future law students, but the important issue now is controlling this virus to reduce and eliminate the illness and deaths. Unfortunately, this critical reality does not get ample examination in a judicial matter or classroom analysis.

254. *Id.*
255. *Id.*
256. *Id.*

[14]—Additional Insured

[a]—In General

It has been long-standing accepted practice that landlords require that they be added as additional insureds on their tenants' liability insurance coverage relating to the tenants' premises and operations or activities on the premises. The value of the coverage clearly depends on the insurance policy language. A careful review of the policy before losses occur is important to assure that the coverage desired is in fact provided for. All too often, a party is merely added as an additional insured. The party added fails to review the policy. Then, when a claim arises, it is discovered that coverage is inadequate or subject to an exclusion or limitation.

With that in mind, no one should simply rely on a certificate of insurance stating that he or she is an additional insured under the relevant policy. Instead, it is important to review the policy itself to assure coverage adequacy and to reveal exclusions, conditions, or endorsements that may significantly impact the additional insured's coverage rights and entitlements.[257]

Changes in the industry endorsement forms for additional insureds may have the effect of limiting coverage to the additional insured. Changes in 2013 resulted in modifications to the additional insured endorsement form that limit the coverage provided to additional insureds.[258] The limits of the additional insured's coverage will not exceed the limit of the insurance coverage that the tenant or contractor is required to maintain in the lease or construction contract, and the naming of a party as an additional insured in a tenant's or contractor's policy may not be enough to give a landlord or property owner comfort in being adequately protected as an additional insured.[259] The landlord or property owner must require that its contract or lease require the tenant or contractor keep CGL insurance with sufficiently high enough limits and coverage types to completely cover what the additional insured endorsement is intended to protect.[260]

By way of background, the additional insured endorsement form used to protect lessors has changed over the past decades. In 1985, for example, in the ISO CG 20 10 11 85, the additional insured endorsement used for construction contracts stated that the party named in the endorsement was also considered to be an insured under the insured's policy regarding liability arising out of activities of the named insured or on

257. May, *supra* note 31.

258. The current versions of the additional insured forms are included below, in this section. For an excellent summary of the 2013 changes, see Moore, *supra* note 32.

259. *Id.* at 1.

260. *Id.*

the named insured's behalf.[261] By 2004, this protection was limited and covered only the additional insured for liability caused in whole or in part by the named insured's actions or omissions or by those acting on behalf of the named insured. Note that the owner's own sole negligence and the sole negligence of other contractors were no longer covered by the contractor's insurance.[262] The endorsement forms for lessors have also changed with limitations put into effect in 1996. These changes cover the additional insured for liability and now exclude occurrences taking place after the named insured ceases being a tenant in the premises and structural alterations, new construction, or demolition operations performed by or on behalf of the additional insured or manager.[263]

The additional insured forms promulgated in 2013 continue this limitation of protection provided to the additional insured. The Additional Insured—Designated Person or Organization Endorsement,[264] Additional Insured—Managers or Lessors of Premises,[265] Additional Insured—Owners, Lessees or Contractors—Scheduled Person or Organization,[266] and Additional Insured—Owners, Lessees or Contractors—Automatic Status When Required in Construction agreements amend in each instance who is an insured in Section II and limit such coverage to "liability for bodily injury, property or personal and advertising injury caused in whole or part by the acts or omissions of those acting on behalf of the Insured and is limited by (i) permitted by law; and (ii) the amount of contractual coverage required to be provided to the additional insured."[267] In the CG 20 11 04 13 endorsement, insurance does not apply to any occurrence taking place after the insured ceases to be a tenant in the premises or structural alterations, new construction, or demolition activities performed by or on behalf of the additional insured.

We go into a further discussion of these issues in Chapter 4A, Determining the Adequacy of Insurance Coverage.

261. *Id.*
262. *Id.*
263. *Id.* at 2. ISO CG 20 11 01 96.
264. ISO CG 20 26 04 13.
265. ISO CG 20 11 04 13.
266. ISO CG 20 01 04 13.
267. ISO CG 20 33 04 13.

Policy Number: **COMMERCIAL GENERAL LIABILITY**
CG 20 11 04 13

THIS ENDORSEMENT CHANGES THE POLICY. PLEASE READ IT CAREFULLY.

ADDITIONAL INSURED – MANAGERS OR LESSORS OF PREMISES

This endorsement modifies insurance provided under the following:

COMMERCIAL GENERAL LIABILITY COVERAGE PART

SCHEDULE

Designation Of Premises (Part Leased To You):
Name Of Person(s) Or Organization(s) (Additional Insured):
Additional Premium: $
Information required to complete this Schedule, if not shown above, will be shown in the Declarations.

A. **Section II – Who Is An Insured** is amended to include as an additional insured the person(s) or organization(s) shown in the Schedule, but only with respect to liability arising out of the ownership, maintenance or use of that part of the premises leased to you and shown in the Schedule and subject to the following additional exclusions:

This insurance does not apply to:

1. Any "occurrence" which takes place after you cease to be a tenant in that premises.

2. Structural alterations, new construction or demolition operations performed by or on behalf of the person(s) or organization(s) shown in the Schedule.

However:

1. The insurance afforded to such additional insured only applies to the extent permitted by law; and

2. If coverage provided to the additional insured is required by a contract or agreement, the insurance afforded to such additional insured will not be broader than that which you are required by the contract or agreement to provide for such additional insured.

B. With respect to the insurance afforded to these additional insureds, the following is added to **Section III – Limits Of Insurance:**

If coverage provided to the additional insured is required by a contract or agreement, the most we will pay on behalf of the additional insured is the amount of insurance:

1. Required by the contract or agreement; or

2. Available under the applicable Limits of Insurance shown in the Declarations;

whichever is less.

This endorsement shall not increase the applicable Limits of Insurance shown in the Declarations.

[b]—Cross-Liability Exclusions

A cross-liability exclusion generally "bars coverage for claims between certain insureds."[268] The exclusion is intended to prevent one insured under a policy from suing another insured under the same policy.

For example, to transfer their risk to other parties, insurers have been increasingly demanding during the application and underwriting process that contractors require that their subcontractors name the contractors as additional insureds on the subcontractors' policies. Similarly, an insurer could require that landlords require that their contractors and managing agents name the landlord as an additional insured on their policies.

The intent behind this requirement is to transfer the contractor's insurer's risk of loss downstream to the subcontractors' policies. A cross-liability exclusion in this situation can seriously impact upstream entities.[269] Cross-liability exclusions are not typically included in standard insurance coverage forms, so they can come as an unpleasant surprise to the additional insured.[270] A careful reading of the policy will reveal these exclusions and allow the parties to devise a coverage solution or at least assure that they are aware of the lack of coverage.

[c]—Assuring Adequate Coverage

One component of an effective insurance risk management review is a close analysis of the various policies. Special attention should be devoted to language regarding "all potentially applicable endorsements and exclusions,"[271] including:

(1) "whether the additional insured coverage is as broad as that specified in the [parties'] agreement";[272]
(2) "whether there is coverage for claims by or against any other insured, including the employees, agents or representatives of any named or additional insureds under the policy."[273]

Upstream entities seeking additional insured coverage should "specify in the governing agreement the desired scope of additional insured coverage and demand that the insurance policy not include any type of cross liability exclusion that would bar

268. May, *supra* note 31.
269. *Id.*
270. *Id.*
271. *Id.*
272. *Id.*
273. *Id.*

claims made by or against an additional insured."[274] Further, the agreement should "obligate the downstream insurer to provide the upstream entity with copies of all policies providing additional insured coverage."[275] A lot of aggravation can be avoided if one in "the additional insured relationship carefully considers whether the coverage is actually what was promised."[276]

[d]—Contractual Indemnification

Traditionally, the prime risk-transfer mechanism used between owners and general contractors or between general contractors and subcontractors has been contractual indemnification. For the most part, the only limitation on this risk-transfer mechanism has been the clarity with which the indemnification provisions were drafted. As states enact "anti-indemnification" statutes, limiting the scope of contractual indemnification, indemnitees look to additional insured coverage to defend and pay for their damages.[277]

Contractual indemnity clauses typically require a party to assume the obligation to cover the loss or damage that the other party may have incurred. Essentially, that one party agrees to assume responsibility for certain liability resulting from third-party claims against the other party to the contract. Even though it has been some time since ISO introduced "acts or omission" wording in its additional insured endorsements, there is not a clear consensus whether acts or omissions requires a finding of negligence on the named insured's part for the additional insured to be given coverage.[278] In some instances, a reference to "fault based" additional insured coverage suggests that bodily injury or property damage alone proximately caused by the named insured is sufficient to result in coverage for the additional insured. The acts or omissions concept may have some flaws. The practitioner should carefully review the proposed policy with his or her risk manager or insurance agent to determine the meaning of acts or omissions under the policy and if there is any state law affecting that interpretation.

One commentator has said that if the phrase acts or omissions means a court must find negligence on the part of the named insured to trigger damage payments for the additional insured, then one of the prime reasons for requiring additional insured status will have been frustrated.[279]

---

274. *Id.*

275. *Id.*

276. *Id.*

277. Craig F. Stanovich, *Additional Insured Issues 2016*, American College of Real Estate (Dec. 2016), *available at* https://www.irmi.com/articles/expert-commentary/additional-insured-issues-2016.

278. *Id.*

279. *Id.*

Chapter 4
Coinsurance

There are two common applications of the term "coinsurance": the coinsurance terms can be expressly stated or implied. Both applications result in insurance protection and recoveries, but from quite different approaches.

[1]—Express Coinsurance

Coinsurance applies to the level of insurance that an owner or tenant is required to maintain on a structure for coverage. The coinsurance clause in a lease requires that a tenant maintain a certain amount of insurance on its property, and the clause may really address a penalty an insurer may impose rather than a requirement as the wording typically states that a tenant not be a "coinsured." Where a tenant does not procure enough insurance for its property, a "coinsurance penalty" may kick in and the insurer may not cover the property loss as originally required or intended. Expressly stated coinsurance requirements in a policy limit the amount that an insured can recover for an underinsured property. Property policies will contain a coinsurance limit to force an insured to keep its policy limits at or near the full, current value of the insured property. The property owner who fails to maintain coverage at or near the full, current value of its insured property will be penalized in an amount proportionate to the underinsured value.

The effect of a coinsurance penalty is illustrated as follows:

Example 1:[1]

$$\frac{\$\text{ Loss} \times \text{Amount of Insurance Carried}}{\text{Amount of Insurance Required} \times (\text{Coinsurance Factor})} = \$\text{ Recovery}$$

1. See Ferrell, Property and Liability Insurance in Lease Transactions at 14–15 (1991).

Hypothetical: An insured landlord owns a building with a replacement cost value of $2,500,000 but elects to insure the building under a policy with a $1,500,000 limit and an 80% coinsurance requirement. A fire occurs with a $700,000 loss. The landlord would recover $525,000 subject to its policy deductibles.

$$\frac{\$\,700{,}000 \times \$1{,}500{,}000}{\$2{,}500{,}000 \times (80\%)} = \$525{,}000$$

A policy with an "agreed amount" endorsement would eliminate the need for coinsurance requirements. These endorsements are more important in instances where a landlord is dependent upon the tenant's insuring the full value of an office building in a triple net arrangement than in multitenant situations where the landlord will be maintaining its own insurance coverage.

[2]—Implied Coinsurance

[a]—In General

The second application of the term "coinsurance" should be referred to as "implied coinsurance" and is distinguishable from expressly stated coinsurance as discussed above. Implied coinsurance coverage of both landlord and tenant occurs when a court determines, upon its examination of facts and circumstances, that the actions or words of one party to a lease (usually the landlord) or the requirements imposed upon the other party (usually the tenant) resulted in the second party's inclusion under the first party's insurance policy. Stated more simply, if at the time a lease was negotiated, a landlord made representations to the tenant that reasonably led the tenant to believe it would be covered under the landlord's insurance policy or imposed certain financial conditions upon the tenant so that the tenant was effectively paying for all or part of the landlord's insurance coverage, the tenant may prevail on a claim that it was entitled to reimbursement for losses covered by the landlord's policy under the doctrine of coinsurance. This is the so-called *Goldman* effect. From this author's research, this is one of the first instances that advanced the theory of implied coinsurance and, as a former judicial law clerk, the author admires the methods in which the judge was able to reach an acceptable decision and conclusion for the parties by digging deeply and creatively into the facts and circumstances of the case

In *General Mills v. Goldman*,[2] one of the employees of the tenant negligently set off a destructive industrial plant fire. The owner's insurance carrier paid him the value of the land and building and then, as subrogee, intervened in the owner's suit against his tenant, General Mills. While the Eighth Circuit found that a lease provision

2. General Mills v. Goldman, 184 F.2d 359 (8th Cir. 1949).

relieved the tenant of the obligation to deliver or yield back the premises "in good condition" at the end of the term if the premises were destroyed by fire, it stretched its reasoning to bar the subrogation action by the landlord's insurer.[3] In ruling for the tenant, the *Goldman* court stated:

It is very clear that in light of all the provisions of the lease, the circumstances of its execution and the understanding about fire insurance coverage to which the lease was related that by the provision that on termination of the lease the tenant would return the property in good condition "loss by fire excepted" the parties meant a loss by fire such as is always meant when men are talking about or figure on the risk of it in business dealings—i.e., "the loss by fire"—which always is insured against in ordinary course and against which the landlords intended here and did take out insurance in an amount greater than the owner's investment.[4]

The lease in *Goldman* required the tenant, General Mills, to return the premises in good condition (loss by fire and ordinary wear excepted) and barred the tenant from doing anything that might lead to an increase in insurance premiums. However, the lease did not specifically require the tenant to obtain fire insurance. The *Goldman* court found that it was the parties' understanding at the time the lease was negotiated that the landlord would assume responsibility for obtaining insurance and that the landlord had indeed insured the premises and had recovered under the policy.[5] In other words, the court held that the tenant was a coinsured under the landlord's policy.

Initially, *Goldman* opened the gates for insurers to bring actions for recovery of fire damage cases caused by negligent tenants. A series of cases followed *Goldman* in which insurers were able to recover against tenants on the basis of a subrogation action.[6] Negligent tenants, and even third parties who sold potentially dangerous materials to tenants, were all targets of these insureds' actions.[7]

Landlords have not been spared either. In *Western Fire Insurance Co. v. Milner Hotels, Inc.*,[8] the tenant's insurer recovered against a landlord-hotel operator for

---

3. In the absence of the "yield up" clause in the lease, the tenant would have been otherwise liable to the landlord's insurer under the subrogation claim.

4. *Goldman*, 184 F.2d at 366.

5. *Id.* at 365–66.

6. *See, e.g.*, the following: Sixth Circuit: Home Insurance Co. v. Hamilton, 295 F.2d 108 (6th Cir. 1968); state courts: Louisiana: Hanover Insurance Co. v. Jacobson-Young, Inc., 294 So. 2d 564 (La. App. 1974); Michigan: Bayley Products, Inc. v. American Plastics Products Co., 30 Mich. App. 590, 186 N.W.2d 813 (1971). For a more exhaustive compilation of cases and authority, see Milton R. Friedman, Friedman on Leases § 9.9 at 529 n.20 (3d ed. 1990).

7. *See, e.g.*, American Guaranty & Liability Insurance Co. v. Little, 328 So. 2d 708 (La. Ct. App. 1976) (sale of stereo receiver without adequate warning that its placement could cause a fire by blocking vents).

8. Western Fire Insurance Co. v. Milner Hotels, Inc., 232 F.2d 779 (8th Cir. 1956).

damage to the tenant's restaurant in the hotel from a fire started in the hotel. Other cases following the *Western Fire Insurance* case have had similar results.

Goldman's rationale of finding a party as a coinsured under the other's policy has been followed by many jurisdictions. Many of these cases have involved leases that expressly required the landlord to furnish insurance for the premises. Some of these cases have protected the negligent tenant even without the expressed requirement that the landlord secure fire insurance.

A number of cases have followed the *Goldman* holding, such as *Rizzuto v. Morris*,[9] in which the court reasoned that (1) it would be an unfair hardship to require a tenant to insure against its own negligence when it is paying, through its rent, for the fire insurance that covers the premises in favor of the landlord; (2) insurance companies expect to pay their insureds for their negligently caused fires and they adjust their rates accordingly;[10] and (3) the ordinary and usual meaning of "loss by fire" includes fires of negligent origin. The *Rizzuto* court concluded,

We do not mean our opinion states that a lessor may never shift to the lessee the burden of insurance against the lessee's negligence. We state only that; [where] there is no clear language or other admissible evidence showing an agreement to the contrary, a lease agreement should be read to place upon the lessor the burden of insuring the premises (as distinguished from a lessee's personal property) against a lessor's and lessee's negligence. Moreover, where the lease has been drawn by the lessor, the language will be strictly construed against the lessor and its insured.[11]

[b]—Commentary[12]

Practice tip: Irrespective of the line of cases following *Goldman* above, I advised clients to first obtain their own insurance coverage rather than rely upon the outcome of cases such as *Goldman*. The benefit of having insurance in place rather than relying on the outcome of as arguably narrow a decision as *Goldman* will undoubtedly be more effective in time, cost, and outcome than having to go through a lengthy and uncertain litigation, especially when the parties need to access any insurance monies to repair damage or rebuild a building. An insurance company has no subrogation claim against its own insured. To allow otherwise would permit the insurer to pass

9. 22 Wash. App. 951, 592 P.2d 688 (1979).

10. In effect, the tenant stands in the shoes of the insured landlord for the limited purpose of defeating a subrogation claim.

11. *Rizzuto*, 22 Wash. App. at 690.

12. This subsection appeared in substantially identical form in A. DiSciullo, *A Guide to Subrogation in Commercial Leases*, Real Estate L.J. (Spring 1992), and is reprinted herein with permission of Warren, Gorham & Lamont.

losses through to its insured and evade its obligations to cover its insured.[13] If it is later determined in court in which, as in *Goldman*, parol evidence was allowed to explain the nature of the agreement between the parties, that insurance was obtained for the mutual benefit of tenant and landlord, the subrogated insurer may not sue the tenant for fire damage resulting from the tenant's negligence.[14] This finding does not require a lease clause or any other writing to support it. However, it is necessary for the court to look at the parties' intent and find some agreement between them to include the tenant under the owner's policy.[15] In some instances, even if the parties merely discussed insurance generally, without any specific reference to fire insurance, the courts have concluded that the lease intended to cover the tenant in the owner's fire policy. These findings have undoubtedly caused apoplexy for the landlord's insurers and their agents. Practitioners should note the uphill efforts the proponent must make to show evidence of this particular party being covered under the other's policy that lends itself to possible proffering of "less than perfect" evidence in the form of unclear writings or even parol evidence that may be relying upon the testimony of witnesses not remembering the specific agreements made through the passage of time or even potential witnesses still being alive at trial, as the author has experienced in his practice.

Experts differ greatly from one another on whether a tenant is presumed to be a coinsured under an owner's policy. Even when the courts have found the tenant to be a coinsured under the landlord's policy for its own leasehold interest, the tenant may still be liable for damage to other parts of the landlord's property.[16] The cases are virtually indistinguishable from one another and serve as equally authoritative precedent for completely opposite conclusions.

In those instances where the tenant is presumed to be a coinsured, the courts' reasoning has been based on the theory that a landlord's expressed covenant to insure is for the benefit of both landlord and tenant. The basis for this conclusion is that

---

13. Chenoweth Motor Co. v. Cotton, 2 Ohio Misc. 123, 124, 207 N.E.2d 412, 413 (1965).

14. *See, e.g.*, West American Insurance Co. v. Pic Way Shoes of Cent. Mich., Inc., 110 Mich. Ct. App. 684, 313 N.W.2d 187, 188 (1981), citing Woodruff v. Wilson Oil Co., 178 Ind. Ct. App. 428, 382 N.E.2d 1009 (1978); Page v. Scott, 263 Ark. 684, 567 S.W.2d, 101, 103 (1978). *See also* Pendlebury v. Western Casualty & Surety Co., 89 Idaho 456, 406 P.2d 129, 136 (1965) (insurer barred from subrogation action against own insured).

15. *See, e.g.*, General Mills, Inc. v. Goldman, 184 F.2d 359 (8th Cir. 1949); Acquisto v. Joe R. Hahn Enter., 95 N.M. 193, 619 P.2d 1237, 1239 (1980); Rizzuto v. Morris, 22 Wash. App. 951, 592 P.2d 688, 690 (1979); Page v. Scott, 263 Ark. 684, 567 S.W.2d 101, 103 (1978). *See also Landlord and Tenant*, 49 Am. Jur. 3d, § 272, at 287 (1970); *Landlord and Tenant*, 51C C.J.S., § 374, at 1000 n.68 (1968).

16. Aetna Ins. Co. v. Craftwall of Idaho, Inc., 757 F.2d 1030 (1985); Agra-By-Products, Inc. v. Agway, Inc. 347 N.W.2d 142, 152 (N.D. 1984) (even where the tenant is a coinsured, it is still liable for amounts in excess of insurance). *Cf.*, Bonneville on the Hill Co. v. Sloane, 572 P.2d 402 (Utah 1977) (once the tenant is found to be a coinsured, it will escape liability for all portions of the landlord's property).

the landlord would not have a section in the lease covering insurance if the insurance were only for the landlord's benefit.[17] Several decisions have taken this reasoning even further. In the absence of an expressed agreement to the contrary, the landlord is presumed to carry insurance for the tenant's benefit.[18] A prominent expert has even suggested adopting a rule barring a landlord's insured from proceeding against a negligent tenant when the lease is ambiguous and the insurance policy is either silent or unclear.[19]

Such presumptions certainly will be disputed, and a number of other courts have rejected this reasoning. There are a host of cases that have rejected this presumption of coinsurance and found the tenant liable for damage resulting from its own negligence in the absence of an expressed provision to the contrary.[20]

These cases and authorities seem to indicate that if the lease does not have a clause naming the tenant as a coinsured, the tenant is responsible for the damages it causes. At least one leading authority agrees.[21] Policy differences, then give a practitioner no clear direction in determining how a court will decide the issue of whether a tenant is a coinsured when the lease does not expressly provide for this. Almost each case becomes a test case, requiring expensive and time-consuming discovery to determine the parties' intent on whether the tenant is covered by the owner's policy.

The published cases on this issue are not easily reconciled.[22] Generally, the courts in the earlier decisions were reluctant to find the tenant to be a coinsured, especially if there was no expressed contractual agreement.[23] This position was consistent with the common law principles that the tenant was liable for its own negligence when the lease did not transfer the responsibility for repairs over the landlord.[24] Cases have been slowly rejecting this position and finding ways to have the tenant considered the landlord's coinsured, taking their cue from the *Goldman* court, which found a way to

---

17. Monsanto Chemical Co. v. American Bitumuls Co., 249 S.W.2d 428, 432 (Mo. 1952); Fry v. Jordan Auto Co., 224 Miss. 445, 80 So. 2d 53, 58 (1955). *Accord*, Newport News Shipbuilding & Drydock Co. v. United States, 34 F.2d 100, 106 (4th Cir. 1929). *See generally* Milton R. Friedman, *Landlords, Tenants and Fires—Insurers' Right of Subrogation*, 43 Cornell L.Q. 225, 228 & n.12 (1957).

18. *See, e.g.*, Alaska Ins. Co. v. RCA Alaska Communications, Inc., 623 F.2d 1216, 1218 (Alaska 1981).

19. R. Keeton, Insurance Law, § 4.4(b) at 210 (1971).

20. *See, e.g.*, Acquisito v. Joe R. Hahn Enter., 95 N.M. 193, 619 P.2d 1237, 1239 (1980) (holding tenant liable because "[i]n the absence of an agreement between the parties specifying which of them will carry fire insurance for the benefit of both parties, or an express clause in the lease relieving a party from his own negligence, each party must bear the risk of loss for his own negligence.").

21. Million, *Real and Personal Property*, 33 N.Y.U. L. Rev. 552, 585 (1985).

22. Aetna Ins. Co. v. Craftwall of Idaho, Inc., 757 F.2d 1030, 1033 (1985).

23. *See, e.g.*, Maistico v. Hot Shoppes, Inc., 287 F.2d 349, 351 (D.C. Cir. 1961); Acquisto v. Joe R. Hahn Enter. 95 N.M. 193, 619 P.2d 1240 (1980). *See generally* Matan, *Liability for Loss by Fire Among Insurer, Tenant and Landlord*, 18 Ohio St. L.J. 423, 425–26 (1957).

24. United States v. Bostwick, 94 U.S. 53, 68, 24 L. Ed. 65 (1876); Miller v. Miller, 217 Miss. 650, 64 So. 2d 739 (1953). *See also* Annot., 10 A.L.R.2d 1023 (1950).

have the tenant covered for its employee's negligence when there was insurance covering the loss.

A novel theory holds that by paying its rent, the tenant has paid for its possible negligence in advance. These cases reason that the rent payments have somehow been adjusted to cover the landlord's expected fire insurance expenses.[25] Some courts have also accepted the notion that when the landlord has insured its building against "losses by fire," its tenants may reasonably expect that all fire losses caused by ordinary negligence will be covered by the owner's insurance even if the lease is silent on the issue of coinsurance.[26] As specious as this reasoning may seem to be, a number of courts have adopted this argument on the grounds that holding a tenant liable would encourage multiple insurance policies on the same building by the landlord and each of its tenants.[27]

Several noted insurance and leasing authorities have seized upon the reasoning of *Rizzuto v. Morris*[28] that insurance companies write their policies with the expectation that they will have to pay their insureds for negligently caused fires and adjust their rates accordingly. These experts believe that subrogation is, essentially, a profit center for insurance companies, since the expected value of the fire losses has already been discounted in the premium charged to the insurer's clients. According to these authorities, subrogation is a windfall for the insurer. It plays no part in the rate schedules (or only a minor one), and no reduction is made in insuring interests, such as that of a secured creditor, when the subrogation right will obviously be worth something. Hence, in such a case, no reason appears for extending subrogation rights to the insurer. Even in the instances when casualty damage is caused by a negligent party, these authorities argue that the insurer should not shift the loss to the tortfeasor since the insurer has already been paid by the insured to cover the risk of any losses caused by the insured's negligence.[29]

25. Liberty Mutual Fire Insurance Co. v. Auto Spring Supply Co., 59 Cal. App. 3d 860, 131 Cal. Rptr. 211, 214–15 (1976); Sutton v. Jondahl, 532 P.2d 478, 482 (Okla. Ct. App. 1975). *See also* Rizzuto v. Morris, 22 Wash. App. 951, 592 P.2d 688, 692 n.3 (1979) (rejecting argument that public policy is violated by allowing a tenant to exculpate himself from liability for his own negligence); Page v. Scott, 263 Ark. 684, 567 S.W.2d, 101, 103–04 (1978). *See* Matan, *supra* note 23, at 432.

26. Alaska Ins. Co. v. RCA Alaska Communications, Inc., 623 F.2d 1216, 1219 (Alaska 1981); Rizzuto v. Morris, 22 Wash. App. 951, 592 P.2d 688, 691 (1979); Sutton v. Jondahl, 532 P.2d 478, 482 (Okla. Ct. App. 1975).

27. Friedman, *supra* note 6, §§ 9.9–9.10.

28. 22 Wash. App. 951, 592 P.2d 688 (1979).

29. E. Patterson, Essentials of Insurance Law 122 (1935). *Accord*, Liberty Mutual Fire Insurance Co. v. Auto Spring Supply Co., 59 Cal. App. 3d 860, 865, 131 Cal. Rptr. 211, 214 (1976), cited in Friedman, *supra* note 6, § 9.9 at 542. *See also* Agra-By-Products, Inc. v. Agway, Inc., 347 N.W.2d 142, 152 (N.D. 1984) ("insurers expect to pay their insureds for negligently caused fires, and they adjust their rates accordingly").

A tenant relying upon the theory of coinsurance will encounter numerous pitfalls, the first being that with the split in authority, no tenant can reasonably expect to be able to predict the outcome of a casualty claim before an exhaustive trial and, at least, an initial appeal. Moreover, releasing the tenant from liability under a coinsurance theory may relieve a tenant for repaying casualty losses in its landlord's building but may not afford protection for damage to adjoining buildings.[30] Finally, the coinsured tenant receives benefits only to the extent of the limits of the landlord's policy. Damage over and above these limits is the tenant's responsibility. The measure of damages assessed against the tenant in at least one case included the replacement cost of rebuilding a building as well as lost profits and other consequential expenses.[31]

30. Hardware Mutual Insurance Co. v. C.A. Snyder, Inc., 242 F.2d 64 (3d Cir. 1957); Sannit v. Aarona, 297 F. Supp. 798 (D. Del. 1969); Agra-By-Products, Inc. v. Agway, Inc., 347 N.W.2d (N.D. 1984).

31. Brown v. Aaron Rents, Inc. 414 F. Supp. 653 (W.D. Ok. 1975).

Chapter 4A
Determining the Adequacy of Insurance Coverage

Commercial leases almost always contain provisions that require the tenant to purchase and maintain insurance, and often require the landlord to purchase and maintain insurance regarding occurrences in common areas.[1] While the scope of these provisions may vary greatly, the goal of insurance is to protect both the landlord and tenant from claims of personal injury or property damage at the leased premises. It is critical to ensure that the policy carries adequate limits based on a current fixed-asset verification.[2]

Landlords and tenants often fail to adequately consider "the effect of certain aspects of the underlying insurance policy,"[3] often looking no further than the summary in a declarations page or certificate evidencing the policy's existence. e parties should review the actual language of underlying insurance policies as part of their risk management strategy. Among the important points to consider when landlords and

1. See Christine Barker, *Insurance broker sold you a worthless policy? Tough luck*, Construction Law Blog (Mar. 17, 2014), http://www.grconstructionlawblog.com/insurance-broker-sold-you-a-worthless-policy-tough-luck (last visited Jan. 31, 2017), discussing *San Diego Assemblers, Inc. v. Work Comp For Less Insurance Services, Inc.*, 220 Cal. App. 4th 1363 (2013), where the court held that an insurance broker is obligated to procure only the insurance requested, not necessarily the insurance the client needs. But see, Jane R. Goldsmith, *Broker may have affirmative duty to advise client*, Phelps Dunbar LLP (April 11, 2014), discussing *Tiara Condominium Ass'n v. Marsh, USA, Inc.*, 2014 WL 109140 (S.D. Fla. 2014), in which the court's opinion may dramatically expand Florida insurance brokers' duties regarding policy selection and coverage under certain circumstances. Following the court's logic, "if a fact-finder determines that a 'special relationship' exists between the broker and client, the broker may have an affirmative duty to recommend the amounts and types of insurance reasonably necessary to protect the client's interests." *Id.* "*Tiara* is the first case in Florida expressly holding that a broker may have an affirmative duty to advise a client when facts suggesting the existence of a 'special relationship' are present." *Id.* Although "persuasive, this opinion is not binding on any Florida court. While its ultimate impact is yet to be determined it certainly will play a role in the analysis of a broker's duty going forward." *Id.*

2. Vincent E. Morgan, *Preparing Your Business for the 2012 Atlantic Hurricane Season*, Perspectives on Insurance Recovery Newsletter (Summer 2012.

3. Grossberg, *Adequacy of Insurance Limits Advanced Considerations for Landlords and Tenants*, Commercial Leasing Law & Strategy, 3 (Law Journal Newsletters July 1, 2011).

tenants make risk management decisions are extent of coverage, requirements, exclusions, deductibles, limitations, internal sublimits that may reduce available proceeds, and the interplay of the policy coverages. Further, some policies also place conditions on coverage based on the location of insured property, only covering property "within a certain distance from a covered location."[4]

[1]—Coverage Layers

Each party should consider the value of multiple insurance coverage layers, including the bottom layer of primary insurance, which is the initial policy triggered by a claim.[5] Then there are a variety of "umbrella" policies, which "provide additional coverage that comes into play only after a predetermined amount of primary coverage has been exhausted. Umbrella policies, unlike other excess coverage insurance policies, may also provide additional primary coverage for gaps or exclusions in the underlying primary policy."[6] Each such policy needs to be carefully evaluated to determine the extent of coverage, requirements, and limitations. Finally, there are excess coverage policies, which often provide coverage only of the same type as was provided by the primary insurance policy.

Among the distinctions between these layers of coverage is that "primary policies typically (though not always) provide protection against the cost of defending the insured party or parties against claims involving covered risks. A general liability policy, for example, may cover the costs of defending litigation against an owner and occupant arising from injuries and other damages caused by alleged negligence or other wrongful acts or omissions that occurred at the leased premises. At the primary layer, these defense costs usually are not charged against the policy limits, which can only be exhausted by the so-called 'indemnity' payments made by the insurance company under the policy for settlements or judgments."[7] This is a significant benefit that may not exist under umbrella or excess coverage policies.

[2]—Defense within Limits Policies

In the mid-1980s, insurers began including so-called "defense within limits" (DWL) language in certain types of insurance policies, including some umbrella and excess policies.[8] "A DWL policy is one where defense costs are charged against and reduce

4. Morgan, *supra* note 2.
5. *Id.*
6. *Id.*
7. *Id.*
8. *Id.*

the policy limits."[9] Several jurisdictions have restricted the use of DWL policies, including Arkansas,[10] Minnesota,[11] Missouri,[12] Montana,[13] New York,[14] and Oregon.[15]

[3]—Enforceability

The enforceability of DWL language will depend on the applicable state law. In the absence of a clear choice of law provision in the insurance policy, a determination of applicable law will have to be made.[16]

"If DWL language is enforceable in your jurisdiction, and depending on the language of your policy, it may be wise to purchase or require additional insurance coverage to cover defense costs and increase limit requirements from a risk management perspective.[17] *This affects the amount of coverage available to the insured because every dollar spent on defense of litigation depletes the policy limits and diminishes the amount of coverage remaining to pay claims.*"[18] Thus, the parties should carefully read the defense language in insurance policies and pay attention to the coverage being purchased by the other party to the lease.[19]

---

9. *Id.*

10. *Id.* at 4, citing Ark. Code § 23-79-307(5)(A), which "requires a separate limit for defense costs to prevent the depletion of indemnity limits, and forbids the approval of any policy in which defense expenditures deplete policy limits, unless a separate limit for defense costs equal to 100% of the annual aggregate limit of liability stated in the policy for judgments or settlements is offered for defense costs or claims expenses to the insured."

11. *Id.*, citing Minn. § 60A.08, subdiv. 13, which "provides that '[n]o insurer shall issue or renew a policy of liability insurance in this state that reduces the limits of liability stated in the policy by the costs of the legal defense,' but excepts 'large commercial risks,' defined as an insured with gross annual revenues of 'at least $10,000,000.'"

12. *Id.*, citing Missouri Insurance Bulletin 98-04, which "allows DWL policies in the state only if approved and in circumstances involving 'sophisticated' insureds."

13. *Id.*, citing Mont. Code § 33-1-502, which "prohibits any provision in a casualty insurance from 'permitting defense costs within limits, except as permitted by the commissioner.'"

14. *Id.*, citing N.Y. Insur. Dept. Reg. § 71.3, which "allows DWL provisions only in certain circumstances, and then defense costs can reduce the policy limits by only 50% unless the insured is given full control of its defense."

15. *Id.*, citing Ore. Code § 742.063, which "provides that a liability policy that includes defense costs within policy limits 'may not be delivered or issued for delivery unless approved by [the] director,' and mandates the inclusion of a statement disclosing that costs of defendingclaims are included in policy limits."

16. *Id.*

17. *Id.*

18. *Id.*

19. *Id.*

[4]—Establishing an Insurance Coverage Plan and Understanding Forms of Coverage

[a]—In General

Even when a company is insured, an unexpected or catastrophic loss can force the company to go out of business. Therefore, it is imperative to understand the risks and how various insurance policies cover those risks to manage them and maintain stability.[20]

First it is necessary to obtain the correct insurance. Merely having an insurance policy does not mean that the insured is sufficiently covered for the casualties and amounts of loss that an insured may sustain. To have the right insurance and form of coverage, each party needs to understand its respective risks and potential amount of loss should an event occur. As such, both landlord and tenant need to understand their respective risks, and this entails each party understanding their agreement, one's own and other's business, and the relationship in which they want to enter or have already entered. Simply covering tangible property itself is usually not enough to make most businesses whole in the aftermath of a natural disaster. Oftentimes restoration will take months to compete so that the company's operations and income stream will be interrupted.

Property and business interruption insurance policies are complex, and the insurance situation of suppliers, customers, and other business partners may directly impact a business as well. For example, even if a business does not suffer direct physical damage to its facilities because of a natural disaster or other loss, if customers or suppliers suffer a loss or damage, that can affect the supply chain or cause an interruption to the business, including a loss of revenue or sales. Thus, insurance to cover business interruption will be an important component of insurance coverage planning. In addition, preparations for hurricanes have caused governmental authorities to order evacuations and business shutdowns, impeding access to business premises and interrupting business operations, utility services, and supply chains. In the aftermath of storms, damage in the form of flooding and widespread power outages may continue for a significant period.

Further, as in any other business situation, it is advisable to ensure that the parties secure and maintain adequate and appropriate insurance for the term of their relationship.[21] The lease agreement should specifically address insurance coverage types, risk allocation, and liability issues, especially regarding potential liability aris-

---

20. Joseph D. Jean, *Is Your Company Prepared for a Disaster? The Property and Business Interruption Insurance Checklist* (Sept. 2011).

21. Adam K. Hollander, *Getting the Most Out of Your Contractual Insurance Provisions*, Barnes & Thornburg LLP (Dec. 2, 2014).

ing from conduct in furtherance of the parties' agreement. If properly drafted, one party's insurance can be a source of additional coverage for the other party in the event that liability arising out of the one party's activities is attributed to the other.[22] Determining the type of coverage and the extent of coverage needed will depend on the nature of the parties' activities and the associated risks. The following are some suggestions to consider when drafting insurance requirements provisions:

> Have your company (and, as necessary, your company's parents, affiliates, subsidiaries, directors and officers) specifically named as an Additional Insured in your counterpart's policies. By doing so, you can minimize the risk of having to claim under your own insurance in the event that you face liability arising out of your counterpart's conduct.
>
> Make sure that the limits of insurance are sufficient to cover any potential exposure and, in no event less than the amount otherwise carried by your counterpart.
>
> Do not allow your counterpart to limit the insurance obligations through sizeable deductibles or self-insured retentions (SIR). If your counterpart cannot secure first dollar coverage, then make it clear that, in the event of a claim, the counterpart is responsible for satisfying the deductible or the SIR.
>
> Draft your insurance requirements so that they are wholly independent of and do not impact or limit any separate indemnity obligations you may otherwise seek to impose on your counterpart.
>
> Expressly state that the required insurance shall not be deemed to release or diminish the liability of your counterpart.
>
> Require your counterpart's insurance to be primary and noncontributory to any coverage you maintain. With such language, in the event that you make a claim as an additional insured, your counterpart's carrier will be prohibited from seeking contribution against your own carrier.
>
> Require your counterpart's carrier to waive any and all rights of recovery, contribution and/or subrogation against you and your insurers. By doing so, in the event that your counterpart faces covered liability based on your conduct (either in whole or in part), its carrier will not be able to seek recovery against you.

22. *Id.*

Require your counterpart's carriers to provide you with advance notice of any policy modification, cancellation and/or nonrenewal.

Have your counterpart specifically schedule your agreement as an Insured Contract. This will enhance the prospect of your counterpart obtaining coverage for any indemnified claim that you may have against it.

Specify that your acceptance of an incomplete policy or your failure to identify a deficiency in the required coverage shall not be construed as a waiver of your counterpart's insurance obligations.[23]

[b]—Establishing a Plan

In addition to determining the correct insurance types and coverage amounts, it is important to have a plan in place to handle each aspect of a claim, including preparing the proof of loss and negotiating the claim with the insurance company.[24] Since most insurance policies require the insurer to preserve and protect insured property from further damage, failure to do so will prejudice the insured's recovery rights. Having a plan in place to assure that proper procedure is followed after a loss is important as well.

[i]—Before a Loss

Well before a loss occurs, it is necessary to understand the terms of existing policies, their coverage, limitations, and exclusions. Among the policies to consider obtaining are property damage, business interruption, contingent business interruption, extended period of liability, logistics and extra expense, sue and labor, civil authority, actual cash value versus replacement cost value, service interruption, flood , and other natural disaster coverage.[25] Each policy may have its own notice requirements, deductible, waiting period, exclusions, and limitations. Terms among policies may conflict. Keeping a list of coverage and basic information like notice of claim requirements, deductibles, and coverage will simplify the claims process should a loss or damage occur. Also, maintaining a list of insured properties (with model numbers and pictures), their values (supported by receipts), and replacement costs will save time when a claim is filed. It is also a good idea to keep copies of the policies and supporting documentation off premises so that they are readily accessible even if the affected premises are destroyed. Further, have an emergency response plan in place and maintain communication with personnel so that they are prepared to take

23. *Id.*
24. *Id.*
25. *Id.*

the steps necessary to preserve and protect the property and handle loss or damage appropriately.

Develop a plan for measuring business interruption losses in the event of a wide-impact catastrophe such as a natural disaster. The timeframe could include pre- and post-disaster business interruption. Having a properly managed insurance recovery process in place can mitigate the impact of the loss on a business.

[ii]—After a Loss

Steps taken in the immediate aftermath of a storm or other natural disaster are "critical to preserving and maximizing a company's insurance recovery, as well as ensuring that the company's business levels return to normal as quickly as possible." From the standpoint of insurance, these steps include the following:

(1) notifying all carriers in accordance with the policies;
(2) forming a claims team, utilizing both internal personnel from the risk management, operations, legal and accounting functions as well as external claim consultants and coverage counsel;
(3) setting up separate accounts to track post-claim losses and expenses incurred in the recovery efforts; and
(4) establishing and observing effective claim management procedures to avoid disputes and streamline the process, such as preservation of the carriers salvage rights, protecting covered property against further loss and seeking advances against the ultimate loss payment.

Commercial property insurance generally provides coverage for physical damage caused to business premises and other property, and it often also covers the loss of profits due to business interruption. Coverage may also extend under commercial property forms or more specialized insurance for supply-chain disruptions, loss of markets, and even liabilities arising from inabilities to meet commercial obligations.[26]

As soon as a potentially covered loss begins, it is necessary to start assessing coverage and quantifying loss. Prompt action is essential. This is especially true when dealing with water damage, which can cause mold and bacterial threats.[27] Immediately obtain and review insurance policies, carefully analyzing them to determine coverage and to assure that notification, proof of loss, and other deadlines are met, and that proper documentation is provided before preparing the proof of loss. Notify the insurance carrier after the loss if your suppliers or customers have been impacted,

26. DeNatale, Foresta, Klein, Levin & Plumer, *Hurricane Irene: Securing Insurance Coveragefor Property Damage and Business Interruption*, Orrick Insurance Practice Group Client Alert (Sept. 6, 2011).

27. See Chapter 6[2] for a further discussion on mold.

even if your property has not been damaged.[28] Following a loss, it will be important to prevent any further damage or injury. It is advisable to attempt to mitigate losses by arranging alternate suppliers/sources and so on to meet your company's needs.[29]

"Carefully and thoroughly document the loss, including increased payroll expenses, overtime, and other increased expenses associated with mitigating losses, extra expense, logistics, travel, etc."[30] Never simply discard damaged property. It is important to keep the property and preserve the area of the loss/damage so that the insurer can inspect it. If it is necessary to remove or discard the property, be sure to take pictures or video so that there is a record of the property damage. Documenting a loss should also include proof of business performance prior to, during, and after loss.[31] Make sure to comply with any and all applicable notice requirements set forth in the policies.

[iii]—The Steps to Take

To secure coverage benefits, it is critical to take prompt, appropriate action, including the following:

(1) **Gather and review all potentially applicable insurance policies and evaluate the scope of coverage.** "The most common policies providing coverage will be first-party property policies, including commercial property, marine property and event cancellation policies. Most property policies are sold on an all-risk basis, meaning that the policy provides coverage for all risks of loss unless the loss is specifically excluded. The key step in evaluating coverage for a hurricane loss under an all-risk policy is to evaluate the policy exclusions."[32]

(2) **Consider coverage for contingent business interruption losses.** Lost income caused by damage to the supplier operations and firm customers may be covered as contingent business interruption loss under the property policy.

(3) **Provide timely notice of loss and proof of loss obligations.** "Commercial insurance typically requires the policyholder to provide notice to the insurer of a loss 'as soon as practicable.' Thereafter, the policyholder is required to file a sworn, detailed 'proof of loss,' often as soon as 60 days after the loss-

---

28. Jean, *supra* note 20.

29. *Id.*

30. *Id.*

31. Steven Gilford & Sheri Drucker Davis, *Insurance Considerations in Hurricanes, Floods and Other Natural Disasters*, Proskauer Client Alert (Sept. 1, 2011), *available at* https://www.proskauer.com/alert/insurance-considerations-in-hurricanes-floods-and-other-natural-disasters.

32. L.D. Simmons, J. Mark Lawless & Pamela A. Hopper, *Hurricane Irma—Commercial Property Damage and Business Interruption Insurance Checklist*, Insurance Recovery Blog (Sept. 22, 2017.

causing event. Any failure to meet these deadlines can lead to disputes with insurers that may compromise your ability to recover or even result in a forfeiture of coverage."[33]

(4) **Document and quantify all losses.** "Insurers require that all claimed losses be quantified in the policyholder's proof of loss. Depending on your policies, coverage may be available not just for destruction or damage to real property, equipment, inventory, furniture, data and records, but also various categories of business interruption, including interruptions continuing days after the storm from lost workdays, civil authority closures, and delays in deliveries. It is critical to begin documenting and quantifying such losses promptly while information is still fresh, ideally with the help of experienced coverage counsel and forensic accountants. Take picture and video to document the damage. Further, the early retention of experts helps to avoid missteps."[34]

(5) **Mitigate losses and protect property from further loss or damage.** "Standard property policies require the insured to mitigate the physical damage and business interruption arising from a catastrophic storm. Ensure that your firm takes these steps."[35]

(6) **Form a team to handle claims.** Include employees and outside experts, such as "outside counsel, independent adjusters and forensic accountants. Claims from catastrophic storms often raise significant coverage issues, and it is important to retain counsel early in the process. Forensic accountants also can be essential in developing and presenting a business interruption claim to a carrier."[36]

(7) **Carefully document communications with insurers and their agents.** Resolution of catastrophe claims can be slow. Detailed records will discourage delays and can be used to position the company to make a bad faith claim later, if necessary.[37]

(8) **Be cautious about internal and external communications about claims and losses.** These communications may be discoverable by the insurance company in litigation, and the way the company characterizes its loss may be used by the carrier against the insured.[38] Have one point of contact with the broker and with the insurer.[39]

---

33. DeNatale, Foresta, Klein, Levin & Plumer, *supra* note 26.
34. *Id.*
35. Simmons, Lawless & Hopper, *supra* note 32.
36. *Id.*
37. *Id.*
38. *Id.*
39. *Id.*

(9) **Keep accounting records and all documents related to property damage and business interruption.** "Key documents to include are: (a) production and sales records; (b) records of cost of goods sold; (c) business forecasts and budgets; (d) inventory records; (e) cost accounting records; and (f) payroll records."[40]

(10) **Keep records of costs incurred to avoid or reduce the loss.** "Key documents to include are: (a) overtime records related to maintaining production at pre-loss levels; (b) price premiums and extra shipping charges to expedite delivery of machinery or inventory; (c) relocation costs; (d) costs incurred in the purchase of generator or replacement power; and (e) costs of notifying customers of a relocation or to maintain customer relationships during down-time."[41]

(11) **Seek partial payments.** "Carriers often seek to delay full payment of the loss by making a minimal 'good faith' payment and claiming that it cannot make full payment until all coverage and claim value issues are resolved. Challenge this approach by insisting that the insurer provide a coverage position in writing, by submitting partial proofs of loss when portions of the claim are quantified, and by demanding payment for the undisputed portion of the claim."[42]

(12) **Be sure to comply with all policy requirements.** Standard requirements include deadlines for submitting proofs of claim and for filing suit if there is a dispute regarding the claim. Time limitations must be strictly adhered to, unless the insurer agrees in writing to an extension.[43]

Insurance coverage may go beyond tangible property damage, covering intangibles, electronic records, and other data. In addition to covering "lost value of property, equipment and inventory," all types of damage that may be covered and the specific policies should be considered.[44] These include the following:

- **Property damage.** Most first-party property policies cover much more than just physical damage to owned property. "Many policies define property damage to include loss of use of your property that has not been physically damaged."[45] The property covered often includes inventory as well as leased property; property in the policyholder's care, custody, or control; and property for which the policyholder is liable or in which the policyholder has an

40. *Id.*
41. *Id.*
42. *Id.*
43. *Id.*
44. DeNatale, Foresta, Klein, Levin & Plumer, *supra* note 26.
45. Gilford & Davis, *supra* note 31.

insurable interest.[46] Many policies also include additional coverage for "debris removal, demolition and increased cost of construction in the event of physical loss to covered property."[47] Costs associated with "expediting repairs are often also included."[48] Further, while such provisions "vary significantly, 'preservation of property' and 'sue and labor' clauses often cover costs incurred to prevent or minimize actual or threatened loss."[49] The causes and type of loss or damage covered by an "all-risk" policy are limited only by the express exclusions in the policy.[50]

- **Business interruption coverage.** Business interruption coverage typically applies to reimburse an insured for "losses sustained due to the total or partial suspension of the policyholder's operations during a period of interruption."[51] While policy wordings and case law interpreting these provisions vary, business interruption policies generally require (1) a loss or damage to insured property to trigger coverage, (2) interruption of the business due to a covered loss, (3) loss of income or profits, and (4) the loss occur within a "period of restoration."[52] Business interruption losses often present complex valuation and calculation challenges. Further coverage may require that the insured "expedite repairs, mitigate losses and/or track expenses in a way that is not consistent with your normal business practice."[53]

Depending on policy language, there may also be coverage for "extra expense" associated with maintaining production while the property is undergoing repair or for "certain expenses incurred before physical damage to property."[54] Covered extra expenses generally include such costs as rent, moving and hauling expenses, overtime, temporary labor, and even advertising. An early evaluation of coverage can help smooth the path to making sure covered expenses are properly captured and presented to insurers. Many policies include coverage for outside professional fees incurred in quantifying the loss.

There may also be "contingent business interruption" coverage triggered by the impairments to a company's "supply chain or markets, even in the absence of direct property damage."[55] Some policies contain "a discrete trigger of business interruption

46. *Id.*
47. *Id.*
48. *Id.*
49. *Id.*
50. *Id.*
51. *Id.*
52. *Id.*
53. *Id.*
54. *Id.*
55. DeNatale, Foresta, Klein, Levin & Plumer, *supra* note 26.

coverage when a civil authority, such as a state or municipal government, has ordered closure."[56] Such "civil authority" coverage may be available for businesses in areas ordered to evacuate due to the risk of flooding or another type of impending disaster.

- **Contingent business interruption/dependent business premises coverage.** A claim for contingent business interruption may arise if the insured's suppliers or customers suffer loss or damage due to the insured's inability to acquire or deliver materials or services.[57] Loss of gross earnings at the insured's premises resulting from a supplier's or customer's inability to "deliver or receive goods or supplies due to damage to its own property" can also be covered, depending on the policy coverage terms.[58] Contingent business interruption coverage protects against losses due to these disruptions.
- **Loss mitigation, prevention, and documentation expenses.** The policyholder should check to see whether his or her policies cover costs of salvage, mitigation of loss, and "extra expenses" incurred in "limiting, documenting and repairing losses."[59] Some business interruption policies have a requirement that the policyholder "take steps to expedite restoration"; the associated expense may be covered expressly under the policy or mandated by law.[60]
- **Supply-chain and service interruption coverage.** Some policy coverage extends to supply-chain interruptions or trade disruptions. Generally, such specialized coverage exists on a "stand-alone basis or by endorsement."[61] There may also be coverage for losses resulting from the disruption of utility services, such as water, power, communications, or similar services, which generally do not require proof of direct damage to the insured's property.[62]

  Damage, loss of income, or extra expenses incurred as a result of service interruption may be covered, such as spoilage of refrigerated goods.[63] This type of coverage typically requires "damage to the property of a supplier of electricity, gas, water, steam, waste disposal, or similar services used by the insured" and sometimes includes requirements that the damage occur within a specified distance of the insured's property.[64] Service interruption coverage may extend to damages and losses resulting from power outages where

56. *Id.*
57. Gilford & Davis, *supra* note 31.
58. *Id.*
59. DeNatale, Foresta, Klein, Levin & Plumer, *supra* note 26.
60. *Id.*
61. *Id.*
62. *Id.*
63. Gilford & Davis, *supra* note 31.
64. *Id.*

power lines brought down by a storm prevent or interrupt normal business operations.[65] Supply-chain and service interruption coverage often have limits in terms of duration and are subject to waiting periods or deductibles.[66] Damages may be extensive when services are interrupted and may include event cancellation, inability to deliver products, office and facilities closures, contractual penalties for noncompletion of orders or late delivery, or loss or damage to covered property.[67]

- **Civil and military coverage/authority access restrictions.** An order by a governmental entity limiting or preventing access to property may trigger insurance coverage.[68] "Some cases have held that no physical damage is required to invoke the civil authority coverage."[69] The most common situations covered are flood, tornadoes, hurricanes, and other natural disasters, where evacuation orders impede access to the insured's property, and "airport closures, beach and waterway closures, curfews, closures of financial exchanges and border closures are each types of civil authority orders that could lead to insurance claims."[70]

  In the aftermath of a disaster, and occasionally beforehand with approaching storms, government authorities may issue evacuation orders and other constraints on access to certain areas.[71] For example, after the September 11 terrorist attacks, sections of Manhattan were closed off for several days. The same was true after Hurricanes Katrina and Rita. "Most commercial property policies provide coverage for losses arising out of prohibitions against access due to orders from a civil or military authority."[72]

- **Ingress/Egress.** Beyond civil authority orders restricting access to property, there may physical damage resulting from natural or man-made disasters that may limit an insured's ability to enter and leave its property.[73] "Ingress/egress clauses can extend the business interruption coverage" and likely require "only property damage 'in the vicinity'" that results in the inability of the insurer or its suppliers or customers to reach the policyholder's premises.[74]

---

65. *Id.*
66. *Id.*
67. *Id.*
68. *Id.*
69. *Id.*
70. *Id.*
71. Morgan, *supra* note 2.
72. *Id.*
73. *Id.*
74. *Id.*

Policyholders must take an active role in determining the adequacy of coverage and, in complex situations, it is advisable to consult insurance coverage counsel for guidance. In each instance, it is important to "[r]ead the policy promptly and confirm that it adequately describes the coverage purchased." For example:

- Are all of the relevant people, companies, property, activities, and locations included within the ambit of the policy?
- Are the limits adequate?
- Is the deductible or self-insured retention too high?
- Is anything excluded from coverage that the policyholder wants or needs to be covered?

Policyholders should ask questions and benefit from the broker's expertise, insight and resources.

[5]—Conclusion

Regardless of the cause, claims arising from natural and/or man-made disasters are likely to raise issues such as causation, trigger, notice requirements, number of occurrences, limits, deductibles, exclusions, insurer defenses, and quantification of loss.[75]

75. *Id.*

Chapter 5
Subrogation and Waivers of Subrogation[1]

Subrogation is a relatively static area in commercial leasing. The few cases on point address the issues of (1) whether the parties have effectively waived subrogation in trying to block an insurer of a casualty victim from proceeding in a subrogation claim against the defending party, (2) the clarity of the terms and the waiver of subrogation, and (3) whether other clauses in the lease can be construed in effect to bring about either a waiver of subrogation or a coinsurance situation.

[1]—Principles of Subrogation Law

Subrogation is an equitable doctrine that allows the substitution of a party in place of a lawful claimant with regard to a demand, claim, or right.[2] It is a derivative right and, as such, the party that exercises the right of subrogation (the subrogee) succeeds to the creditor's rights (the subrogor) in relation to the debt.[3] A subrogee stands in the shoes of a subrogor and succeeds to, but has no greater rights than, those that the subrogor initially had. The subrogee is also subject to all defenses that a third- party tortfeasor might assert against the subrogor.

Only after its early applications in debtor-creditor law and surety law were subrogation principles applied to insurance law. The rules with respect to subrogation and work of subrogation are fairly well-settled. Generally, an insurance company will be able to bring a subrogation action against the party causing the injury or damage unless the parties have completely and clearly waived the subrogation rights of their insurers.[4]

---

1. Chapter 5 appeared in substantially identical form in A. DiSciullo, *A Guide to Subrogation inCommercial Leases*, Real Estate L.J. (Spring 1992), and is reprinted herein with permission of Warren & Lamont, Boston, MA.
2. *Black's Law Dictionary* (4th ed. 1972).
3. 83 C.J.S. *Subrogation* § 1.
4. *See* Verdier v. Marshallville Equity Co., 70 Ohio App. 43, 446 N.E.2d 636 (1980).

There are some few exceptions to the general rule stated in the preceding paragraph, and the practitioner should be aware that his or her case may fall into one of these very rare instances where an insurer would still be able to preserve its subrogation rights against a party. Two New Jersey cases at the turn of the last century established the principle that if the insurance company settled for less than the full amount of the alleged liability, subrogation rights were not barred by a settlement with a tortfeasor.[5] These cases also established the principle that when an insurance company failed to recognize a waiver, an insurer was not prevented from proceeding against a tortfeasor even though subrogation had been waived in the contract.[6]

Practice tip: The practitioner is advised to research his or her current state law and cases to see if this nuance exists in that state.

[2]—Waivers of Subrogation

Waivers of subrogation are generally recognized. They must, however, be clear and the insurance company given adequate notice of this contractual waiver. Protecting against a subsequent subrogation action is too important to be left later to judicial interpretation. The lease should clearly cover wavier of an insurer's subrogation rights. Since insurers contemplate the parties waiving subrogation, this waiver is already reflected in the expected risks to be encountered by the insurer and encompassed in its premiums. With waivers of subrogation being generally accepted practice in commercial lease transactions, risk taking by landlord and tenant becomes more predictable; risk shifting that otherwise would have eventually gone to the negligent party is ultimately absorbed by the insured's carrier.

Waiver of subrogation has considerable benefits for the insurance companies as well. They need only calculate the expected probability of their own insured's losses and the additional cost of the losses they might incur in subrogation claims against their insureds.

Most fire policies contain an endorsement that allows the insured to waive in advance its rights to recover against third parties for losses to its insured property. Such an endorsement means that the landlord's right to recover for its tenant's fault will rest with the landlord. Presumably, the landlord has required the tenant to obtain a fire policy with a similar endorsement so that any rights the tenant might have to recover from the landlord stay with the tenant.

---

5. Camden Fire Ins. Ass'n v. Prezioso, 93 N.J. Eq. 318, 116 A. 694 (1924); Fire Ass'n of Philadelphia v. Wells, 83 N.J. Eq. 484, 90 A. 244, *rev'd* 84 N.J. Eq. 484, 94 A. 619 (1915).

6. *Camden Fire Ins. Ass'n*, 93 N.J. 318, 116 A, 694, and *Fire Ass'n of Philadelphia*, 83 N.J. Eq. 484, 90 A. 244.

This alternative, however, does not prevent the insurer from asserting any right it might have to recover its losses from a tortfeasor. A better approach would be to pass responsibility over to the insurer. This can be done by both obtaining an endorsement from the insurance company to waive its recovery rights and by inserting a clause in the lease to this effect. The following is an example of such a clause:

Example 1:

To the extent not prohibited by or violative of any policy of fire or extended coverage insurance issued to Landlord or to Tenant, Landlord and Tenant hereby waive the right to maintain a direct action against the other for damages arising out of such other's negligence or otherwise tortious acts or omissions, but only to the extent that the cost of repairing such damage is covered by insurance or would have been covered by insurance proceeds payable under any policy required to be maintained under this Lease, but not so maintained. Each policy of such insurance shall, if obtainable from the insurer without additional expense either, (i) contain a waiver of subrogation by insurer against Tenant and Landlord, as the case may be, or (ii) include the name of the Landlord or Tenant, as the case may be, as an additional insured, but not as a party to whom any loss shall be made payable. If the inclusion of either said provisions would involve an additional expense, either party, at its expense, may require such provisions to be inserted in the other's policy. In the event a party is unable to obtain such a waiver, it shall immediately notify the other of this inability. In the absence of such notification, each party shall be deemed to have obtained such waiver of subrogation.

Under the suggested clause, the landlord and tenant each waive their respective rights against one another and are required to obtain a waiver of subrogation from their insurance companies. Alternatively, a landlord and tenant may elect to have the other named as an additional insured in its own policy, effectively preventing the insurer from bringing a subrogation action since the insurer is barred from collecting against its own insured. In the last two sentences, the paragraph creates the presumption of the existence of a waiver of subrogation in the absence of notification to the other that a party is unable to obtain such an endorsement. While this last portion is intended to give a party the comfort that it will not face a subrogation action by the other party's insurer, the clause has not been litigated extensively. Presumably, the party that fails to notify the other will be liable under a breach of contract theory for any damages awarded to a subrogee. However, the effectiveness of this cause of action may be questionable if the defaulting party is either bankrupt or insolvent.

A properly drafted waiver of subrogation clause will ideally rule out a later subrogation action by an insurance company against a negligent party and thoroughly cover all instances in which coverage is intended. Several decisions have upheld these clauses.

Most cases involving waiver of subrogation clauses arise when insurers unsuccessfully attempt to go after a tortfeasor. In *Safeco Insurance Co. v. Capri*,[7] the owner recovered from his insurance company for the loss caused by fire damages to the tenant's leased premises. The insurer then sued the tenant in a subrogation claim for negligently causing the fire. The tenant argued that he could not be sued because the owner had taken out a policy to protect himself and the tenant. The court ruled that the tenant was an implied coinsured under the insurance policy.[8] As such, the insurer could not sue him. Insofar as the tenant had expected to be covered by the owner's policy when he signed the lease, nothing in the lease made him liable for negligently causing the fire.[9]

However, not all courts have followed this theme. In *Zurich-American Insurance Co. v. Eckert*,[10] the federal district court held that the insurer was entitled to subrogation against a tenant despite a lease provision requiring a waiver of subrogation. The insurer had no knowledge of such a provision in the lease, while its policy specifically provided for subrogation. The lease stated that each party's insurance policy would "contain waivers of the right of subrogation against Lessor and Lessee."[11] The lease, however, did not address this situation where the insurers were not notified of the waiver.

The *Zurich* case gives rise to concern to protected parties that they cannot merely rely on a lease provision requiring waiver of subrogation if the insurer has not agreed. The rule in the states where this issue has been determined seems to be that the insurer is not bound by a waiver of subrogation to which it is not a party and of which it is not aware.[12] A simple solution for this anomaly is that each protected party should obtain a certificate from its insurer stating that the insurer has agreed to the waiver of subrogation similar to the representations commonly contained in the certificate of insurance.

Insurers generally do not charge landlords or tenants extra for the waiver of subrogation endorsement. These clauses give the most extensive protection possible. A tenant should, however, be aware that a waiver of subrogation will not protect it from damage to another tenant's property and should insure itself for this possibility. On

---

7. Safeco Insurance Co. v. Capri, 101 Nev. 429, 705 P.2d 659 (Nev. 1986).

8. See Chapter 4 for a discussion of coinsurance.

9. *See also* Crowell v. Housing Authority of Dallas, 495 S.W.2d 8887 (1973); Fishel's Fine Furniture v. Rose Fruit Market, 474 S.W.2d 539 (1971); International Insurance Co. v. Medical-Professional Building of Corpus Christi, 405 S.W.2d 867 (1966). These particular courts found generally that a waiver of subrogation rights between the parties precluded the insurer from exercising a subrogation claim

10. Zurich-American Insurance Co., v. Eckert, 770 F. Supp. 269 (E.D. Pa. 1991).

11. *Id.* at 270.

12. *See* I.C.C. Industries v. GATX Terminals Corp., 690 F. Supp. 1282, 1286 (S.D.N.Y. 1988).

the other hand, if a landlord obtains waivers from all of its tenants, it should be fully protected.

In a 1997 case, the New York State Court of Appeals, the highest court in that state, affirmed that clearly stated waivers of subrogation clauses contained in the parties' lease can preclude the negligence claims of the subrogated insurance carriers.[13] The court held that the broad applicability of the waiver of subrogation clauses in each of the parties' leases precluded the negligence claims of both parties' subrogated insurance carriers. Sections 8 and 9 of the lease between the parties allowed the tenant to seek reimbursement for property losses caused by the landlord's negligence and to set forth waiver of subrogation rights, respectively. In May 1993 a fire damaged the leased premises and the tenant's property. The origins of the fire were never discovered. The tenant's insurance company paid the tenant's claims for personal property and business interruption losses while the landlord's insurer paid the defendant's losses, which included the building and lost rent.

Then each insurer started a subrogation action against the other insurer's insured. The tenant's insurer's action against the landlord alleged that the landlord had been negligent in failing to maintain the sprinkler system, thereby greatly increasing the tenant's fire and water damage. The landlord's insurer brought a negligence action against the tenant.

In affirming the appellate division's orders upholding the supreme court's dismissal of each of the respective actions, the court of appeals noted that the lease language clearly and unambiguously found that the landlord and tenant had anticipated such an eventuality when they negotiated and executed the lease. In Section 9(e) they had "releas[ed] and waiv[ed] all rights of recovery against the other or any one claiming through or under each of them by way of subrogation or otherwise."[14] The court noted that in the same clause, the tenant had acknowledged that the landlord would not carry insurance on the tenant's personal property and that the landlord would not be required to repair or replace any of the tenant's property. Moreover, Section 8 of the lease broadly and plainly relieved the landlord from liability for any damage to the tenant's property unless the damage was caused by the negligence of the landlord, its agents, servants, or employees.

Such clear and customary language should have dissuaded the insurers from bringing their respective subrogation claims. It did not, and the court inevitably concluded that the lease language clearly applied the waivers to each of the parties' respective claims but also fell within well-established principles holding that waivers

13. Kaf-Kaf, Inc. v. Rodless Decorations, Inc. and a companion matter, Rodless Decorations, Inc. v. Kaf-Kaf, Inc., decided October 16, 1997, and reported in the New York Law Journal, pp. 25 and 26 (N.Y. App. Oct. 17, 1997).

14. *Id.*

of subrogation clauses cannot be enforced beyond the scope of the specific context in which the clause appears.[15] The court found that the pertinent clauses—while taken from a standard loft lease frequently used in office situations—reflected the parties' intention to look first to their insurers for recovery of their casualty losses and that each party in seeking recovery from the other clearly ignored the express provisions of the waiver of subrogation clause.

Interestingly, the court noted that in fixing premiums, insurers presumably consider that they have permitted their insureds to waive their subrogation rights and thus a waiver of subrogation clause will be upheld to preclude the negligence claims of a party's subrogated insurance carrier when the meaning and context of the waiver are so clearly expressed in the agreement.

Landlords and tenants should negotiate "which risks, and damages are included in their waiver of subrogation clause. Should the waiver be limited to: (i) the extent insurance proceeds are received, (ii) the risks that are required to be insured under the lease (whether or not actually insured); or (iii) for all claims, on the theory that each party takes its own risk in deciding what and how much insurance to carry?"[16]

Before agreeing to subrogation, however, the landlord and tenant "should each confirm with their insurers that their policies will allow them to waive their respective insurer's rights against the other party and should confirm the waiver limits negotiated between the parties, since a waiver might otherwise impair the insurance coverage. While request for a waiver of subrogation clause on a property insurance policy is not uncommon and most insurers will not object; a request for a waiver on a liability policy is not as widely granted."[17]

Often, as part of a mutual waiver of subrogation, the landlord and tenant will include a direct waiver of claims provision in their lease. Under such a provision, "each party (as a prospective injured party) directly waives claims it may have against the other based on the policies and for negotiated limits. This is a broader protection than a simple waiver of subrogation, because it means that neither the party nor its insurer will seek recovery for insured claims."[18]

To assure the highest level of protection, each party should review the other party's insurance policy to make sure that "the other party's insurer included the waiver of subrogation language in the insurance policy or that the other party's insurance policy permits waiver of subrogation by the insured."[19]

15. *Id.*, citing S.S.D.W. Co. v. Brisk Waterproofing Co., 76 N.Y.2d 228, 556 N.E.2d 1097, 1990 N.Y. LEXIS 1359, 557 N.Y.S.2d 290 (1990).

16. Salinger & Rebbe, *The Importance of a Waiver of Subrogation Clause in a Commercial Lease* (Jan. 30, 2012).

17. *Id.*

18. *Id.*

19. *Id.*

Chapter 6
Indemnification and Exculpatory Clauses[1]

[1]—Generally

Even before the Eighth Circuit's 1950 decision in *General Mills v. Goldman*,[2] landlords and tenants contracted away their liability through exculpatory and indemnification clauses. In the typical clause, the landlord requires the tenant to indemnify or protect the landlord against losses or damages for any actions that may be brought later against the landlord by third parties due to activities on the tenant's premises or due to the tenant's activities.[3]

Indemnification provisions are usually triggered by actions brought by customers, contractors, employees, and invitees using or working at the tenant's leased premises. These actions typically name both the tenant and the landlord with the tenant assuming the costs of the landlord's defense. Exculpatory clauses take this concept even further. They require the tenant to absolve a landlord from any fault regarding damages or injuries to the tenant even if they are due to the landlord's own negligence or willful actions.[4] Together, these clauses are an attempt by landlords and tenants to protect themselves from liability from direct or vicarious actions.

As expected, tenants and courts have not universally accepted these provisions. An indemnification clause can be dangerous for a tenant since it may be tantamount to being an exculpatory clause. This will result in closer and stricter examination of the clause but, if enforceable, will result in the tenant waiving away almost all of its property and liability protection.

1. For a good primer on insurance clauses in leases, see Wesch & Rowe, *What Every Leasing Attorney Needs to Know about Insurance: Ask for What You Want, Then Make Sure the Insurance Covers What You Need*, Prop. & Probate 40–44 (March/April 2008).

2. General Mills v. Goldman, 184 F.2d 359 (8th Cir. 1950), *cert. denied* 340 U.S. 947 (1951).

3. Tenants may also ask for a similar protection from their landlords.

4. Often there are mutual indemnification provisions in a lease, but exculpatory clauses almost always run to the landlord's benefit.

Indemnification clauses present other problems as well. It is doubtful whether indemnification covers a protected party's liability for punitive damages. Because the courts have not definitively ruled in this area, the respective liability of the protected party (the indemnitee) and protecting party (the indemnitor) for their shared activities has to be determined on a case-by-case basis.

In *Hartford Fire Insurance Co. v. Chicago Tunnel Terminal Co.*, the court found the tenant liable to the landlord's insurer for a fire and explosion of unknown origin.[5] The tenant's liability was based on its agreement in the lease to indemnify and hold the lessor harmless from all losses irrespective of the cause of the fire. Taken with the potential exculpatory effects of an indemnification clause, a tenant who is then agreeing to indemnify and hold a landlord harmless from third-party liability may unwittingly become virtually an insurer for the landlord. The result would make the tenant liable for casualties for which it was not even remotely responsible.

When the indemnification provisions work properly, the tenant will usually hold the landlord harmless for the landlord's costs of defending a lawsuit and for any judgment arising from the action or will itself assume the defense of the action.[6] These provisions are usually accompanied by an agreement to defend the landlord against any claims covered by the indemnity.

Frequently, the tenant will request the same protection from the landlord. Commentators are divided as to the effectiveness of this mutual indemnification. One commentator who criticizes the proponents of mutual indemnification points out that

> (1) these proponents do not fully consider the unfairness of the landlord shifting liability to the tenant by an indemnity clause; (2) there may be better standards than using a negligence standard in this risk shifting; and (3) carving exceptions to the indemnity for injury or damage caused by the landlord's negligence is superficial and may be counterproductive.[7]

If indemnification provisions, even mutual ones, give tenants and landlords pause for concern, then exculpatory clauses are even more troublesome. The usual exculpatory clause goes much further than an indemnification provision. Accordingly, it can be that much more damaging to a tenant if used to support an insurer's subrogation action against a lessor for fire damage or another casualty. The typical exculpatory clause attempts to relieve the landlord from all fault and any liability to the tenant. This waiver includes damages and injuries that are usually the landlord's

---

5. Hartford Fire Insurance Co. v. Chicago Tunnel Terminal Co., 12 Ill. App. 2d 539, 139 N.E.2d770 (1956).

6. See sample indemnification clause and discussion in Chapter 6, *infra.*

7. Grant, *Subrogation, Indemnification and Exculpation in the Context of Commercial Leases*, ABA Enforceability of Subrogation and Indemnity Clause program, Atlanta, Georgia 1991.

responsibility, such as damages from leaking roofs, as well as from causes that are both within and beyond the landlord's control. These clauses address both tort and contractual liability.

It is long-standing law that the landlord can contractually exculpate itself from liability in commercial office leases. Even so, these clauses will be strictly construed against the landlord or other exculpated party. It is therefore important that the lawyer drafting the clause do so carefully to avoid any gaps in the protection. For instance, it has been held that where an exculpatory clause in a lease exempts the landlord for liability for damage resulting from the landlord's carelessness, negligence, or improper contract, but fails to exculpate the landlord for liability for damage resulting from the defective design and construction of major structural components of the building, the landlord is not protected from liability for water damages to its tenant's computer system caused by the defective design of the roof.

[a]—The Pollution Exclusion

[i]—The History

Before discussing coverage for pollution-related injury, it is worth considering the history of the pollution exclusion. Issues regarding pollution coverage and exclusions came to a head because of the events of September 11, 2001. The World Trade Center disaster gave rise to a host of insurance and tort litigations, with cases not resolved in federal courts in New York for over a decade.

Among the insurance issues born of the disaster were those that "concerned the interplay between the absolute pollution exclusion, which is contained in many of the commercial general liability and excess insurance policies issued to defendants in the underlying personal injury actions, and the disbursement of contaminants into the air caused by the destruction of two massive buildings. On one hand, defendants sought to have their commercial insurance policies defend and, if necessary, indemnify them for the personal injury claims brought by rescue, recovery and cleanup workers. On the other hand, insurers with policies containing the pollution exclusion often disclaimed or reserved rights based on that exclusion and other policy provisions."[8]

Before 1970, insurance policies rarely contained an exclusion for pollution-related harm.[9] As toxic tort claims began more popular, the industry recognized the need for a pollution exclusion.

---

8. Schiffer, *Terrorism and the Pollution Exclusion*, Insurance Coverage Law Bulletin 1 (Law Journal Newsletters Oct. 2012).

9. *Id.*, citing Lathrop, *What Is the Pollution Exclusion?*, 2 Toxic Torts Practice Guide, § 32:8 (2011).

In 1970, the Insurance Services Office (ISO) released an exclusion that came to be known as the "1970-form" or the "sudden and accidental" pollution exclusion, which was widely adopted by the insurance industry.[10] The form read as follows:

> This Policy Shall Not Apply: To bodily injury or property damage arising out of the discharge, dispersal, release or escape of smoke, vapors, soot, fumes, acids, alkalis, toxic chemicals, liquids or gases, waste materials or other irritants, contaminants or pollutants into or upon land, the atmosphere or any watercourse or body of water; but this exclusion does not apply if such discharge, dispersal, release or escape is sudden and accidental.[11]

What constitutes "sudden and accidental" became a hotly debated issue with the adoption of environmental legislation throughout the 1970s and 1980s. "While the majority of states concluded that 'sudden' denoted a temporal element requiring an abrupt, time-limited discharge, others ruled that 'sudden' was an ambiguous term that could mean 'unexpected' in this context."[12]

Responding to all the litigation over the 1970-form's pollution exclusion, the insurance industry adopted a new version of the exclusion that "came to be known the absolute pollution exclusion."[13] This version was adopted in the early 1980s and made its way into most liability policies by the mid-1980s.[14] The following is the most commonly used exclusion language:

> Pollution
>
> (1) "Bodily injury" or "property damage" arising out of the actual, alleged or threatened discharge, dispersal, seepage, migration, release or escape of "pollutants":
>
>> (a) At or from any premises, site or location which is or was at any time owned or occupied by, or rented or loaned to, any insured. However, this subparagraph does not apply to:
>>
>>> (i) "Bodily injury" if sustained within a building and caused by smoke, fumes, vapor or soot produced by or originating from equipment that is used to heat, cool or dehumidify the building, or equipment that is used to heat water for personal use, by the building's occupants or their guests;
>>>
>>> (ii) "Bodily injury" or "property damage" for which you may be held liable, if you are a contractor and the owner or lessee of such premises, site or location has been added to your policy as an additional insured with respect to your

10. *Id.* at 3.
11. *Id.*
12. *Id.*
13. *Id.*
14. *Id.*

ongoing operations performed for that additional insured at that premises, site or location and such premises, site or location is not and never was owned or occupied by, or rented or loaned to, any insured, other than that additional insured; or

(iii) "Bodily injury" or "property damage" arising out of heat, smoke or fumes from a "hostile fire";

(b) At or from any premises, site or location which is or was at any time used by or for any insured or others for the handling, storage, disposal, processing, or treatment of waste;

(c) Which are or were at any time transported, handled, stored, treated, disposed of, or processed as waste by or for:

(i) Any insured; or

(ii) Any person or organization for whom you may be legally responsible; or

(d) At or from any premises, site or location on which any insured or any contractors or subcontractors working directly or indirectly on any insured's behalf are performing operations if the 'pollutants' are brought on or to the premises, site or location in connection with such operations by such insured, contractor or subcontractor. However, this subparagraph does not apply to:

(i) "Bodily injury" or "property damage" arising out of the escape of fuels, lubricants or other operating fluids which are needed to perform the normal electrical, hydraulic or mechanical functions necessary for the operation of "mobile equipment" or its parts, if such fuels, lubricants or other operating fluids escape from a vehicle part designed to hold, store or receive them. This exception does not apply if the "bodily injury" or "property damage" arises out of the intentional discharge, dispersal or release of the fuels, lubricants or other operating fluids, or if such fuels, lubricants or other operating fluids are brought on or to the premises, site or location with the intent that they be discharged, dispersed or released as part of the operations being performed by such insured, contractor or subcontractor;

(ii) "Bodily injury" or "property damage" sustained within a building and caused by the release of gases, fumes or vapors from materials brought into that building in connection with operations being performed by you or on your behalf by a contractor or subcontractor; or

(iii) "Bodily injury" or "property damage" arising out of heat, smoke or fumes from a "hostile fire";

(e) At or from any premises, site or location on which any insured or any contractors or subcontractors working directly or indirectly on any insured's behalf are performing operations if the operations are to test for, monitor, clean up, remove, contain, treat, detoxify or neutralize, or in any way respond to, or assess the effects of, "pollutants."

(2) Any loss, cost or expense arising out of any:

(a) Request, demand, order or statutory or regulatory requirement that any insured or others test for, monitor, clean up, remove, contain, treat, detoxify or neutralize, or in any way respond to, or assess the effects of, "pollutants"; or

(b) Claim or "suit" by or on behalf of a governmental authority for damages because of testing for, monitoring, cleaning up, removing, containing, treating, detoxifying or neutralizing, or in any way responding to, or assessing the effects of, "pollutants".

This paragraph, however, does not apply to liability for damages because of "property damage" that the insured would have in the absence of a request, demand, order or statutory or regulatory requirement, or a claim or "suit" by or on behalf of a governmental authority.[15]

The standard policy defines "pollutant" as "any solid, liquid, gaseous or thermal irritant or contaminant, including smoke, vapor, soot, fumes, acids, alkalis, chemicals and waste." "Waste" includes "materials to be recycled, reconditioned or reclaimed." Variants of the absolute pollution exclusion exist.[16]

Despite efforts to clearly exclude pollution from coverage, ambiguities still exist and have been litigated.[17] Among the more important issues raised are "the breadth of the terms 'pollutant' and 'irritant,' whether the exclusion only applies to traditional cases of environmental pollution, and how to treat an intervening cause of injury such as a lack of safety equipment."[18]

[ii]—Terrorist Acts and the Pollution Exclusion

"The interplay between the pollution exclusion and exposure to contaminants caused by acts of terrorism may arise in varying contexts from bio-terrorism and other sorts of malicious pollution to the destruction of massive office towers," like the World Trade Center, "or other structures made up of materials that may be considered pollution when pulverized and disbursed through the air."[19]

In the aftermath of the World Trade Center disaster, the City of New York set up a relatively modest insurance program to protect itself and contractors employed to handle the cleanup. The program included general liability coverage for bodily

15. *Id.* at 3–4.
16. *Id.*
17. *Id.*
18. *Id.*
19. *Id.*

injuries sustained in the course of the cleanup efforts.[20] The City of New York was overwhelmed when hundreds of rescue and cleanup workers filed claims. The claims "alleged, among other things, that the plaintiffs had been injured by the toxic air hanging over the site, and that the city and the contractors had failed to properly protect these individuals by not providing necessary equipment, supervision and training."[21] Over the years, the claims reached into the thousands. In late 2004, the city established a new insurance company, the World Trade Center Captive Insurance Company (WTC Captive) using federal funds.[22] The various lawsuits were consolidated for pre-trial discovery in the Southern District of New York.[23]

"After defending the respiratory claims cases for more than two years, the WTC Captive brought a declaratory judgment action seeking to hold the primary carrier and the excess insurers responsible for the defense of these cases, and seeking reimbursement of the substantial legal fees paid to date."[24] The primary insurer settled with the WTC Captive. With just the excess insurers as remaining defendants, "in 2008, the court granted partial summary judgment to the WTC Captive on the excess insurers' duty to defend and directed the parties to determine the amount due from the excess insurers to the WTC Captive for defense costs."[25]

The district court sided with the WTC Captive, concluding that the excess insurers failed to satisfy their burden of establishing that "all claims related to the respiratory claims were within the scope of the exclusion."[26] The court dealt only with the duty to defend. It never ruled on whether the pollution exclusion applied or whether the excess insurers would be required ultimately to pay the respiratory claims.[27] "The issue was rendered moot by a settlement between the excess insurers and the WTC Captive before an appeals court could rule."[28]

---

20. *Id.*, citing Schiffer & Chakraborty, *Exploring Latest Developments in the U.S. and What They Hold for the UK and European Markets*, C5 11th Annual Reinsurance Claims Conference (April 24–25, 2008).

21. *Id.*

22. *Id.*

23. *See* The World Trade Center Disaster Site Litigation, 21 MC 100, New York Law Journal, 1202486082749 at *1 (S.D.N.Y. March 11, 2011).

24. Schiffer, *supra* note 8, referencing WTC Captive Insurance Co. v. Liberty Mutual Fire Insurance Co., No. 07 Civ. 1209 (S.D.N.Y. 2008) (Hellerstein, J.).

25. *Id.*, discussing WTC Captive Insurance Co., Inc. v. Liberty Mutual Fire Insurance Co., 549 F. Supp. 2d 555 (S.D.N.Y. 2008).

26. *Id.* at 5.

27. *Id.*

28. *Id.*

[iii]—Arguments that the Pollution Exclusion Applies Only to Traditional Environmental Pollution Cases

To properly exclude a terrorism-related pollution claim, "the insurer must demonstrate that all of the allegations of a complaint fall entirely within the exclusion and are subject to no other interpretation."[29]

According to one commentator:

> In the context of "terrorism pollution," satisfying this burden might prove difficult, simply because the exclusion was not written with terror-related pollution in mind. As such, it can be argued that the exclusion may be reasonably interpreted in a way that removes this sort of pollution from the protections of the exclusion. Under this line of reasoning, the standard pollution exclusion applies only to typical cases of environmental pollution involving the failure to abate or contain pollution, which were clearly contemplated when the exclusions were drafted. Conversely, terror-related pollution cases tend to revolve around improper cleanup techniques and are brought by those tasked with the cleanup, and therefore might be seen by courts as being focused around theories of workplace safety obligations rather than any sort of pollution rules.[30]

According to the Second Circuit, "it is appropriate to construe that standard pollution exclusion clause in light of its general purpose, which is to exclude coverage for environmental pollution."[31] More recently, the Seventh Circuit stated that "even if pollutants are the source of damages, the exclusion will not apply if the method of dispersal is not one that would be characterized as an incident of environmental pollution."[32] A few courts have concluded that workplace safety claims are not covered by the standard pollution exclusion.[33]

---

29. *Id.*, citing and discussing State of New York v. Blank, 27 F.3d 783, 790 (2d Cir. 1994). *See also* state courts: Colorado: City of Englewood v. Commercial Union Assurance Cos., 940 P.2d 948 (Col. App. 1996); New York: Frontier Insulation Contractors, Inc. v. Merchants Mutual Insurance Co., 91 N.Y.2d 169, 175, 667 N.Y.S.2d 982, 984–85 (1997).

30. Schiffer, *supra* note 8, citing and discussing *State of New York v. Blank*, 27 F.3d 783, 790 (2d Cir. 1994).

31. *Id.*, citing Stoney Run Co. v. Prudential LMI Commercial Insurance Co., 47 F.3d 34, 37 (2d Cir. 1995), and also citing MacKinnon v. Truck Insurance Exchange, 31 Cal. 4th 635, 3 Cal. Rptr. 3d 228, 73 P.3d 1205 (2003), *as modified on denial of rehearing* (Sept. 17, 2003) (the absolute pollution exclusion is limited to injuries arising from events commonly thought of as environmental pollution).

32. *Id.*, referencing and discussing Scottsdale Indemnity Co. v. Village of Crestwood, 11-2385, 2012 WL 769730, at *2 (7th Cir. March 12, 2012).

33. *Id.* at 6, citing National Union Fire Insurance Co. v. American Re-Insurance Co., 351 F. Supp. 2d 201, 209 (S.D.N.Y. 2005) (applying Ohio law) (ruling that the pollution exclusion did not apply to employees exposed to metalworking fluids, reasoning that a court would be remiss to simply look at the bare words of the exclusion "and apply it to situations that do not remotely resemble traditional environmental contamination"); Calvert Insurance Co. v. S&L Realty Corp., 926 F. Supp. 44, 47 (S.D.N.Y. 1996) (exclusion does not apply where action is "based not only on an alleged pollutant, but on various

Another argument is that the exclusion should not apply if it does not explicitly include all the materials associated with pollution upon which the claim is based.

[iv]—Arguments for Excluding "Terrorism Pollution"

There are courts that argue that the standard pollution exclusion is intended to be absolute, and that the exclusions terms are "broad, clear and unambiguous."[34] According to these courts, there is "nothing in the plain meaning of the exclusion that limits it solely to cases of environmental pollution, and the exclusion would therefore be applicable in the terrorism-related pollution context."[35]

These courts take the view that the standard pollution exclusion simply and broadly excludes from coverage all injuries "arising out of" pollution. Since this language is "straightforward and unambiguous," terror-related pollution would fall directly under the purview of the exclusion.[36] "As long as there is a causal link between the injury and the risk to which the policy refers, the exclusion would apply. . . . Although the injuries may be alleged to have been caused by a lack of proper safety equipment or other workplace safety concerns, none of the workplace safety issues or injuries would exist but for the polluted environment. As such, it can be argued that in most terrorism-related pollution cases, the injury will 'arise out' of the polluted environment, and the pollution exclusion should therefore apply."[37]

There are a number of other factors that suggest that the "particulates resulting from the collapse of a building" fall within the definition of "pollutant."[38] For instance, the courts in the WTC Captive case actually used some variation of the words "pollutant" and "contaminant" when they described the "conditions that the

---

allegedly negligent acts and omissions of the insured"); Schumann v. State, 160 Misc. 2d 802, 806, 610 N.Y.S.2d 987, 989–90 (Ct. Cl. 1994) (exclusion does not apply where "injury arises not from pollution to the atmosphere but from obliging others to work with inadequate protection in an atmosphere known to be polluted").

34. *Id.* at 7, citing, e.g., Second Circuit: West World Insurance Co. v. Stack Oil, Inc., 922 F.2d 118, 121 (2d Cir. 1990); Eleventh Circuit: West American Insurance Co. v. Band & Desenberg, 925 F. Supp. 758, 761 (M.D. Fla. 1996), *aff'd* 138 F.3d 1428 (11th Cir. 1998); state courts: Maryland: Alcolac Inc. v. California Union Insurance Co., 716 F. Supp. 1546, 1549 (D. Md. 1989); New York: Budofsky v. Hartford Insurance Co., 147 Misc. 2d 691, 695 (N.Y. Sup. Ct. 1990).

35. *Id.*

36. *Id.*

37. *Id.*

38. *Id.*

victims were exposed to."[39] This supports the argument that the particulates involved were considered pollutants "under the plain meaning of the term."[40]

Beyond that, "federal, state and local environmental agencies were called upon to monitor the effects of these materials on the atmosphere," which "suggests that these materials were clearly considered potential environmental pollutants by the relevant authorities,"[41] making it reasonable to assume that they were included in the standard pollution exclusion.[42]

[v]—Expectations for the Future

In some ways, events after 9/11 have mitigated the impact of this issue. The insurance industry reacted to the disaster by drafting new contract language to avoid coverage in the future, and it lobbied the U.S. government "to shoulder some of the burden associated with insuring injury and damage caused by terrorist acts."[43] In late 2001, the ISO drafted a "terrorism exclusion," designing it to "exclude injury or damage caused directly or indirectly by terrorism."[44] "By February 2002, forty-five states, plus the District of Columbia, Puerto Rico and Guam, had approved the terrorism exclusion."[45]

"While the industry worked on implementing terrorism exclusions in new policies and policies to be renewed, Congress was holding hearings on the feasibility and desirability of a federal backstop program under which the federal government would provide coverage for damage related to terrorism."[46]

While these developments make it "unlikely that the legal questions surrounding the interplay of terrorism and the pollution exclusion will be much of an issue going forward . . . not all of the cases brought in the aftermath of September 11th have

39. *Id.*, citing *In re* World Trade Center Disaster Site Litigation, 456 F. Supp. 2d 523 ("Thousands of workers . . . risked their lives from shifting debris, fires, smoke, and acrid and polluted air. . . ."); McNally v. Port Authority of New York and New Jersey, 414 F.3d 352, 358–59 (2d Cir. 2005) (stating that respiratory plaintiffs' were exposed to "toxins and other contaminants").

40. *Id.*

41. *Id.*

42. *Id.*

43. *Id.*, citing Jeff Woodward, *The ISO Terrorism Exclusions: Background and Analysis*, IRMI (Feb. 2002), *available at* https://www.irmi.com/expert/articles/2002/woodward02.aspx. The Terrorism Risk Insurance Act of 2002 (TRIA) "nullified all existing terrorism exclusions, and required all property and casualty insurers to offer their customers terrorism insurance." See Chapter 3[5] *infra* for a detailed discussion of TRIA and the Terrorism Risk Insurance Extension Act of 2005 (TRIEA).

44. Schiffer, *supra* note 8, citing Jeff Woodward, *The ISO Terrorism Exclusions: Background and Analysis*, IRMI (Feb. 2002), *available at* http://www.irmi.com/expert/articles/2002/woodward02.aspx.

45. *Id.*

46. *Id.*, referencing R. Allyn, *The Fall and Rise of Terrorism Insurance Coverage Since September 11, 2001*, 29 Wm. Mitchell L. Rev. 821 (2002–2003).

settled, and it is possible that a court may have to reach this issue at some point."[47] So it still remains to be seen whether the exclusion will be interpreted narrowly or broadly.

[b]—Pollution Legal Liability Insurance

This type of insurance is designed to cover claims arising from pollution conditions on, within, or under covered areas. It covers clean-up costs as well as bodily injury and property damage. Business interruption and extra expense coverage are also available. Limits usually range from $1 million to $100 million, with deductibles of $10,000 and up per incident. Unless specifically scheduled, the following key exclusions exist: preexisting conditions known to the insured, intentional concealment, and underground storage tanks (USTs). Terms of coverage are usually one to five years.[48]

[c]—Commercial Pollution Legal Liability Insurance Update

This is a form of insurance available since December 1998. It covers on-site cleanups of pollution conditions at an insured property discovered by an insured and reported to the carrier during the policy period. The author is not aware of many carriers offering this form of coverage. The target market includes light manufacturing, biotech, and research and developments companies, as well as medical and educational facilities. The minimum premium is $5,000. This insurance covers off-site waste disposal from a set date forward ("Retroactive Date"). Limits, deductibles, and terms are similar to those offered for pollution legal liability insurance. Key exclusions are preexisting conditions known to the insured and preexisting conditions that the insured *reasonably* could have expected would give rise to a claim under the policy.

[d]—Commercial Real Estate Pollution Legal Liability Insurance

This form of environmental liability policy is targeted to owners of real estate and buyers and sellers of real estate. It is designed to benefit landlords, tenants, buyers, and sellers of properties on which there are offices or warehousing operations or even light manufacturing. The premium is approximately $1,200 to $1,500 for a policy with a five-year term and possibly twice that amount for a ten-year term. The policy is designed to cover monetary awards or settlements of compensatory damages, defense costs, and cleanup costs caused by pollution conditions on, under, or beyond the boundaries of the insured property that the insured legally becomes obligated

47. *Id.*
48. *Id.* at 8.

to pay as a result of an award or settlement. The policy covers the cost to clean up a pollution condition discovered on the insured property during the policy period.[49] Limits are $1 million and up, with a $5,000 deductible. Key exclusions are preexisting conditions known to the insured and preexisting conditions that the insured reasonably could have expected would give rise to a claim under the policy.

[e]—Property Transfer Insurance

Property transfer insurance is designed to cover claims arising with respect to specifically listed property for preexisting unknown contamination and existing known contamination below reportable levels. The limits are $1 million to $10 million, with a $10,000 deductible. This type of policy excludes preexisting known contamination and deliberate, intentional, or willful noncompliance with laws, and underground storage tanks (USTs). The term is generally three to five years. The coverage is actually a form of pollution legal liability coverage, which is marketed to those involved in a property transfer situation.[50]

[f]—Brownfields Restoration and Development Insurance

Brownfields insurance is designed to cover properties with known environmental problems on which there is a planned remediation and a planned development. It contains both property transfer type coverage and "cleanup cap" coverage. It can also include business interruption coverage and extra costs coverage. Limits are $1 million and up. Some insurers only insure up to $75 million. Deductibles are $5,000 and up. Key exclusions are clean-up costs. However, an increase in the cost of a specifically insured cleanup plan is covered. There are also exclusions for preexisting known contamination that is not disclosed to the insurer and dishonest or deliberate intentional noncompliance with law. In this respect, this insurance coverage is similar to other types of coverage.[51]

[g]—"Cleanup Cap" or "Stop Gap" Insurance

This type of insurance is designed to cover an increase in the costs associated with a known cleanup. Prerequisites require that the insured have a governmental-approved cleanup plan in place or a cleanup plan approved by an insurance company.[52] Coverage comes into effect when the cost to perform the work is more than original

49. *Id.* at 10.
50. *Id.* at 11.
51. *Id.* at 13.
52. *Id.* at 12.

estimates. This insurance does not cover the cost to clean up any other contamination discovered during the insured cleanup. Coverage ends when the project is completed, and the insured receives a No Further Action Letter or equivalent documentation from the governmental agency overseeing the cleanup. Limits range from $1 million to $10 million. Generally, there is a self-insured retention, which is usually the estimate for the approved cleanup plus between 3 percent and 10 percent of these cleanup costs. A key exclusion is legal fees incurred in governmental negotiations, and the coverage applies only to the increased cost of the specifically insured approved cleanup.

[h]—Closure/Post-Closure Insurance

This insurance is designed to cover regulated facilities such as solid waste landfills, hazardous waste treatment and disposal facilities, and other environmentally sensitive facilities. It is added coverage that insures against a premature closure of a facility and regulatory agencies. Limits are $1 million and up, with deductibles of $25,000 and up. Liability coverage or associated defense costs are key exclusions.

[i]—Secured Creditor Impaired Property Insurance

This insurance is being marketed as a substitute for a Phase I audit, and the per-property premium will be less than the costs of having a consultant prepare the Phase I. An environmental questionnaire is used in place of an audit.[53]

[j]—Contractor's Pollution Liability and Errors and Omissions Insurance

This type of policy is designed to provide for bodily injury and property damage that arise out of covered operations performed by the insured contractor or consultant on a third party's real property and for pollution arising from professional services rendered by the insured contractors or consultant. It covers a property owner if there is extra contamination caused during a remediation or exploratory project.

[k]—Finite Risk Coverage

This untraditional insurance coverage is fully funded by the insured and administered by the insurance companies. Basically, the carrier looks to the insured to pay a premium equal to the discounted value of the cleanup. It is designed to meet the

53. *Id.* at 15.

insured's particular needs. The term can be beyond ten years to even twenty or thirty years.[54]

[2]—Mold: The Associated Risks and Insurance Coverage[55]

[a]—Introduction

Risks associated with the presence of mold and the damage it may cause have become serious insurance coverage concerns.[56] Mold claims have grown dramatically since the early 2000s. Policyholders have been seeking insurance recoveries for property damage losses, including removal costs[57] and the cost of alternative business accommodations,[58] as well as damages for lost rent.[59] Tenants have claimed to develop medical problems when their offices became contaminated by mold.

54. *Id.* at 18.

55. The author wishes to thank Nancy C.L. Stein, a principal in the law firm of Stein & Stein, 585 Stewart Avenue, Garden City, New York, for her assistance in researching and preparing the materials in this section.

56. Note that the Building Owners and Managers Association (BOMA) "supports laws, regulations and policies that will ensure that adequate insurance coverage for mold claims is available to the commercial real estate industry at a fair and reasonable cost," but states that "[b]uilding codes and standards designed to address mold and moisture should be developed through the industry standards consensus processes," not by governments. BOMA of Metropolitan Detroit, *Advocacy Issues: Mold.*

57. John H. Mathias, John D. Shugrue & Thomas A. Marrinson, Insurance Coverage Disputes § 11.01[8] (Law Journal Press 1996), citing Fifth Circuit: Maynard v. Lloyd's, 2002 WL 1461923, at *2–3 (N.D. Tex. 2002); Lexington Insurance Co. v. Unity Waterford-Fair Oaks, Ltd., 2001 WL 694582, at *1 (N.D. Tex. 2001); state courts: Arizona: Hatley v. Century-National Insurance Co., No. CV 2000-006713 (Ariz. Super. Nov. 5, 2001), *reprinted in* 15 Mealey's Litigation Report: Bad Faith (Dec. 5, 2001); Washington: Bowers v. Farmers Insurance Exchange, 99 Wash. App. 41, 43–44, 991 P.2d 734, 736 (2000).

58. *Id.*, citing Arizona: Hatley v. Century-National Insurance Co., No. CV 2000-006713 (Ariz. Super. Nov. 5, 2001), *reprinted in* 15 Mealey's Litigation Report: Bad Faith (Dec. 5, 2001); Texas: Home Insurance Co. v. Dennis D., 2000 WL 144115, at *6 (Tex. App. 2000).

59. *Id.*, citing Ninth Circuit: Factory Mutual Insurance Co. v. Estate of James Campbell, No. 01-7518 (C.D. Cal. March 18, 2002), *reprinted in* 1 Mealey's Litigation Report: California Insurance (April 16, 2002); state courts: Washington: Bowers v. Farmers Insurance Exchange, 99 Wash. App. 41, 43–44, 991 P.2d 734, 736 (2000).

Among the injuries alleged are general respiratory problems,[60] mold-induced asthma,[61] and damage to the lungs.[62] In some circumstances, claimants have sought recovery for reactive airways dysfunction disease and cognitive impairment.[63] Some claimants have been able to recover for these bodily injuries by asserting that the injuries resulted from "the first-party property insurer's negligence in identifying or repairing the mold problem or bad faith breach of the insurance agreement."[64] Damage to the property caused by mold may be covered by commercial all-risks property insurance policies,[65] landlords' insurance policies,[66] and other first-party property policies.[67] "Mold-related property damage may be covered if it was caused by a covered peril."[68] Just one example of mold damage is caused by water.[69]

---

60. Fifth Circuit: Maynard v. Lloyd's, 2002 WL 1461923, at *2–3 (N.D. Tex. 2002); state courts: Texas: Ballard v. Fire Insurance Exchange, No. 99-05252 (Tex. Dist. Oct. 30, 2001) (claiming general health problems caused by *Stachtbotrys Atra* mold), *reprinted in* 15 Mealey's Litigation Report: Bad Faith (Nov. 7, 2001).

61. Strader v. Grange Mutual Insurance Co., 179 Ore. App. 329, 331–32, 39 P.3d 903, 905 (Ore. App. 2002).

62. Hatley v. Century-National Insurance Co., No. CV 2000-006713 (Ariz. Super. Nov. 5, 2001), *reprinted in* 15 Mealey's Litigation Report: Bad Faith (Dec. 5, 2001).

63. Mathias, Shugrue & Marrinson, *supra* note 57, citing Traub v. Great American Insurance, No. 1995-C-153 (Pa. Comm. July 3, 2002), *reprinted in* 2 Mealey's Litigation Report: Mold, No. 8 (Aug. 2002).

64. *Id.*, citing Arizona: Hatley v. Century-National Insurance Co., No. CV 2000-006713 (Ariz. Super. Nov. 5, 2001), reprinted in 15 Mealey's Litigation Report: Bad Faith (Dec. 5, 2001); Pennsylvania: Traub v. Great American Insurance, No. 1995-C-153 (Pa. Comm. July 3, 2002), reprinted in 2 Mealey's Litigation Report: Mold (Aug. 2002); Texas: Ballard v. Fire Insurance Exchange, No. 99-05252 (Tex. Dist. Oct. 30, 2002), *reprinted in* 15 Mealey's Litigation Report: Bad Faith (Nov. 7, 2001).

65. Columbiaknit, Inc. v. Affiliated FM Insurance Co., 1999 WL 619100, at *8 (D. Ore. 1999) (commercial all-risks property insurance covered mold damage to garments stored in leaking warehouse).

66. *See* state courts: Ohio: Belich v. Westfield Insurance Co., 2000 Ohio App. Lexis 6212 (Ohio App. 2000) (discussing commercial landlord's property insurance coverage); Washington: Bowers v. Farmers Insurance Exchange, 99 Wash. App. 41, 43, 991 P.2d 734, 736 (Wash. App. 2000) (noting that plaintiff was covered under a "Landlord's Protection Package insurance policy"); Wisconsin: Ramsey v. Landmark American Insurance Co., No. C5-01-7827 (Minn. Dist. July 24, 2002), *reprinted in* 2 Mealey's Litigation Report: Mold, No. 8 (Aug. 2002) (noting that plaintiff was covered under "Owner's, Landlord's and Tenant's" insurance policy).

67. See the discussion in Mathias, Shugrue & Marrinson, *supra* note 57, § 11.01[8].

68. *Id.*, citing Bowers v. Farmers Insurance Exchange, 99 Wash. App. 41, 47, 991 P.2d 734, 738 (Wash. App. 2000) ("When the insured can identify an insured peril as the proximate cause, there is coverage 'even if subsequent events in the causal chain are specifically excluded from coverage.'"), quoting Findlay v. United Pacific Insurance Co., 78 Wash. App. 17, 20, 895 P.2d 32 (Wash. App. 1995). *But see* Cooper v. American Family Mutual Insurance Co., 184 F. Supp. 2d 960 (D. Ariz. 2002) (holding that the efficient proximate cause rule would not be enforced due to specific mold exclusion).

69. See Ninth Circuit: Anderson v. Allstate Insurance Co., 45 Fed. Appx. 754, 757, 2002 WL 2021617, at *2 (9th Cir. 2002) (upholding jury award for mold damage caused by ruptured pipe); Columbiaknit, Inc. v. Affiliated FM Insurance Co., 1999 WL 619100 (D. Ore. 1999) (holding that mold

[b]—Insurance Coverage Mold Exclusions

Despite the fact that mold claims have really only been asserted during the 2000s, such claims have resulted in almost as much exposure as asbestos claims.[70] In fact, in the year 2002, there were approximately 300,000 mold claims.[71] The risks associated with "exclusions for mold losses expose insurance buyers to a greater degree of risk than being uninsured for fire claims."[72]

In an attempt to limit their exposure to the potential of multimillion dollar verdicts, the insurance companies have formally excluded coverage for mold-related injuries and damage.[73] In other instances, they have imposed a variety of limits, "including the creation of mold exclusions, the application of previously existing pollution exclusions and other exclusions, the creation of sub-limits of liability for mold

---

damage to garments was covered by corporation's all-risks policy insofar as it was caused by water infiltration); state courts: Texas: Home Insurance Co. v. Dennis D., 2000 WL 144115, at *1 (Tex. App. 2000) (holding that the insurance policy did cover mold damage despite the policy's specific mold exclusion because the mold growth was directly caused by otherwise covered water damage and thus fell within the policy's ensuing loss provision).

70. David J. Dybdahl, *Mold Risk Management and Insurance Strategies* (2003). *See also* David J. Dybdahl & Steven J. Lemon, *The Risk Advisor's Survival Guide to Mold Exclusions*, 15 Envtl. Claims J. 1 (Winter 2003).

71. Dybdahl, *supra* note 70, and Dybdahl & Lemon, *supra* note 70.

72. David J. Dybdahl, *New Insurance Exclusions for Terrorism and Mold Create Unprecedented Levels of Uninsured Risks for Property Managers, Property Owners and Lenders or Sorry We Forgot to Tell You.*

73. *See* Alexander J. Bandza, *Illinois Appellate Court Rejects Insurer Contention That "Broad and General" Pollution Exclusion Barred Mold-Related Claims*, Spotlight Newsletter Resource Center (Jan. 2016) https://jenner.com/resource_centers/update/1411#resource_center_article_14775 (last visited April 6, 2016), discussing *In re* Liquidation of Legion Indemnity Company, 2015 Ill. App. (1st) 140452 (Ill. App. Nov. 10, 2015). "Certain jurisdictions interpret the pollution exclusion more expansively than others, but a recent Illinois decision interpreting Texas law suggests that this expansiveness has its limits." The court considered whether a commercial general liability policy's pollution exclusion applied to mold-related claims. "The policy included specific exclusions for asbestos and lead contamination as well as a generic 'Pollution and Health Hazard' exclusion that excluded, among other things, 'contamination of the environment by any pollutant that is introduced at anytime, anywhere, or in any way.' The trial court held that mold fell within this broad definition and, therefore, the 'Pollution and Health Hazard' exclusion barred coverage for mold-related claims. The First District reversed, stressing that courts must interpret exclusions narrowly and in favor of coverage, [noting] that the policy did not specifically exclude mold- or fungi-related claims. The court then rejected that the policy exclusion applied, reasoning that the exclusion and its definitions used such 'broad and general language' that '***anything***—solid, liquid, gas or substance—that would potentially cause injury to a person would be excluded from coverage.' In the First District's view, such a reading would render the policy 'illusory.' In reaching its conclusion, the court acknowledged that Legion had later issued several other insurance policies that 'unambiguously' excluded mold or fungi from coverage, but it stressed that the existence of such revised policies was not determinative" (emphasis in original).

claims, and other provisions."[74] There are, however, a group of specialized underwriters still issuing policies. There are not clear answers on whether these exclusions and limits will be upheld since the legislative, regulatory, and judicial responses have been mixed and are still evolving.[75]

Considering these exclusions and limitations, what can claimants expect? Is adequate insurance coverage available? The fact is that there are mold policies, but they are often limited in terms of the nature of the damage, what caused the damage, and the injured parties or premises. A variety of interrelated factual and legal issues will come into play to exclude, limit, or allow coverage. Policyholders should expect their insurers to argue against coverage and need to be prepared. Additionally, insurers are also protecting themselves by imposing higher deductibles and maximum payouts. Specific insurance covering mold damage may not be the only source of recovery. "A policyholder should consider whether the mold problem gives rise to a claim under its own first party property coverage, a contractor's insurance program, general liability coverage, worker's compensation, professional liability insurance or other insurance."[76]

Many factors have contributed to the rise of mold claims, including changes in building materials and techniques, energy efficiency, poor workmanship in new buildings, scientific developments that have made it easier to discover the damages and mold as the cause, coverage in the press, and the success of cases brought claiming damages as a result of exposure to mold.[77]

In the past, insurance policies were written to exclude coverage for pollution damage. The standard policy stated, "This insurance does not apply to bodily injury or property damage arising out of the actual, alleged or threatened discharge, disposal, release or escape of pollutants at or from the premises."[78]

This type of exclusion is called an absolute pollution exclusion. Insurers faced with mold-related damage claims often argue that the policy's pollution exclusion

---

74. Summers, *How to Maximize Insurance Coverage for Mold Damage* (Howrey Newsletter March 2, 2009).

75. *Id.*

76. *Id.*

77. Dybdahl, *supra* note 70. According to this article, $20 billion in damages were paid based on asbestos claims as of the time the article was written, while $15 billion had been paid on mold claims as of that date. *See also* Dybdahl & Lemon, *supra* note 70. The authors of this article note that mold has become a much more significant problem with the buildings constructed during the 1980s and thereafter. The airtight construction increases the likelihood of mold damage, and the recycled wood is a breeding ground for mold. *Id.* at 16.

78. John Larkin, *How Mold Can Ruin a Business: What Steps You Need to Take*, 45 Water Conditioning & Purification 101 (Feb. 2003).

bars coverage.[79] "Insurers have argued that mold and fungus spores are airborne pollutants and thus fall within the exclusion from coverage."[80] Some courts have held that mold and fungus do not fall under the general definition of pollutants contained in many pollution exclusions.[81] These courts reason that "the broad 'catch-all' language of a pollution exclusion cannot be interpreted to include 'every conceivable solid, liquid or gaseous contaminant or irritant.'"[82] One court held that "a pollution exclusion did not bar coverage for mold damage because the clause was ambiguous—opining that if the insurer had 'intended to exclude coverage for exposure to fungi, it would have listed them expressly in the definition of "pollutant" or set out separate exclusions for them as it did for asbestos and lead paint.'"[83]

Some policyholders have also tried to defeat the pollution exclusion defense by arguing that the "sudden and accidental" exception allows coverage for mold damage.[84] One court held that the "growth of the molds, fungus, mildew, etc. were unexpected and unintended," thus triggering the "sudden and accidental" exception and rendering the pollution exclusion inapplicable.[85]

[c]—Exceptions to the Mold Exclusions

While in the absence of a specific mold exclusion, mold claims may still be denied under the terms of a standard policy containing a pollution exclusion provision, such provisions tend not to be the safest way protect the insurers. Claimants are stating that mold and the resulting damage and injury do not fit in that exclusion, and the courts are listening. Many are "hesitant about applying the standard pollution exclusions," reasoning that mold "may not constitute the type of 'pollutant' to which the exclusion is directed."[86]

---

79. Mathias, Shugrue & Marrinson, *supra* note 57, citing Fifth Circuit: Lexington Insurance Co. v. Unity Waterford-Fair Oaks, Ltd., 2002 WL 356756, at *1–2 (N.D. Tex. 2002); Eleventh Circuit: Stillman v. Travelers Insurance Co., 88 F.3d 911, 914 (11th Cir. 1996); state courts: Minnesota: Ramsey v. Landmark American Insurance Co., No. C5-01-7827 (Minn. Dist. July 24, 2002), *reprinted in* 2 Mealey's Litigation Report: Mold (Aug. 2002); Wisconsin: Leverence v. United States Fidelity & Guaranty, 158 Wis. 2d 64, 96–97, 462 N.W.2d 218, 232 (1990).

80. *Id.*

81. *Id.*, citing Ramsey v. Landmark American Insurance Co., No. C5-01-7827 (Minn. Dist. July 24, 2002), *reprinted in* 2 Mealey's Litigation Report: Mold (Aug. 2002).

82. *Id. See, e.g.*, Ramsey v. Landmark American Insurance Co., No. C5-01-7827 (Minn. Dist. July 24, 2002), *reprinted in* 2 Mealey's Litigation Report: Mold, at 20 (Aug. 2002).

83. Mathias, Shugrue & Marrinson, *supra* note 57, § 11.01[8][b].

84. *Id.*, citing Leverence v. United States Fidelity & Guaranty, 158 Wis .2d 64, 96–97, 462 N.W.2d 218, 232 (1990).

85. *Id.*

86. Larkin, *supra* note 78.

One commentator has noted that mold-related damage and injury should not be subject to the absolute pollution exclusion because:

(1) "Mold does not release or escape within the intent of the pollution exclusion."[87]

(2) "Mold is not a waste."

(3) Water is the "proximate cause of mold," and water does not fit the policy definition of pollutant.

(4) Mold occurs naturally. It is a living thing and does not fit the definition of pollutant in an insurance policy.

(5) Some "environmental impairment liability insurance policies specifically exclude naturally occurring substances from the definition of 'Pollutants' in their environmental insurance contract." This demonstrates that the underwriters thought that these "naturally occurring substances [like mold] were not excluded under the absolute pollution exclusion in the general liability insurance policy."

(6) Mold was only addressed as a separate loss event in late 2001.

(7) If mold were already excluded in the standard pollution exclusion provision, there would be no need for a separate mold exclusion provision in newly issued liability insurance policies.[88]

Another commentator noted that since water damage usually is not the result of pollution, it follows that it is "not the release, discharge or dispersal of a pollutant."[89] Therefore, it can be effectively argued that the standard pollution exclusion in general liability policies may not apply. In that case, the insurance company will be liable for repairing the damage caused by the mold. It can also be argued that the insurance company should be responsible for clean up since it is really the repair of the damage

87. David J. Dybdahl, *Managing Mold Related Risks, After the Mold Exclusions Become Effective*, 4–5. *See also* Mathias, Shugrue & Marrinson, *supra* note 57, § 11.01[8][b], citing Lexington Insurance Co. v. Unity Waterford-Fair Oaks, Ltd., 2002 WL 356756, at *2–3 (N.D. Tex. 2002). The policyholder in the *Lexington Insurance* case unsuccessful attempted such an argument, claiming that the "pollution exclusion does not apply to claims for mold damage because mold and fungi are never 'dispersed, discharged or released' and thus fall outside the scope of the pollution exclusion even if they are considered pollutants." *Id.* According to the policyholder, "the mold that caused the extensive damage to the [property] 'was simply already present and thrived because of the moisture.'" *Id.*, citing 2002 WL 356756, at *2. The court rejected the policyholder's argument, reasoning "that the mold that was the cause of the damage at issue was dispersed within the covered properties and, consequently, that the damage caused thereby falls within the scope of the Pollution and Contamination Exclusion contained in the policy." *Id.*

88. Dybdahl, *supra* note 87.

89. Larkin, *supra* note 78.

to the property that is being undertaken.[90] The fact that the mold will now be gone, causing no further injury or damage, is merely an added benefit.[91]

[d]—Avoiding Liability—Allocating Responsibility

To avoid these liability problems, nearly all insurance companies have now specifically excluded mold coverage.[92] Facing the risk of liability and responsibility for mold remediation, the exclusion of coverage for mold-based claims means the risks associated with mold now must be allocated. Who will bear the risk for such claims—the landlord, the tenant, the property owner, the property manager, lenders? How will the risk be allocated? How can the risk be reduced? The parties will need to shop around for coverage. Some policies may cover damage at a price. It is also possible to obtain environmental insurance or a stand-alone (separate) mold coverage policy. Likely these options will be quite costly.

Environmental impairment liability insurance may be available to property owners, tenants, and lenders. This type of policy covers "bodily injury, property damage, remediation expenses and defense" and may also cover contractual liability, business interruption, extra expense, and non-owned disposal sites."[93] Landlords (and building owners) will now need to take specific steps to limit their exposure to liability.

All leases should reflect the fact that mold is excluded from coverage. The landlord (or owner) will want to shift the responsibility for obtaining coverage for mold damage and injury to the tenant (or purchaser) or at least shift responsibility for detecting and monitoring visible or known mold problems. Why should the landlord bear sole responsibility if the tenant was aware of a problem and failed to report it promptly? It seems only fair that the additional damage should be the tenant's responsibility. Whoever ends up as the responsible party will want to make certain to have a policy that specifically covers mold-related injuries and damage. There is also the possibility of self-insurance. If the landlord is unable to obtain coverage at an affordable price, self-insurance may be his or her only, or at least best, option.

By 2003, nearly all newly issued property and liability insurance policies excluded mold, microbial matter, and fungus.[94] These exclusions applied to new loss events incurred during the policy period.[95] However, since most companies have occurrence-based liability insurance policies, such policies should provide coverage for any

---

90. *Id.*

91. *Id.*

92. A number of states have allowed insurers to specifically exclude mold coverage in their policies. Other states have allowed limitations on coverage. *Id.* at 103.

93. Dybdahl, *supra* note 70.

94. Dybdahl, *supra* note 87.

95. *Id.* at 3.

event that took place when the policy was in force.[96] This would include "continuous or repeated exposure to the cause of the loss."[97]

Determining when the loss or damage occurred is not always a simple matter, and that date will have a direct impact on whether the claim is or is not covered by a particular policy. For example, in the case of mold caused by water damage, is the date of loss when the mold develops, when the leak or other water entered the building, when the mold was discovered, or some other date? In fact, it would seem that the damage occurs over time. The mold condition develops and worsens unless the damage is properly repaired. When did the mold reach such a point that it creates a health and safety hazard? How will the damages be measured? The best way to insure against the damage or loss is to purchase a policy specifically covering mold. It is possible to buy an environmental policy that is modified to cover loss, damage, or injury resulting from mold.[98]

[e]—The Effect of the Mold Exclusion in the Claims-Made Liability Insurance Context

The effect of the mold exclusion is very different in the claims-made liability insurance context. In a claims-made policy, the mold exclusion on the policy renewal "is, in effect, a full prior acts and prospective work exclusion for all mold related damage claims."[99] This retroactive gap in coverage must be addressed. The parties will want to provide some form of protection during that gap period.

[f]—Types of Claims

In addition to the different types of coverage, there are a variety of claims that may be brought depending on who suffers the damage, loss, or injury.

[i]—First-Party Claims

If the policyholder is injured or suffers a loss, he or she would file a first-party claim. Such claims may be covered by renter's, commercial property, or builder's risk insurance. The terms of these policies vary, even within a particular type and certainly from state to state. "However, most modern policies contain some form of mold and/or pollution exclusion that the insurer will claim precludes coverage."[100]

---

96. *Id.*
97. *Id.*
98. *Id.* at 4. *See also* Dybdahl & Lemon, *supra* note 70; Dybdahl, *supra* note 70.
99. Dybdahl, *supra* note 87.
100. Summers, *supra* note 74.

Whether and to what extent such exclusions will bar or limit coverage for a particular mold problem will be based on the facts at issue, the policy terms, and the applicable law. The policyholder must fully understand all of these before asserting that a particular claim should be covered.

The insuring agreements for such policies typically provide that the insurer will pay for direct physical loss from covered perils or for damage to property arising from a covered peril. The policies can be all-risk or specified peril policies. "Whether mold damage is covered can seem like a chicken-and-egg proposition. The insurers are likely to argue that mold damage is not a covered peril and any consequences similarly are not covered. However, if the damage is caused by a covered peril (e.g., roof leaks, wind-driven rain, or accidental discharge from a plumbing system) and mold is the consequence of the covered peril, the policyholder has a better argument for coverage."[101]

Courts have not been consistent in applying the insuring agreements and exclusions to mold claims.[102] Therefore, familiarizing yourself with your jurisdiction's approach and decisions will be important in presenting and establishing your claim. "Three important concepts to consider are the 'wear and tear' exclusions, the 'ensuing loss' doctrine and 'efficient proximate cause.' Some courts have enforced 'wear and tear' exclusions to preclude coverage for mold naturally occurring over time as a result of high humidity and other general climatic conditions."[103] In such cases, there is not a single covered event that can be said to have caused the mold and resulting damage. The "wear and tear" analysis is very fact specific. When asserting a mold claim under a policy with a "wear and tear" exclusion, "the policyholder should be prepared to offer proof of a covered peril that resulted in the mold."[104]

Some courts have found coverage for mold damage when the damage is an ensuing loss of a covered peril, even where there is a specific mold exclusion in the policy. Other courts relied on the doctrine of efficient proximate cause to find coverage for mold despite mold exclusions. In such cases, the claimant will have to show that the "efficient proximate cause of the mold is a covered peril rather than an excluded peril such as wear and tear."[105]

[ii]—Third-Party Claims

Damages resulting from mold can also be asserted by third parties, such as guests or visitors to the premises. The specific language of liability policies varies from policy

---

101. *Id.*
102. *Id.*
103. *Id.*
104. *Id.*
105. *Id.*

to policy and from state to state. Therefore, it is important to understand the specific policy terms and the holding of the courts in the applicable jurisdiction to determine what will likely be covered, excluded, or limited.[106] Typically, the "insuring agreements of liability policies provide that the insurance company will pay 'all sums the insured becomes legally obligated to pay as damages' or that it will reimburse the ultimate net loss sustained by the policyholder."[107]

The law regarding the applicability and enforceability of mold exclusions in liability policies is unclear at this time. "In policies that do not contain specific mold exclusions, insurers have asserted that pollution exclusions bar coverage, relying by analogy on indoor air quality cases that involved lead paint, carbon monoxide and other contaminants. There are countless cases both in favor of coverage and restricting coverage for policyholders and insurers to cite by analogy to pollution cases."[108] In light of the lack of clarity in the law, taking steps to maximize the likelihood of coverage takes on added importance.

[g]—Maximizing Insurance Coverage for Mold

There are some practical steps that can be taken to maximize coverage. First, research mold. Understand the potential liability, the types of damage, and the facts and nature of mold. Investigate the available policy types, coverages, limitations, allowances, and exclusions. While the policy might not provide full coverage, the extent of coverage should be clear. Hire an expert who, if necessary when a potential or actual problem is detected, can explain the types of damage, long-term effects, and whether the damage occurred over a short or long period of time. Review your policy or policies. Different policies have different terms and will vary in their applicability and extent of coverage. Filing requirements and deadlines must be met. The policy deadlines may be substantially shorter than those available under a statute of limitations.[109]

It is important to provide written notice to all potential insurers as soon as a potential claim exists.[110] Records should be maintained of all the claims filed, related correspondence, and oral communications as well "records of activities undertaken by [the] insurer, including dates, the names of insurer representatives involved, requests for follow-up information and so on."[111] These records will be very important if the claim is litigated. In the case of a dispute, the policy will determine if it will be sub-

106. Common exclusions include mold exclusions, pollution exclusions, and owned-property exclusions. *Id.*

107. *Id.*

108. *Id.*

109. *Id.*

110. *Id.*

111. *Id.*

mitted to arbitration, mediation, or some other form of alternative dispute resolution or if the dispute will go directly to litigation.

[h]—Concluding Comment

Basically, mold exclusions will force parties to make claims under their liability policies instead of under property insurance. For the time being, while the exclusions on liability insurance policies will eliminate insurance coverage for new occurrences, "most businesses will still have some residual liability insurance protection in place."[112]

Certainly, during the construction phase, it makes sense to hire an industrial hygienist to examine the plans, property, and actual construction to ascertain and advise with respect to mold and other such environmental concerns.

Considering the escalating insurance costs, litigation, and evidence of the dangers caused by mold and other indoor environmental problems, better air quality and prevention of sick building syndrome[113] need to be addressed by landlords, building owners, and tenants. Landlords and building owners will want to adopt strict measures to prevent mold and have a plan set up for treating mold and correcting the damage when mold appears.[114] These measures and any plan of action must be clearly communicated to the members of the landlord's and owner's management team. Considering the potential damage claims and resulting potential liability, it is advisable for landlords to address mold-related issues specifically in their leases.[115]

[3]—Notifying the Insurer about Material Changes in Circumstance

Landlords and property owners have a duty to notify building insurers and keep them updated with respect to all material changes in circumstance relating to the insured property. Failure to provide such notice may result in reduced or denied coverage. The insurer has to be provided with all material facts that might influence its decision to insure or the amount of the premium it will charge.

For example, the reporting of sprinkler impairments is generally a condition set forth in a building's insurance policy. Failing to notify the insurer of an inoperable system will likely be considered a breach or violation of the condition and may result in nonpayment for any loss or damage or even cancellation of the policy. A material

---

112. *Id.*

113. See § 13.06[3] Commercial Leases *supra* for a discussion of sick building syndrome.

114. Roy Harris, *Mold Spreads*, CFO Magazine 2 (Sept. 2003).

115. Jones & Weinberg, *Using Lease Provisions to Address Mold Growth*, 16 Commercial Leasing Law & Strategy 1 (Law Journal Newsletters Jan. 2004).

change in circumstances may also include a change in use of the premises. For example, if the premises were used simply as an office and are now being used to store combustibles or tons of paper, the risk of fire and the extent of damage that could result are substantially increased so that the property owner would have to notify the insurer of the changed use. If a building is a single-occupancy tenant and the tenant abandons the property, that is a significant change in circumstances in that it presents an increased the risk of damage to the building by trespassers.

Further, adding walls and creating a number of office spaces in a formerly open-space office could be considered material changes in circumstance that would trigger the owner's responsibility to notify the insurance company.

[4]—Defective Construction

A hotly debated issue today is whether defective construction constitutes an "occurrence" and therefore may be covered under a liability insurance policy.[116] "Standard general liability insurance policies provide coverage for, among other things, 'property damage' caused by an 'occurrence.'"[117] "Occurrence" is generally defined as "an accident, including continuous or repeated exposure to substantially the same general harmful conditions."[118] The courts are split on whether defective construction falls within the general definition of "occurrence."

[a]—Whether Construction Defects Qualify as "Occurrences"

Courts tend to reach one of three conclusions when considering whether construction defects qualify as "occurrences" in construction defect coverage cases.[119] The first point of view is that they do not qualify because neither the defective work nor the resulting damage were "the result of an 'accident' (i.e., an 'occurrence')."[120] These courts "typically hold that construction defects are the natural consequence of performing substandard work and focus on the intentional nature of the act of construction as opposed to whether the resulting 'property damage' was expected or intended."[121] "The guiding principle underlying this view is that liability policies

---

116. Aaron Mandel & Stevi Raab, *Is Defective Construction an "Occurrence"? The Answer Isn't So Concrete*, Construction Defect Coverage Quarterly (Feb. 2013). See Chapter 3 regarding additional named insureds, coverage, and liability limitations under subcontractor policies.

117. Mandel & Raab, *supra* note 116, referencing ISO Form CG 00 01 10 01, § I.1.b(1).

118. *Id.* § V.13.

119. *See* Stephen M. Prignano & Nora A. Valenza-Frost, *Recent Developments in Coverage for Construction Defect Claims* (Jan. 31, 2014).

120. Mandel and Raab, *supra* note 116, referencing ISO Form CG 00 01 10 01, at § V.13.

121. *Id.*

do not protect against foreseeable business risks the insured can mitigate, and that to hold construction defects are 'occurrences' would impermissibly convert liability insurance policies into performance bonds (which generally have considerably higher premiums per dollar of coverage than liability policies) and liability insurers into guarantors of an insured's work."[122]

The second point of view is that "defective construction work itself is not covered because it is not the result of an 'occurrence,' but that the resulting damage may be covered because it was fortuitous and unintended."[123] In one such case, an owner of seven gas stations sued the supplier of concrete used to construct the gas stations "on the ground that the concrete was defective and damaged nearby asphalt." The supplier's general liability insurers denied coverage stating that the owner's claims did not allege "property damage" or an "occurrence."[124] The case went to trial and then appeal, where the appellate court held that "while the damage to the concrete itself was not covered, the damage to the asphalt was because it was neither expected nor intended and, therefore, an 'occurrence.'"[125]

The third point of view is that "*all* liabilities—including damage to the work itself—are covered because defective construction work itself is accidental and the insured rarely expects construction defects."[126] These decisions appear simply to favor finding coverage, transforming liability policies into performance bonds.[127]

[b]—Addressing the Construction Defect "Occurrence" Issue through Legislation

Considering these varied court interpretations of the "occurrence" issue, some state legislatures have passed laws in an attempt to clarify how "occurrence" should be

122. *Id.*, citing and noting as an example American Home Assurance Co. v. Trumbull Corp., No. GD-11-006886 (Pa. Ct. Com. Pl. Allegheny Co. Oct. 10, 2012). According to the court, liability insurance policies do not cover damage resulting from faulty workmanship because "faulty workmanship can never constitute an accident."

123. *Id.*, citing Westfield Ins. Co. v. Custom Agri System, Inc., 979 N.E.2d 269 (Ohio 2012).

124. *Id.*

125. *Id.*

126. *Id.*, citing and discussing Florida: U.S. Fire Insurance Co. v. J.S.U.B., 979 So. 2d 871 (Fla. 2007) (concluding that the costs of repairing a subcontractor's use of poor soil, improper soil compaction, and testing were covered under a liability policy); Tennessee: Travelers Indemnification Co. of America v. Moore & Assocs., Inc., 216 S.W.3d 302, 308 (Tenn. 2007); Texas: Lamar Homes, Inc. v. Mid-Continent Casualty Co., 242 S.W.3d 1 (Tex. 2007) (finding coverage for damage to a building's foundation, sheetrock, and stone veneer allegedly caused by the builder's defective construction of a house's foundation).

127. *Id.*

interpreted when determining coverage for construction defect claims.[128] These include Colorado,[129] Arkansas,[130] South Carolina,[131] and Hawaii.[132]

Colorado's state legislature was the first to address the "occurrence" issue. Effective May 21, 2010, Section 13-20-808 of the Colorado Code applies only to insurance policies issued after the statute's effective date.[133] The statute provides that "a court interpreting a liability insurance policy 'shall presume that the work of a construction professional that results in property damage, *including damage to the work itself or other work*, is an accident unless the property damage is intended and expected by the insured.'"[134] Section 808 broadened existing law, replacing the "more limited Colorado common law, which held that only 'unforeseeable damage to non-defective property arising from faulty workmanship' qualified as an 'occurrence' under liability insurance policies."[135] Despite the emphasized language, nothing in Section 808 "requires coverage for damage to an insured's own work unless otherwise provided in the insurance policy," and nothing in Section 808 "creates insurance coverage that is not included in the insurance policy."[136] Basically, under Colorado's statute, "damage to the insured's work itself qualifies as an 'occurrence' unless the subject policy expressly provides otherwise."[137] The practitioner should be aware, then, that despite statutory protection, states have allowed individual insurance policies to override or nullify this protection, a practice quite common in instances where state statutory protection may be nullified by the specific agreement made between an insured and its insurer. Thus, the practitioner's first read, especially in a commercial policy where such nullifications of state protection are offered, should be of the policy itself and not necessarily rely upon the state's statutes, in the relatively rare instance where that state's laws actually address the issue itself.

Arkansas's state legislature was the next to address the "occurrence" issue, enacting Section 23-79-155 on March 23, 2011.[138] Prior to its enactment, "Arkansas courts held that "'faulty workmanship is not an accident,' although it was unclear whether coverage was available for the cost of repairing damage to property other than the

128. Mandel & Raab, *supra* note 116.

129. Colorado: Col. Code § 13-20-808, effective May 21, 2010.

130. Arkansas: Ark. Code § 23-79-155 (March 23, 2011).

131. South Carolina: S.C. Code § 38-61-70 (May 2011).

132. Hawaii: Haw. Code § 431:1-217 (June 3, 2011).

133. Mandel & Raab, *supra* note 116, discussing Col. Code § 13-20-808, effective May 21, 2010.

134. Mandel and Raab, *supra* note 116.

135. *Id.*, citing Greystone Constr., Inc. v. Nat'l Fire & Marine Ins. Co., 661 F.3d 1272 (10th Cir. 2011).

136. Mandel & Raab, *supra* note 116.

137. *Id.*

138. *Id.*, discussing Ark. Code § 23-79-155 (March 23, 2011).

defective work itself."[139] Section 23-79-155 clarifies the law, requiring that "commercial general liability policies sold in Arkansas define 'occurrence' to include 'property damage or bodily injury resulting from faulty workmanship.'"[140] The statute does not seem to address specifically whether *damage to the insured's work* itself is covered (although it is unlikely).[141] It also does not restrict policy exclusions typically applied in construction defect coverage cases, so that it appears that existing Arkansas case law interpreting those exclusions remains good law.[142]

In May 2011, South Carolina's state legislature enacted its own law addressing the occurrence issue.[143] "In addition to the traditional 'occurrence' definition contained in the ISO Form, Section 70 provides that commercial general liability policies issued in South Carolina 'shall contain or be deemed to contain a definition of "occurrence" that includes . . . property damage or bodily injury resulting from faulty workmanship, exclusive of the faulty workmanship itself.'"[144] In other words, the statute "expressly provides that damage to the insured's work itself is not an 'occurrence.'"[145] Section 38-61-70 of the South Carolina Code clarified case law, "which held that faulty workmanship was not an 'occurrence' where the resulting damage was a natural and expected consequence of the faulty work rather than a fortuitous event."[146] The statute "applies to insurance policies issued on or after May 17, 2011."[147]

Finally, Hawaii's state legislature addressed the "occurrence" issue in construction defect cases, enacting Section 431:1-217 on June 3, 2011.[148] The statute was enacted as an express response to a Hawaii Court of Appeals decision in which "the court denied coverage for both defects in the insured's own work and resulting 'property damage' caused by faulty workmanship on the ground that faulty workmanship claims arise out of contract breaches as opposed to 'occurrences.'"[149]

Instead of seeking to reinstate the coverage that the legislature alleged was eliminated by the court of appeals decision and define "occurrence" in the construction defect coverage context, the statute merely provided that "the meaning of the term

139. *Id.*, citing Essex Ins. Co. v. Holder, 261 S.W.3d 456 (Ark. 2007) (defective workmanship alone "resulting in damages only to the work product itself" does not qualify as an "occurrence under a CGL policy").

140. *Id.*, citing Ark. Code § 23-79-155(a).

141. *Id.*

142. *Id.*

143. S.C. Code § 38-61-70.

144. Mandel & Raab, *supra* note 116.

145. *Id.*

146. *Id.*

147. *Id.*

148. *Id.*, discussing Hawaii Code § 431:1-217.

149. *Id.*, citing and discussing Group Builders, Inc. v. Admiral Insurance Co., 231 P.3d 67 (Haw. App. 2010).

'occurrence' shall be construed in accordance with the law as it existed at the time that the insurance policy was issued."[150] Therefore, it seems that even under Section 431:1-217, insurance policies issued after that court's decision "are subject to its holding that construction defect claims are not covered under liability policies because they do not arise out of 'occurrences.'"[151] The Hawaii statute "simply refers parties back to the case law," and coverage depends on when the applicable policy was issued.[152]

[c]—Case Law Regarding Faulty Workmanship and the Occurrence Issue

Courts are just beginning to rule on the faulty workmanship and "occurrence" issue. After a number of decisions against policyholders regarding whether general liability policies can ever provide coverage for construction liabilities, some courts have held that there is coverage "in certain circumstances" for such liabilities.[153] And currently the majority of courts are taking the view that unexpected and unintentional damage caused by negligent workmanship qualifies as an insured "occurrence."

Relying on the subcontractor exception to the "your work" exclusion, the Second Circuit, reversing the district court, ruled that a general liability policy provides coverage for liability sustained by a swimming pool installer on account of cracks that developed in the pools following installation.

The policyholder successfully argued that "the language of the exception to the 'own work' exclusion for work 'performed on [the insured's] behalf by a subcontractor' demonstrated that in some circumstances the insured's own work is covered."[154] Agreeing with that argument, the Second Circuit held "as coverage is limited by the policy to 'occurrences' and defects in the insured's own work in some circumstances are covered, these policies . . . unmistakably include defects in the insured's own work within the category of an 'occurrence.'"[155] The Second Circuit left the question of whether the "subcontractor" exception applied for the court to decide on remand.

The North Dakota Supreme Court soon after "overruled an earlier decision and held that property damage caused by faulty workmanship may constitute an 'occurrence' if the faulty work was 'unexpected' and not intended by the insured, and the property damage was not anticipated or intentional, so that neither the cause nor

150. *Id.*, citing Haw. Rev. Stat. § 431:1-217(a).

151. *Id.*

152. *Id.*

153. John B. Berringer, *Faulty Workmanship Can Be an Accident*, Reed Smith (April 22, 2013).

154. *Id.*

155. *Id.*, citing Scottsdale Insurance v. R. I. Pools, 11-3529-cv (2d Cir. March 21, 2013).

the harm was anticipated, intended or expected."[156] Reviewing the commercial general liability (CGL) policy drafting history, including the "subcontractor exception" to the "exclusion from coverage of damages to an insured's own 'work,'" the court noted that CGL policies were broadened to provide coverage for defective construction claims where the defective work was performed by the insured's subcontractor.[157]

Another court, this time in New York, lent further support to what appears to be a pro-policyholder trend "when it affirmed a lower court decision that 'faulty workmanship' can be an 'occurrence' where it damages property other than to the policyholder's own work."[158] "While recognizing that an earlier decision of the same court had held that CGL policies 'do not insure against faulty workmanship in the work product itself,' the . . . court held that such policies 'do insure against property damage caused by faulty workmanship to something *other than* the work product.'"[159]

Still another court addressed the issue. In July 2013, the Georgia Supreme Court decided two important certified questions from the Eleventh Circuit "that affirm and expand the rights of property owners and policyholders seeking insurance coverage for construction defects under standard commercial general liability (CGL) insurance policies."[160] Specifically, the court held that "[t]o constitute an 'occurrence' under a CGL policy, it is not necessary that there be damage to property other than the

156. *Id.*, citing K&L Homes v. American Family Mutual Insurance Co., 2013 N.D. 57 (April 5, 2013), which stated that this is consistent with our definition of "accident" for purposes of a CGL policy. *But see* Zurich American Insurance Company v. R.M. Shoemaker Company, No. 12-2268, 2013 WL 1224104 (3d Cir. March 27, 2013), where the court came out with the opposite result. There, applying Pennsylvania law, the court "affirmed the district court's summary judgment order holding that a general liability insurer had no duty to defend or indemnify a policyholder in a lawsuit seeking damages resulting from faulty workmanship of the policyholder's subcontractor. 2013 WL 1224104, at *4." Virginia L. White-Mahaffey & Erica L. Gerson, *Two Cases Analyze Faulty Workmanship Claims under CGL Policies, with Contrary Results* (April 12, 2013).

157. Berringer, *supra* note 153, citing K&L Homes v. American Family Mutual Insurance Co., 2013 N.D. 57 (April 5, 2013), which stated that this is consistent with our definition of "accident" for purposes of a CGL policy. *But see* Zurich American Insurance Company v. R.M. Shoemaker Company, No. 12-2268, 2013 WL 1224104 (3d Cir. March 27, 2013), where the court came out with the opposite result. There, applying Pennsylvania law, the court "affirmed the district court's summary judgment order holding that a general liability insurer had no duty to defend or indemnify a policyholder in a lawsuit seeking damages resulting from faulty workmanship of the policyholder's subcontractor. 2013 WL 1224104, at *4." White-Mahaffey & Gerson, *supra* note 156.

158. Berringer, *supra* note 153,

159. *Id.*, discussing I.J. White Corp. v. Columbia Casualty Co., 2013 N.Y. Slip Op 02500 (N.Y. App. Div. First Dept. April 16, 2013).

160. *Insurance Coverage Update: Georgia Supreme Court Rules on Insurance Coverage for Construction Defects*, Thompson Hine (July 22, 2013), discussing Taylor Morrison Services, Inc. v. HDI-Gerling Insurance Co., S13Q0462 (Ga. Sup. July 12, 2013).

insured's work itself" and that "[c]laims for breach of warranty, but typically not for fraud, may constitute an occurrence and may be covered."[161]

These decisions reverse a trend by "some courts to find coverage under CGL policies where the underlying damage is allegedly caused by faulty workmanship,"[162] reasoning that the underlying claims did not result from an "accident" because defects in work are "foreseeable" or are not "fortuitous."[163] The pro-policyholder cases recognized that "contractors and manufacturers often rely on subcontractors to perform some or all of their 'work,' and that insurance plays a key role in protecting a policyholder from damages caused by a subcontractor's negligence, which—from the standpoint of the insured—is 'accidental.'"[164]

However, cases with the opposite results include a Third Circuit case where the court, applying Pennsylvania law, "affirmed the district court's summary judgment order holding that a general liability insurer had no duty to defend or indemnify a policyholder in a lawsuit seeking damages resulting from faulty workmanship of the policyholder's subcontractor."[165]

The divergent viewpoints expressed by the courts indicate that "litigation will persist on the question of whether, absent a pertinent exclusion, coverage exists under a commercial general liability policy for faulty workmanship of a policyholder's subcontractor."[166]

[d]—What the Future Holds

Whether coverage for construction defects exists under a CGL policy will depend on the policy language and the law of the particular jurisdiction.[167] The Colorado, Arkansas, South Carolina, and Hawaii legislatures all attempted to clarify whether claims arising out of defective construction work can qualify as an "occurrence," which will, "at least *potentially* trigger coverage—under general liability insurance policies."[168] Until the courts issue opinions addressing the statutes, their ultimate effect will not be known. It remains to be seen how other legislatures will address the "occurrence" issue considering these early statutes. However, if they side with Colorado, adopting the line that both defective construction work and resulting "property

161. *Id.*
162. Berringer, *supra* note 153.
163. *Id.*
164. *Id.*
165. White-Mahaffey & Gerson, *supra* note 156, citing and discussing Zurich American Insurance Company v. R.M. Shoemaker Company, No. 12-2268, 2013 WL 1224104 (3d Cir. March 27, 2013).
166. *Id.*
167. *See* Prignano & Valenza-Frost, *supra* note 119.
168. Mandel & Raab, *supra* note 116.

damage" are the result of "occurrences," liability insurers will respond accordingly. Faced with uncertainty and the fact that courts and legislatures continue to reach different conclusions regarding coverage, it can be expected that insurers will recraft their policies to limit their liability. They will likely include broad exclusions for faulty workmanship rather than rely on how "occurrence" will be defined and interpreted.[169] Insurers will also likely include more specific exclusions to preclude the "coverage for 'property damage' to an insured's own work."[170] Alternatively, or additionally, insurers may charge higher premiums for construction industry policies in those states, "and/or issue policies only in excess of significant self-insured retentions (SIR) because they would now be forced to provide coverage for risks that they never intended to take on, and that liability policies traditionally do not cover."[171] However unlikely, in extreme cases, insurers may just stop issuing policies to covering construction.

Over time, as more courts analyze, interpret, and apply these and similar laws, it will become clearer how the laws will impact the real estate, construction, and liability insurance industries.[172] In the meantime, when purchasing insurance to protect against losses stemming from the "faulty workmanship" of subcontractors, policyholders should make sure that their coverage includes the "subcontractor" exception to the "your work" exclusion.[173] They should also consider "seeking an endorsement that clarifies the 'occurrence' definition by providing that the term 'occurrence' includes faulty or negligent workmanship by subcontractors. Similarly, just because a claim is couched as a breach of contract does not automatically mean that general liability coverage is unavailable."[174] "Ultimately, 'the question whether the insured's liability for defects in its own work is covered turns on whether the subcontractor exception applies.'"[175]

---

169. *See* Prignano & Valenza-Frost, *supra* note 119.
170. Mandel & Raab, *supra* note 116.
171. *Id.*
172. *Id.*
173. Berringer, supra note 153.
174. *Id.*
175. Thomson, *Defects in an Insured's Own Work Are "Unmistakably Included" in the Definition of 'Occurrence' in CGL Policy, Rules Second Circuit*, Gavel 2 Gavel (April 22, 2013).

Chapter 7
The "No Fault" Approach

[1]—In General

Recently, some notable authorities in the commercial leasing field have advanced the position that by combining certain lease provisions on insurance, indemnification, and subrogation, the parties can achieve a "no fault" indemnification in the lease. The no fault scheme essentially shifts liability and property damage risk (without regard to fault) to the parties most able and willing to carry these risks, namely the landlord and tenant's insurance carriers. While the no fault indemnification is not absolute (some liability remains), it is clearer, much fairer, and more user-friendly than the shifting of risk for liability and damage onto the landlord and tenant themselves, which is what typically occurs in most commercial lease negotiations.

One prominent commentator and commercial real estate attorney speaks most eloquently on this topic. He states, "A simple solution to the problem of negotiation on indemnity clauses is to convert the lease, as to indemnity, to no fault. Resistance to this proposition—as efficacious as it sounds—is nearly universal. Someday, I hope to have the reasons explained to me."[1]

The theory of no fault is simple. The risk of loss for any given damage or claim of damage falls on the party who is obligated to carry the insurance for such a loss under the terms of the lease. For example, as one commentator explains, if the landlord is obligated to carry an "all-risk" policy for the building, it does not matter why the building burned down.[2] Except for certain exclusions, the landlord is then declared to be the responsible party.

---

1. Martin I. Zangel, Negotiating Commercial Real Estate Leases 157 (1991). The authors could not agree more. If a risk is insurable at commercially acceptable rates, carefully and fully insure it, waive direct actions and claims one against the other, waive subrogation rights, and get on with it. Look only to insurance. Nothing seems clearer than when each party is required to maintain insurance and there is a huge reservoir of insurers who most likely calculated in their premiums the cost of covering catastrophic damage caused by either their insured or the other party. That many still resist no fault protection does not make sense.

2. *Id.*

No fault has clear advantages to both parties, particularly the landlord, since most of the insurance obligations rest with the tenant. Liability, property, and insurance for tenant's improvements installed by the tenant are typically all a tenant's obligations. The landlord is usually obligated to carry property insurance only for the building and will be obligated to indemnify the tenant from any claims arising out of damage to the building. Except for the common areas, which the landlord is required to keep and maintain, the parties should be able to have simple no fault handling of normally insurable claims. Excluded from normal insurance are those casualties that are caused by gross negligence and those that the courts in a particular state will forbid indemnification of, such as a party's own acts of negligence or injuries and damage caused by a party's willful acts.

There may be some types of exculpatory clauses that have the potential to defeat even a no fault approach. Landlords may attempt to completely exculpate themselves or excessively limit the extent of their liability even for the negligence of their own work, for failure to respond to the tenant's needs or fulfill their own obligations under the lease.[3] Take, for example, the situation where a plumber negligently tightened a value on a high-pressure water column, therefore shutting off pressure on lower floors. As a result, a valve exploded, flooding several floors. Due to an exculpatory clause in the lease, the landlord was able to avoid paying for the resulting damage.[4]

What are some of the reasons mitigating against no fault? Some carriers claim that premiums are based on the landlord's loss history. With a switch to no fault, the party takes on the obligation for losses that may not be its fault but rather are the fault of another party. However, a protected party can protect itself against this result by providing examples of its own exemplary loss record and stipulating that the no fault provisions will not apply if the other protected party does not keep an exemplary loss record.

One of the leading commercial leasing lawyers in the country makes one of the few persuasive arguments for retaining exculpatory clauses.[5] He states that due to the IRS regulations, landlords use partnership and noncorporate entities to enter into leases. Under these types of structures, the landlords are not able to avail themselves of the protection of the corporate shield. Therefore, they need the protection of exculpatory clauses against a tenant that might be able to bring an action or obtain a judgment against a landlord, possibly decimating the landlord vehicle and going against the individual partners comprising the ownership.[6]

---

3. John B. Wood, Navigating the Dangerous Shoals of Commercial Leases 39–40 (1991) (on file with author).

4. *Id.*

5. Halper, *Can You Find a Fair Lease?*, 14 Real Estate L.J. 99 (Fall 1985).

6. *Id.* In the exculpatory clause to which this commentator refers (which may in many respects be a limitation of liability clause going to judgment rather than liability in the first place), the most serious

The better, clearer, and easier way, however, is the no fault scheme. A mutually satisfactory end can be achieved by clearly stating the intent of the parties to the lease, setting up a scheme of mutual waiver of subrogations and mutual indemnifications for items that can be indemnified, by striking out exculpation clauses and setting up strong insurance clauses.

[2]—A Sample No Fault Clause

The following is an example of a no fault clause prepared by the late Sid Saltz, a prominent real estate attorney:[7]

Example 3

VI. RISK ALLOCATION AND INSURANCE

6.0. Allocation of Risks. The parties desire, to the extent permitted by law, to allocate certain risks of personal injury, bodily injury or property damage, and risks of loss of real or personal property by reason of fire, explosion or other casualty, and to provide for the responsibility for insuring those risks. It is the intent of the parties that, to the extent any event is insured for or required herein to be insured for, any loss, cost, damage or expense, arising from such event, including, without limitation, the expense of defense against claims or suits, be covered by insurance, without regard to the fault of Tenant, its officers, employees or agents ("Tenant Protected Parties"), and without regard to the fault of Landlord, its beneficiaries (if Landlord is an Illinois land trust), Agent, their respective partners, shareholders, members, agents, directors, officers and employees ("Landlord Protected Parties"). As between Landlord Protected Parties and Tenant Protected Parties, such risks are allocated as follows:

(a) Tenant shall bear the risk of bodily injury, personal injury or death, or damage to property, of third persons occasioned by events occurring on or about the Leased Premises, regardless of the party at fault. Said risks shall be insured as provided in Section 6.1(a).

(b) Landlord shall bear the risk of bodily injury, personal injury, or death or damage to the property of third persons occasioned by events occurring on or about the Real Estate (other than premises leased to tenants), provided such event is occasioned by the wrongful act or omission of any of Landlord Protected Parties. Said risk shall be insured against as provided in Section 6.2(a).

---

harm a lawsuit ever does is to take the landlord's interest in the real estate. He suggests inducing the tenant to go along with the clause by providing "that the tenant will have the right to make deductions from rent to recoup the cost of curing a failure by the landlord to comply with his obligations under the lease." He notes, however, that this concession should be limited to protect the landlord.

7. Excerpts from no fault clause prepared by Sidney G. Saltz, Esq. of Chicago, IL. Copyright 1995.

(c) Tenant shall bear the risk of damage to Tenant's contents, trade fixtures, machinery, equipment, furniture and furnishings in the Leased Premises arising out of loss by the events required to be insured against pursuant to Section 6.1(b).

(d) Landlord shall bear the risk of damage to the building on the Real Estate arising out of loss by events required to be insured against pursuant to Section 6.2(b).

Notwithstanding the foregoing, provided the party required to carry insurance under Section 6.1(a) or Section 6.2(a) hereof does not default in its obligation to do so, if and to the extent that any loss occasioned by any event of the type described in Section 6.1(a) or Section 6.2(b) exceeds the coverage or the amount of insurance required to be carried under said Sections or such greater coverage or amount of insurance as is actually carried, or results from an event not required to be insured against or not actually insured against, the party at fault shall pay the amount not actually covered.

6.1. Tenant's Insurance. Tenant shall procure and maintain policies of insurance, at its own cost and expense, insuring:

(a) the Landlord Protected Parties (as "named insureds"), and Landlord's mortgagee, if any, of which Tenant is given written notice, and Tenant Protected Parties, from all claims, demands or actions made by or on behalf of any person or persons, firm or corporation and arising from, related to or connected with the Leased Premises, for bodily injury to or personal injury to or death of any person, or more than one (1) person, or for damage to property in an amount of not less than $3,000,000.00 combined single limit per occurrence/aggregate. Said insurance shall be written on an "occurrence" basis and not on a "claims made" basis. If at any time during the term of this Lease, Tenant owns or rents more than one location, the policy shall contain an endorsement to the effect that the aggregate limit in the policy shall apply separately to each location owned or rented by Tenant. Landlord shall have the right, exercisable by giving written notice thereof to Tenant, to require Tenant to increase such limit if, in Landlord's reasonable judgment, the amount thereof is insufficient to protect the Landlord Protected Parties and Tenant Protected Parties from judgments which might result from such claims, demands or actions. If Tenant is unable, despite reasonable efforts in good faith, to cause its liability insurer to insure the Landlord Protected Parties as "named insureds", Tenant shall nevertheless cause the Landlord Protected Parties to be insured as "additional insureds" and in such event, Tenant will protect, indemnify and save harmless the Landlord Protected Parties from and against any and all liabilities, obligations, claims, damages, penalties, causes of action, costs and expenses (including without limitation reasonable attorney's fees and expenses) imposed upon or incurred by or asserted against the Landlord Protected Parties, or any of them, by reason of any bodily injury to or personal injury to or death of any person or more than one person or for damage to property, occurring on or about the Leased Premises, caused by any party including, without limitation, any Landlord Protected Party, to the extent of the amount of the insurance required to be carried under this Section 6.1(a) or such greater amount of insurance as is actually carried. Tenant shall cause its liability insurance to include contractual liability coverage fully covering the indemnity hereinabove set forth.

(b) All contents and Tenant's trade fixtures, machinery, equipment, furniture and furnishings in the Leased Premises to the extent of at least ninety percent (90%) of their replacement cost under Standard Fire and Extended Coverage Policy and all other risks of direct physical loss as insured against under Special Form ("all risk" coverage). Said insurance shall contain an endorsement waiving the insurer's right of subrogation against any Landlord Protected Party, provided that such waiver of the right of subrogation shall not be operative in any case where the effect thereof is to invalidate such insurance coverage or increase the cost thereof (except that Landlord shall have the right, within thirty (30) days following written notice, to pay such increased cost, thereby keeping such waiver in full force and effect.

(c) Tenant Protected Parties from all worker's compensation claims.

(d) Landlord and Tenant against breakage of all plate glass utilized in the improvements on the Leased Premises.

6.2. Landlord's Insurance. Landlord shall procure and maintain policies of insurance insuring:

(a) All claims, demands or actions made by or on behalf of any person or persons, firm or corporation and arising from, related to or connected with the Real Estate, other than premises leased to tenants, for bodily injury to or personal injury to or death of any person, or more than one (1) person, or for damage to property in an amount of not less than $3,000,000.00 combined single limit per occurrence/aggregate. Said insurance shall be written on an "occurrence" basis and not on a "claims made" basis. If at any time during the term of this Lease, Landlord owns more than one location, the policy shall contain an endorsement to the effect that the aggregate limit in the policy shall apply separately to each location owned by Landlord.

(b) The improvements at any time situated upon the Leased Premises against loss or damage by fire, lightning, windstorm, hailstorm, aircraft, vehicles, smoke, explosion, riot or civil commotion as provided by the Standard Fire and Extended Coverage Policy and all other risks of direct physical loss as insured against under Special Form ("all risk" coverage). The insurance coverage shall be for not less than 90% of the full replacement cost of such improvements with agreed amount endorsement. Landlord shall be named as the insured and all proceeds of insurance shall be payable to Landlord. Said insurance shall contain an endorsement waiving the insurer's right of subrogation against any Tenant Protected Party, provided that such waiver of the right of subrogation shall not be operative in any case where the effect thereof is to invalidate such insurance coverage or increase the cost thereof (except that Tenant shall have the right, within thirty (30) days following written notice, to pay such increased cost, thereby keeping such waiver in full force and effect).

(c) Landlord's business income, protecting Landlord from loss of rents and other charges during the period while the Leased Premises are untenantable due to fire or other casualty (for the period reasonably determined by Landlord).

(d) Flood or earthquake insurance whenever, in the reasonable judgment of Landlord, such protection is necessary and it is available at commercially reasonable cost.

6.3. Form of Insurance. All of the aforesaid insurance shall be in responsible companies. As to Tenant's insurance, the insurer and the form, substance and amount (where not stated above) shall be satisfactory from time to time to Landlord and any mortgagee of Landlord and shall unconditionally provide that it is not subject to cancellation or non-renewal except after at least thirty (30) days' prior written notice to Landlord and any mortgagee of Landlord. Originals of Tenant's insurance policies (or certificates thereof) satisfactory to Landlord, together with satisfactory evidence of payment of the premiums thereon, shall be deposited with Landlord at the Commencement Date and renewals thereof not less than thirty (30) days prior to the end of the term of such coverage.

This clause achieves a number of desired goals when drafting a commercial lease. It is very well written and clear in its intent. Section 6.0, entitled "Allocation of Risks," explicitly states the parties' intent to allocate the risks normally incurred in a commercial leasing transaction between the parties, and where possible, to shift those risks to an insurer.

This opening section achieves several purposes. First, by clearly stating the contractual intent of the parties at the outset, the provision reduces the possibility of the clause being misinterpreted by strangers to the deal or by the parties themselves at some later date. Second, a clearly drafted clause stating the intent of the parties reduces the possibility of ambiguity in the interpretation of the entire provision. Thus, the parties may avoid the need later to find the persons who originally negotiated the deal, if indeed they can be found, in order to determine what the parties intended to do when they negotiated this provision. In the authors' experience, even if the original negotiators later surface for depositions or trial testimony, their recollections of a particular transaction are often so vague that their testimony is of little or no use in interpreting a particular clause. Even if this testimony is supported by notes or memoranda made contemporaneously with the transaction, it is the authors' experience that a clearly drafted provision is much more useful in constructing the contractual intention of the landlord and the tenant than later recollections that can become muddied or biased with the passage of time.

Having acknowledged the risk allocation that is inherent in any lease negotiation, Section 6.0 then defines the risks that will be apportioned between the landlord and tenant and the way those risks will be shared. Overall, subsections 6.0(a) through (d) attempt to apportion the risk fairly to the party most able to bear that risk or the party who receives the most beneficial use of the area or property for which it is responsible. Thus, the tenant bears the risk for injury and damage occurring on or about the leased premises (of which the tenant is the sole occupant and beneficiary under subsection (a)), as well as for damages to its contents, trade fixtures, and other property on the leased premises under subsection (c). Similarly, the landlord bears the risk of loss for injuries and damages arising out of events in the "building" (outside the leased premises) and on the "property" under subsections (b) and (d). Each party agrees to indemnify the other for third-party claims in the areas for which they are responsible under subsections (a) through (d). The result of this clause is that each party has the responsibility of bearing the risk or expense for property or events most within control of that party.

This is the first step in establishing a no fault framework. In the acknowledgment of risk allocation, the identification of risks that a party can best handle and by setting a mutual indemnification scheme, the parties have begun the process of shifting the casualty and liability risk to the parties in the business of handling such risks—the insurers. So long as the landlord and tenant maintain the insurance required in Sections 6.1 and 6.2, subject to periodic review for adequacy of coverage, the parties should not have to worry about incurring any liability beyond that for which they have contracted.[8]

The parties' insurance requirements are remarkably similar in the spirit and intent of a no fault scheme. Each party is required to insure the other party and itself from liability and property damage claims with at least a $3 million combined single limit policy. The insurance is to be written on an occurrence basis rather than a claims-made basis so that the protection runs from the originating event. Each party is also required to at least ask its insurer to name the other party as the "named insured" or, being unable to do that, as an "additional insured." The effect of adding the other as an insured is to cut off any possibility of a subrogation action against a party responsible for generating the claim by an insurer paying out on a claim, thus ending the action at the insurer's doorstep. Subsections 6.1(b) and 6.2(b) mirror one another in requiring the tenant's and landlord's property carrier to include an endorsement in which the insurer waives any subrogation rights against the other party, achieving

8. Note that the insurance amounts should be adequate to cover any claims since there is an exception for this preliminary no fault scheme. In the last paragraph of Section 6.0, the party at fault is responsible for paying the amount of any damages or claims not actually insured.

the same result on property claims as is achieved in liability claims under subsections 6.1(a) and 6.2(a).

The insurance requirements are not exact mirror images of one another, however. Under subsection 6.1(a), the landlord has the right to require the tenant to increase its liability limits if the amounts are insufficient to cover the parties from possible claims, damages, or actions, in the landlord's reasonable judgment. The tenant does not have a reciprocal right to have the landlord increase its insurance. The provision is also not clear as to the extent of protection that a tenant receives from exposure for damage to the entire building or property due to a fire or other casualty caused by the negligence of the tenant or one of its employees, contractors, customers, or agents. It is in this area that the real exposure can occur to the tenant. If the building or property are not adequately insured by the landlord, then the tenant may find itself liable for paying the balance of the costs to replace or restore the building or property not covered by the landlord's policy.

Overall, this risk allocation and waiver of claims provision is a thorough attempt at creating a fair apportionment of the risks and liability between the parties in the event of fire or another casualty. The provision clearly states its intent, allocates responsibilities, and finds ways to place the liabilities on the parties intended by the landlord and tenant to incur it.

Chapter 8
Arbitration of Insurance Disputes

[1]—In General

Increasingly, insurers are requiring mandatory arbitration of coverage disputes, imposing choice of venue and choice of law provisions to give themselves an advantage when disputes arise. Policyholders need to be aware of these restrictions and attempt to negotiate and remove them. Failing to do so may result in reduced or eliminated coverage and will certainly "provide the insurer with significant tactical advantages."[1]

Frequently, insurers will impose mandatory arbitration in an effort to keep insurance coverage disputes out of court. Recognizing that courts will enforce standard contract rules of interpretation, viewing exclusions narrowly and resolving ambiguities in the insureds' favor, insurers are increasingly seeking mandatory arbitration of disputes. Arbitration generally will limit opportunities for discovery, especially regarding extra-contractual claims, such as bad faith.[2] Further, there are fewer opportunities to appeal arbitration decisions than court decisions. Also, insurers have more leeway in arguing inconsistent positions in arbitrated cases, since arbitrations are private proceedings without a public record. The right to recover attorneys' fees may also be limited in arbitration.

[2]—States Limiting Arbitration of Insurance Policies

Recognizing the limitations of arbitration, "26 states have enacted statutes that restrict arbitration provisions in insurance policies."[3] Note that California, New Jersey, and

1. Lynda A. Bennett & Ryan J. Cooper, *Policyholders Beware: Mandatory Arbitration, Choice of Law and Choice of Venue Provisions May Restrict Insurance Coverage Rights* (March 20, 2013).

2. *Id.*

3. *Id.* See, e.g., *Washington Department of Transportation v. James River Insurance Co.*, 292 P.3d 118 (Wash. 2013) (*en banc*), where the Washington Supreme Court upheld the lower court's denial of a motion to compel arbitration of an insurance coverage dispute on grounds that such disputes are not arbitrable as a matter of state and federal law. The Washington Supreme Court "voided an insurance policy's arbitration provision because it violated a Washington statute that prohibits insurance policies from 'depriving the courts of [Washington] of the jurisdiction of action against the insurer.'" The court

New York do not have statutes that restrict arbitration provisions in commercial liability and casualty insurance policies.

In certain instances, "a policyholder can insist that an arbitration provision be removed through an endorsement."[4] In other cases, the policyholder can seek removal of an arbitration provision upon renewal or "seek coverage from another insurer that will not require mandatory arbitration of coverage disputes."[5] When a claim involves operations between or among states, the arbitration provision must be reviewed to determine whether it is enforceable under the laws of each state connected to the claim, "including where the claim arose and where the policy was issued."[6]

[3]—Venue Provisions

Recognizing that certain jurisdictions are known as either pro-policyholder or pro-insured regarding insurance coverage disputes, insurers will seek to include a choice of venue provision in their policies, of course selecting a pro-insurer jurisdiction. Since courts tend to enforce choice of venue provisions, it is best for policyholders to attempt to negotiate the removal of choice of venue provisions when they purchase their insurance policy in order to avoid giving the insurer a strategic advantage.

[4]—Choice of Law Provisions

Courts also tend to strictly enforce choice of law provisions, so policyholders should try to negotiate their removal. With no "universal interpretation of insurance policies used by courts across the United States," the choice of law can mean that the very same provision may be interpreted quite differently, depending on the applicable law, and "can mean the difference between a claim being covered or denied."[7]

Absent a choice of law provision, "courts generally evaluate all potentially applicable law and then apply the law that has the greatest connection to the particular claim presented. To avoid narrowing the options available to establishing coverage for a claim in the first place, policyholders should not agree to a choice of law provision in their policies."[8]

---

also held that the Federal Arbitration Act, 9 U.S.C. §§ 1 *et seq.*, did not apply because the McCarran-Ferguson Act, 15 U.S.C. §§ 1011–15, prevents federal law from preempting state insurance laws. The Federal Arbitration Act typically preempts state restrictions on arbitration.

4. Bennett & Cooper, *supra* note 1.
5. *Id.*
6. *Id.*
7. *Id.*
8. *Id.*

Chapter 9
Final Thoughts

In striving to reach a "no fault" position with respect to liability for fire damage or other casualties, landlords and tenants should be aware of the numerous steps necessary to achieve this result. Each party must realize the pitfalls of such devices as indemnification and exculpatory provisions and, especially, the ramifications of a subrogation action in the event of a casualty.

While a growing number of states have placed restrictions on unrestrained exculpation and indemnification provisions in commercial transactions, neither a tenant nor a landlord should rely upon a court overturning an exculpatory or indemnification clause in a commercial lease in order to defeat a claim for damages from the protected party. The courts and legislatures are still not uniformly clear on their interpretation of these clauses and have, in some instances, retreated from their former positions of viewing these provisions with a jaded eye.

A tenant who believes that it is automatically covered on a landlord's policy as a coinsured when the lease does not expressly provide this coverage is not entitled to any sympathy when it is later liable for fire loss. The cases are much too sparse on the point to find such comfort. If a common thread is apparent from these cases, it is that the courts may stretch their reasoning to extend fire coverage to a tenant whose negligence has caused fire damage to a building when the building is insured by the owner. However, the courts will not always do this.

While this reasoning is partially based on some experts' opinion that subrogation presents a windfall to the insurance companies, the application of coinsurance is better suited for residential leasing situations.[1] Subsequent cases may start to chip away at this notion of coinsurance in commercial leases; however, tenants should take notice and structure their insurance and casualty clauses accordingly.

Subrogation can still defeat all precautions taken by landlords and tenants in establishing a "no fault" liability scheme in their leases. Insurers can still swoop in

1. In residential leasing, the bargaining positions are usually mismatched, and the resulting liability is much more catastrophic to the negligent tenant than in commercial transactions where the parties have relatively equal bargaining positions, better access to competent representations, and better opportunities for comprehensive insurance coverage.

after a casualty on a subrogation claim and recoup their losses against a negligent party. The only sure way of deflecting these actions is through (1) a waiver of subrogation clause in the lease, (2) a clear and concise waiver of direct actions or claims of landlord and tenant against each other, and (3) obtaining certificates of mutual waiver of the insurer's rights of subrogation recovery from each insurance carrier. The waivers must, however, be clear, explicit, and binding upon the landlord's and tenant's respective insurance companies. Only then will the ominous threat of a subrogation action be dissipated as it properly should be in a risk-free commercial transaction rather than later taking center stage after casualty strikes.

Lease language is key in determining the parties' insurance obligations. Courts are not inclined to impose responsibility upon a party unless such responsibility was clearly intended by the parties.[2] Therefore, when reviewing the terms of a lease, it is a good idea "for counsel to consult with the client's insurance broker or risk manager regarding the insurance obligations in a lease, and to have him or her review not only the provisions regarding insurance, but also the provisions pertaining to damage and destruction, indemnification, waivers and releases and obligations for compliance with laws."[3]

---

2. *See, e.g.*, TAG 380 LLC v. ComMet 380, Inc., New York Law Journal, p. 22 col. 1 (N.Y. App. Div. Feb. 20, 2007), where the court refused to extend the lease's insurance coverage provision to require terrorism insurance. The New York Appellate Division reversed a lower court finding and held that a 1989 lease that required the tenant to acquire insurance covering "fire, explosion and physical contact of an aircraft" with the property did not extend to require coverage for damage resulting from acts of terrorism. The court reasoned that an insurance policy "should not be extended beyond its plain meaning to include perils not specifically covered by its provisions." *Id.*

3. Jay L. Paxton, *Insurance and Commercial Leases: Critical Provisions in Uncertain Times*, in Meyer, Rusche, Sarasek & Wood, 1 *Negotiating Commercial Leases: How Owners & Corporate Occupants Can Avoid Costly Errors*, No. 2941, 907, 910 (PLI/Real Estate Fall 2004).

Index